Business Intelligence Career Master Plan

Launch and advance your BI career with proven techniques and actionable insights

Eduardo Chavez

Danny Moncada

BIRMINGHAM—MUMBAI

Business Intelligence Career Master Plan

Group Product Manager: Kaustubh Manglurkar

Publishing Product Manager: Arindam Majumder

Book Project Manager: Kirti Pisat

Content Development Editor: Manikandan Kurup

Technical Editor: Kavyashree K S

Copy Editor: Safis Editing

Proofreader: Safis Editing

Indexer: Pratik Shirodkar

Production Designer: Joshua Misquitta

DevRel Marketing Coordinator: Nivedita Singh

Cover design: Angel Cristerna

First published: July 2023

Production reference: 1100823

Published by Packt Publishing Ltd.

Grosvenor House

11 St Paul's Square

Birmingham

B3 1RB, UK.

ISBN 978-1-80107-795-8

www.packtpub.com

To my mother, Irma, who was the main pillar of my growth; Carolina, Ania, and Alicia, my sister and nieces - they are my purpose in this life; Donald Yerbic for all his support; to all the great professors I've absorbed knowledge from - Gilberto Alapizco, Roberto Aramburo, Jose Antonio Garcia at Tecnologico de Monterrey, and Yicheng Song, De Liu, and Ravi Bapna at University of Minnesota. Matt Nuttall, Brian Krupski, and Paul Volkmuth for always believing in me. And to my friends, who kept me alive and inspired me during my most challenging times, especially Angel Cristerna, Alejandro Caro, Abdel Vargas, Grace Burgos, and Yuleth, and of course my co-author Danny Moncada.

– Eduardo R. Chavez Herrera

To my mother, Dora, and father, Ariel, thank you for sacrificing so much for Marilyn and me, so that we could have a better life in the US. You have both shown us the true meaning of fearlessness, generosity, compassion, love, respect, and perseverance, and have given so much of yourselves to the world around you. To my sister, Marilyn, and nephew, Luciano, your big bro and tío will always be here for you. To my abuelito Jose, you are in my heart always and forever. To the Moncada and Marin families, you all live in my heart always and forever, and I hope I have made you proud. To my coauthor, Eduardo Chavez, I will treasure our friendship for the rest of my days, and you have my eternal gratitude for this opportunity of a lifetime to co-author this book with you. To all the people in my life who told me my potential was limitless and that I could do whatever I put my mind to, I finally listened. To anyone that offered encouragement or support for this book, this is for you. Y para todos los Colombianos y gente Latina: nunca dejen de brillar que el mundo necesita de su luz.

– Danny Moncada

Foreword

It gives me great pleasure to introduce *Business Intelligence Career Master Plan* to the world. Written by two seasoned analytics and business intelligence professionals, Eduardo Chavez and Danny Moncada, this book is a well-laid-out roadmap for anyone looking to enter and flourish in the field of business intelligence, or BI as we call it. As we know there is a lot of hype around BI, and many companies struggle to extract meaningful intelligence from their data. A substantial portion of the variance in extracting business value from data is explained by heterogeneity in the people and processes around it. More often than not, I find different employees, different business units, and different teams using different language around business intelligence within a firm. This causes unnecessary friction and leads to suboptimal use of resources. It is also linked to burnout and employee churn.

In simple but insightful terms, Eduardo and Danny lay down the foundation of the field of business intelligence so that there is a common language and understanding that gets professionals to work together to create business value. The book serves as a guide for anyone looking to enter the BI profession and advance through it to other layers, such as analytics and AI. Using real-world examples and stories from their experiences, they showcase essential concepts in a jargon-free manner. Readers of this book can expect to gain an intuitive understanding of key BI skills such as data modeling, data visualization, data analysis, and data warehousing.

I want to congratulate them for putting together this fine career roadmap and I look forward to seeing the book have a positive impact on the BI community.

Ravi Bapna

Curtis L. Carlson Chair Professor in Business Analytics and Information Systems

Academic Director, Carlson Analytics Lab, and Analytics for Good Institute

Carlson School of Management

University of Minnesota

Minneapolis, MN 55455

Contributors

About the authors

Eduardo Chavez is a Business Intelligence professional with over 18 years of industry experience and hails from Mazatlan, Mexico. He is a certified GCP professional data engineer who has extensively engaged with leading cloud platforms such GCP, Oracle, Azure, and AWS. With a bachelor's degree in information systems and three master's degrees, including IT, business administration, and business analytics, Eduardo specializes in SQL, semantic layers, and data modeling. He has worked for prominent private companies like Accenture, Oracle, and Google, as well as the University of Minnesota in the public sector. Eduardo is known for advocating the rapid development cycle, emphasizing late binding data warehousing, rapid prototyping, and a top-down approach.

Danny Moncada is a seasoned Business Intelligence professional with 15 years of experience, excelling in project implementations related to database administration, data analysis, and data engineering. He has contributed his expertise to renowned companies like Cigna Healthcare, Indeed, IOTAS, as well as the University of Minnesota in the non-profit sector. In 2020, Danny completed his M.S. in Business Analytics from the Carlson School of Management, where he was recognized as the most helpful student by his peers. He has achieved numerous certifications, including Python programming from NYU, data engineering, big data, and machine learning on GCP, Google Business Intelligence, and most recently, Google Advanced Data Analytics from Coursera. Danny's specialties lie in data visualization, analysis, and data warehousing.

About the reviewers

Brandon Acosta has been working in the realm of data for seven years now. While data has always been an interesting topic to him, it wasn't until completing his B.S. in computer science that he learned the real-world value of data. From there, his first several years of experience in the industry were as a business analyst in small and large company settings. This led him to an interest in the engineering aspect of data, where he was then able to pursue a role in data engineering. Although his current title is data engineer, he, like most working on a small data team, covers a wide range of the BI spectrum. As he continues to hone his skills as a data engineer, he hopes to work his way into predictive analytics and begin a role in data science.

Atul Kadlag, a seasoned professional in the business intelligence, data, and analytics industry, possesses diverse experience across different technologies and a proven track record of success. A self-motivated learner, he has excelled at working at various multinational companies for more than 15 years, leading transformative initiatives in business intelligence, data warehouses, and data analytics. Atul has immense experience in handling end-to-end projects in business intelligence and data warehouse technologies. Atul is dedicated to driving positive change and inspiring others through continuous learning, making a lasting impact in the data industry. His expertise involves SQL, Python, and business intelligence and data warehousing technologies.

Chandan Kalra's journey in the business intelligence and analytics industry spans over 20 impactful years, marked by an impressive portfolio of work across ERP, business intelligence, and consulting for Fortune 100 behemoths. His expertise doesn't stop at just knowing the theoretical, but delves deep into the practical. Whether it's dissecting convoluted data or strategizing for multinational corporations, he has done it all. His ability to translate complex data concepts into digestible content comes from years of understanding the subtleties of the business world. His seasoned perspective, enriched by the practical wisdom of handling raw data and converting it into powerful strategic insights, brings a depth of understanding that sets him apart. No doubt, he is a unique guiding voice in the literary landscape of business analytics and technology.

Table of Contents

3

How to Talk Data   39

4

How To Crack the BI Interview Process   63

5

Business Intelligence Landscape   91

6

Improving Data Proficiency or Subject Matter Expertise   131

7

Business Intelligence Education   167

8

Beyond Business Intelligence   179

9

Hands-On Data Wrangling and Data Visualization   195

Preface

The path to entering the field of **business intelligence** (**BI**) is both vast and challenging to navigate. Throughout our experience in various BI roles, we have encountered individuals with diverse skill sets and backgrounds. This spectrum ranges from highly skilled **machine learning** (**ML**) and AI engineers holding PhDs in statistics and mathematics to graduate students transitioning from academia to pursue careers as business analysts. Through this book, we aim to convey to you that there is no single predefined path to follow. Numerous different routes can lead to the same destination, depending on your area of expertise, level of interest in various subject areas, and proficiency in both technical and soft skills.

We have two main objectives in this book. The first is to help business professionals understand the foundations of BI in a way that is tool and technology-agnostic. Our second objective is to show the process of starting and advancing in BI. Furthermore, we aim to provide insight into the broader realms beyond BI, encompassing data exploration, business analytics, and data science.

Who this book is for

This book is for BI professionals who are passionate about data and its complexities, have some foundational knowledge of BI, and would like to become more proficient in BI tools and technologies to advance their career in any BI organization.

We extend a warm welcome to readers, analysts, and developers of all skill levels and backgrounds. Whether you are a seasoned ML engineer well-versed in implementing ML pipelines seeking to delve into data visualization, or a business analyst looking to transition into data engineering, we acknowledge and value the individuality and diversity of each reader's expertise, level of interest in various subject areas, and proficiency in technical and soft skills.

What this book covers

Chapter 1, *Breaking into the BI World*, offers a general overview of BI, an introduction to BI roles, and an overview of BI technologies and entering the BI space.

Chapter 2, *How to Become Proficient in Analyzing Data*, explores how to build a taxonomy of data sources, using the right tools to explore data, and understanding an organization's data needs.

Chapter 3, *How to Talk Data, delves into presenting your findings*, talking with business stakeholders, data visualization basics, and telling a story with data

Chapter 4, *How to Crack the BI Interview Process*, examines the tips and tricks to find the right BI interview and techniques to approach common BI interview questions

Chapter 5, Business Intelligence Landscape, looks at the current state of the BI landscape, including common tools, the most effective technologies to study, and the differences between BI roles.

Chapter 6, Improving Data Proficiency or Subject Matter Expertise, explores data behavior in different business units and leveraging online tools to increase and improve BI skills.

Chapter 7, Business Intelligence Education, delves into certifications, academic programs, training courses, and books to continue your BI education.

Chapter 8, Beyond Business Intelligence, examines business analytics, data science, and data exploration.

Chapter 9, Hands-On Data Wrangling and Data Visualization, looks at simple data wrangling, visualization, and dashboard exercises with Python and Tableau.

To get the most out of this book

This book caters to developers and business analysts who possess a foundational understanding of data analysis tools and are enthusiastic about delving into the intricacies of data. It offers an opportunity to enhance proficiency in these tools, thereby enabling career growth within any BI organization. A fundamental grasp of tools such as Microsoft Excel, working knowledge of SQL, Python, and Tableau, and experience with major cloud providers such as AWS or GCP are basic requirements. However, the most crucial prerequisite is the capacity to extract valuable business insights from data and a genuine eagerness to embrace and master challenging new concepts.

Software/hardware covered in the book	Operating system requirements
Python	Windows or macOS
Tableau	Windows or macOS

If you are using the digital version of this book, we advise you to type the code yourself or access the code from the book's GitHub repository (a link is available in the next section). Doing so will help you avoid any potential errors related to the copying and pasting of code.

Within this book, you will find clear, detailed explanations of vital concepts, along with real-world examples that demonstrate their practical application. By delving into the taxonomy of BI and data within an organization, you will develop a comprehensive understanding of the subject matter, providing a solid foundation for your journey.

Download the example code files

You can download the example code files for this book from GitHub at https://github.com/PacktPublishing/Business-Intelligence-Career-Master-Plan. If there is an update to the code, it will be updated in GitHub.

We also have other code bundles from our rich catalog of books and videos available at https://github.com/PacktPublishing/. Check them out!

Conventions used

There are several text conventions used throughout this book.

Code in text: Indicates code words in text, database table names, folder names, filenames, file extensions, pathnames, dummy URLs, user input, and Twitter handles. Here is an example: "Inspect the first five rows of the dataset using the `head()` function."

A block of code is set as follows:

```
def plot_salary_distribution(df):
    plt.figure(figsize=(10, 6))
    sns.histplot(data=df, x='Average Salary', kde=True)
    plt.title('Distribution of Salaries')
    plt.xlabel('Average Salary')
    plt.ylabel('Count')
    plt.show()
```

When we wish to draw your attention to a particular part of a code block, the relevant lines or items are set in bold:

```
Biotech & Pharmaceuticals               66
IT Services                             61
Unknown Industry                        60
Computer Hardware & Software            56
Aerospace & Defense                     46
Enterprise Software & Network Solutions 43
```

Bold: Indicates a new term, an important word, or words that you see on screen. For instance, words in menus or dialog boxes appear in bold. Here is an example: " Drag the **Longitude** and **Latitude** marks into **Columns** and **Rows**, respectively."

> **Tips or important notes**
> Appear like this.

Get in touch

Feedback from our readers is always welcome.

General feedback: If you have questions about any aspect of this book, email us at customercare@packtpub.com and mention the book title in the subject of your message.

Errata: Although we have taken every care to ensure the accuracy of our content, mistakes do happen. If you have found a mistake in this book, we would be grateful if you would report this to us. Please visit www.packtpub.com/support/errata and fill in the form.

Piracy: If you come across any illegal copies of our works in any form on the internet, we would be grateful if you would provide us with the location address or website name. Please contact us at copyright@packt.com with a link to the material.

If you are interested in becoming an author: If there is a topic that you have expertise in and you are interested in either writing or contributing to a book, please visit authors.packtpub.com.

Share your thoughts

Once you've read *Business Intelligence Career Master Plan*, we'd love to hear your thoughts! Scan the QR code below to go straight to the Amazon review page for this book and share your feedback.

https://packt.link/r/1801077959

Your review is important to us and the tech community and will help us make sure we're delivering excellent quality content.

Download a free PDF copy of this book

Thanks for purchasing this book!

Do you like to read on the go but are unable to carry your print books everywhere?

Is your eBook purchase not compatible with the device of your choice?

Don't worry, now with every Packt book you get a DRM-free PDF version of that book at no cost.

Read anywhere, any place, on any device. Search, copy, and paste code from your favorite technical books directly into your application.

The perks don't stop there, you can get exclusive access to discounts, newsletters, and great free content in your inbox daily

Follow these simple steps to get the benefits:

1. Scan the QR code or visit the link below

https://packt.link/free-ebook/978-1-80107-795-8

2. Submit your proof of purchase
3. That's it! We'll send your free PDF and other benefits to your email directly

1
Breaking into the BI World

This book follows the philosophy of the *path of least resistance*, which states that in nature and physics, organisms and elements always try to find the shortest, most efficient way to their destination.

Imagine that you are standing in front of a large skyscraper in downtown Manhattan called "Business Intelligence." As you look up at it, you can see floor after floor as it slowly reaches into the clouds and out of your immediate eyeline. While it can be very awe-inspiring and daunting, the building, just like every other one, has many entrances – one entrance at the front, one at the back, and some on the sides of the building. And like many buildings with proper security protocols, each of those entrances require different keys to enter and exit the building. Once you step inside, you will notice right away that there are a myriad of different rooms and workspaces.

Now that we have set the scene, we can begin discussing how this relates to entering the **Business Intelligence (BI)** world. In this chapter, we will explore entering the BI world (the skyscraper), what background you may come from (the various entrances to the building), what skills you require to be successful (the keys to open the doors), and what career paths or roles you may find once you are (the myriad of rooms and workspaces).

Now, you might be thinking to yourself – how do they even know to let me in the building? How do I prove that I belong and have the capabilities to even get in? The short answer is, you don't… yet. But our goal is to show you that even if you may not have the "right" title like a PhD in statistics and mathematics (don't worry, we don't either), you might have the right skills and experience to get you a key to the kingdom, and you didn't even know it. How do we start? Well, let's dive right in, shall we? It's probably a little cold out there; it is Manhattan, after all!

Where to start?

If you are reading this book, good chances are that you have been exposed to BI or have some notion about its capabilities and benefits, but let's begin by establishing a common concept – BI is like a powerful telescope that helps a business look deep into its operations and the surrounding market. It's a set of techniques and tools that turn raw data – such as sales numbers, customer feedback, or supply chain info – into easy-to-understand, actionable insights.

Think of it like this – if a business is a ship sailing in the sea, BI is the captain's map and compass. It helps the business understand where it's currently docked, which direction it's heading in, and what obstacles might be in the way. It does so by analyzing the company's own data (like looking at the ship's logbook) and also data from the market (like watching the weather and sea currents).

BI can help answer questions such as, *"What products are selling best? Who are our most valuable customers? How can we reduce costs? Which market should we enter next?"* This allows businesses to make smarter decisions and better plan for the future. However, embarking on a journey into BI can indeed be a lengthy process. It requires patience and dedication, as the multitude of potential paths to success can sometimes make the journey seem perplexing.

A good starting point is to examine the background of other people that enter and exit the building every day, which is "everyday" BI professionals, such as the two co-authors of this book. What sets us apart from the rest of the population going about their day in downtown Manhattan? While we all come from a diverse set of backgrounds and experiences, there are certain common themes and skills that seem to come up again and again – among them, problem solving, analytical thinking, the ability to think through challenging concepts logically and conceptually, proficiency with computers, communication skills, and business acumen.

Another thing to point out is that many professionals work in different areas of a business before starting in BI. It's quite common to find accountants, business administrators, marketing experts, and other skilled professionals looking to break into BI because they all have the same goal in common – making their business unit more efficient and data-driven. What makes these professionals similar is they came from a common path, which is a background molded by and refined by time spent working in the business. Accountants spend their days crunching numbers and building reports to deliver to senior leadership, business administrators rely heavily on metrics and **key performance indicators (KPIs)** to help improve their decision-making, and marketing experts use tracking tools to analyze trends for their company's conversion rate and cost per sales. What can we infer from the preceding examples? In these business professionals' search to improve their companies and business units' goals, they take a winding path up 5th Avenue and through Central Park and then end up at the front door of our imaginary skyscraper, but they are now ready to give BI the chance to not only be leveraged as a tool for their organizations but also, even more critically, become a possible career progression for themselves.

At the other end of the BI spectrum, we have IT professionals, composed of programmers, server administrators, QA testers, database developers, and administrators, among many others, whose relationship to data and technology is not casual but much more intimate and nuanced. IT professionals have in-depth knowledge of the ins and outs of how data flows through a building; like plumbers working at a water treatment facility, they very carefully calculate and monitor the flow of data as if it were water going through pipes. Programmers understand and adhere to strict computing principles and understand the importance of CPU usage when developing programs. Server administrators design systems to minimize system bottlenecks and maintain a secure platform for their customer base. Database developers have expertise in handling tables with millions of records, updated at different intervals, and experience using a wide-ranging collection of database technologies. These potential candidates take a different path through lower Manhattan and enter the skyscraper through the *back door*, preferring to dedicate their careers to BI from a technical point of view.

Now that we've covered the front and back entrances to BI, you might be asking, what are the side doors to enter the building? For us, BI as a career represents a commitment to concepts and technologies that take time (sometimes *years*) to master and may not be in line with the career you originally chose or your original career path. Here's an example – let's say you are the **Chief Medical Officer (CMO)** at a hospital in a major metropolitan area, such as Chicago, and your HR generalist has made you aware that the hospital faces a major challenge in scheduling enough qualified nurses to cover all the shifts required to treat patients throughout the day. The most experienced nurses with the most amount of medical training are allocated the night shift, which typically does not have as much activity as during the day. Your suspicion is proven right by reviewing historical trends of the number of lives saved when the hospital had the proper coverage for day shifts. If you, as the CMO, had the right data, the right BI platform, and experienced IT professionals, you *might* be able to obtain some answers – but what if you could combine that with your domain expertise and years of experience leading the hospital? With your knowledge, a more accurate optimization algorithm could be built to allocate nurses accordingly. However, does this mean you want to become a BI analyst for life? These are the side doors of BI, and we'll discuss more about BI as a tool in the upcoming *Non-technical data analysis* section.

As we mentioned and demonstrated previously, there's no one way to enter the BI world. In fact, there are so many different possible paths that it can almost seem like a maze, and you end up feeling like a business professional getting lost in downtown Manhattan on the way to an important client visit. While it can feel like organized chaos at times, there's also a *great* deal of opportunity for growth and career progression, and the barrier to entry is much lower than in other professions, such as medicine or law. What we hope to demonstrate is that having a willingness to learn and master some basic skills and concepts can lead you not only to the skyscraper but also through the long and winding journey up to the top. So, let's get started by diving into what those skills entail and what tools you'll need in your BI journey.

BI roles

As you might have surmised, there's a variety of different BI roles; what those roles have in common is the need to have some polished skills if you want to perform and be successful at them. It is important to assess *which* of the following skills you may have, and be honest in your assessment of your proficiency in each skill. We would also like to emphasize that the skills we cover here are *not* meant to be viewed as an exhaustive list, but we've specifically picked the set of skills we would like to emphasize because they have the biggest impact on any BI organization. We encourage you to keep track of and continually practice and hone these skills, as they require dedication and focus to keep sharp.

While some of these skills require years of training or years of practice to fully master, there are a few where the length of time isn't as important as the use of your brain agility. One such skill is data analysis, which you can develop through different mental exercises – that is, using your imagination to try to picture and create mental visualizations of data. In BI organizations, professionals are often encouraged to use different data visualization tools and perform exploratory data analysis at their own discretion and direction. However, being able to identify how your organization's data is structured and *then* determining what the best approach is to shape the data to the appropriate dimensions, level of granularity, and what its final "shape" looks like will help you when defining the appropriate business requirements, or when writing the correct algorithm/query that will produce the final output you need.

Here are some tips on how to develop proficiency in data analysis. These are not meant to be taken in any special order, and nor should this be viewed as a comprehensive list:

- Start by asking some simple questions to determine the purpose of your data. Here are some sample questions to think through:

  - What does the data describe?

  - What entity does it represent?

  - What relationships are present between data points (if any)? What types of relationships are being captured?

  - What field or fields are the individual pieces that make every record unique?

  - Can you visualize those fields and ascertain their relationship with the rest of the columns? Do they matter?

  - Is there any "white noise" or random variance present in the data?

  - Is there any metadata available for analysis?

  - Can you determine the purpose of the data?

  - How and where was the data created? Gather data about the systems, servers, databases, and so on.

  - In what format is the data being stored?

- Follow this up by wrapping some general statistics around your data. You might try building commonly used, simple data visualizations as a starting point. For example, you can use techniques such as the following:

  - Building a bar chart or histogram for discrete data

  - Creating histograms to determine the distribution of continuous data

  - Uncovering patterns or trends using a scatterplot or heatmap

  - Creating box plots containing mean and percentiles, and adding KPIs with metrics such as standard deviation, mode, max, and mins

- Our final suggestion is to do a "deep dive" and systematically pick apart a few records from your dataset. For example, you could start by finding out how many distinct values each variable in your dataset has to determine how large of a distribution you are working with. You could follow this up by grouping the most important columns in the dataset and determining the meaning behind the values they store. To provide a little more context, here's an example. Let's say your dataset has a column labeled `STATUS` that contains four unique values, `[P0, P1, P2, P3]`, and another column labeled `IS_CURRENT`, with two distinct values of `[1, 0]`. You might select one row of data containing `STATUS` of `P1` and an `IS_CURRENT` value of `0`, and try to figure out what information this conveys. Then, get confirmation from a subject matter expert in your organization.

- Finally, you can take one additional next step and analyze a few rows of data (or maybe just one row, depending on the complexity of the dataset). Take the time to trace the route that a single record takes along your dataset and find out where it ends. Once you have that route mapped out, use the lessons learned from your initial exploration of the dataset combined with your intuition to narrate the story of that single record. The goal of going through this extensive exercise is to extrapolate your analysis to a *much* larger dataset and, with the help of technology, apply algorithms that perform the same steps you took on a localized dataset.

Problem solving

As a BI professional, having the ability to solve problems quickly and creatively is an incredibly important skill to successfully carry out complex BI projects. In our estimation, this is one skill that is the thread that ties all of the others together. Problem solving has many components to it, and the first involves the ability to *identify* and *understand* both potential problems and areas of improvement, and then couple that with developing and applying practical, cost-effective solutions based on data analysis.

Additionally, problem solving requires critical thinking, an ability to evaluate alternatives, and the courage to implement creative solutions quickly and effectively (especially if the problem is time-sensitive!). Problem solving also requires the ability to adapt to changing situations and make quick, effective decisions in an uncertain environment. Problem solving also requires the ability to collaborate with other departments and make data-driven decisions.

In the context of BI, it's important to combine that problem solving mindset with advanced data analysis and machine learning techniques to help you identify patterns and trends in large datasets, using the insights gained from that analysis to make informed decisions and improve operational efficiency and the effectiveness of business processes.

To summarize, problem solving is essential for success in challenging BI projects and requires a combination of technical skills, leadership, and critical thinking.

To help you develop your problem solving skills, we suggest trying the following in your day-to-day roles:

- **Practice makes perfect**: Take some time in your week to solve problems regularly to improve your skills (e.g., a crossword puzzle, Wordle, or a programming challenge)

- **Break down complex problems**: Divide large-scale, wide-reaching problems into smaller, more manageable parts first

- **Seek different perspectives**: Work on the problem from different angles and assess a variety of solutions

- **Collaborate with others**: Work with others to gain new insights and come up with innovative solutions

- **Think critically and creatively**: Try to develop unconventional solutions and "think outside the box"

- **Learn from failure**: Reflect on mistakes and failures and use them as opportunities for growth and improvement

- **Inform yourself**: Stay updated on new developments and the best practices in your field

- **Be patient and persistent**: Remember that developing effective problem solving skills takes time and continuous effort

Specific industry knowledge and subject matter expertise

There is no denying that domain expertise – that is, knowledge of a business – is the light that guides you in the dark. Subject matter experts are the ones that know what to look for and what to measure. For all of you who have no technical background but a great deal of business knowledge, you are also a great candidate to become proficient in BI, since you are capable of defining metrics that would make a business area, organization, or even an industry perform well. You also would be able to ascertain how data looks to make correct decisions. Learning about the specifics of a particular industry is out of the scope of this book, but we encourage you to evaluate yourself if you consider you have the required experience in your particular field. The more extensive your domain/industry knowledge, the greater the benefit for you as a BI expert.

Communication skills

Communication skills are extremely important in the context of BI. BI involves gathering and analyzing data to inform business decisions, and effective communication is crucial to convey the insights and recommendations that result from this analysis. Some of the skills you will need to develop in order to succeed in communicating about BI projects are as follows:

- **Clear presentation of findings**: BI professionals must be able to clearly present complex data insights and recommendations to both technical and non-technical stakeholders in a way that is easily understandable and digestible

- **Collaboration**: BI often requires collaboration with cross-functional teams, and effective communication skills are necessary to ensure that all stakeholders are on the same page and work toward a common goal

- **Influencing decision-makers**: Effective communication is crucial in convincing decision-makers to adopt recommendations based on data insights
- **Building relationships**: Strong communication skills can help BI professionals build strong relationships with stakeholders, which can be valuable in obtaining buy-in for their recommendations and insights

Communication skills play a critical role in the success of BI initiatives and can greatly impact the effectiveness and impact of data-driven decision making.

To help you enhance your communication skills, we suggest attempting the following techniques:

- **Practice active listening**: Give your full attention to the speaker, ask questions for clarification, and avoid interrupting
- **Speak clearly and concisely**: Use simple language, avoid technical jargon, and get to the point quickly
- **Improve your writing skills**: Write clearly and concisely, and proofread for clarity and accuracy (leverage technology wherever possible, making sure to use your word processing software's built-in spelling and grammar check)
- **Learn to adjust your communication style**: Adapt your communication style to different audiences and situations
- **Seek feedback**: Ask for feedback from others on your communication skills, and be open to constructive criticism
- **Use effective body language**: Be mindful of your body language because non-verbal communication can greatly impact the effectiveness of getting your point across, so use appropriate visual cues to help reinforce your message
- **Take courses or workshops**: Consider taking courses (online or in-person) or workshops to improve your communication skills, such as public speaking or persuasive writing
- **Observe and learn from others**: Pay attention to how great communicators deliver their message effectively, and try to incorporate what you learn into your own communication style

Developing strong, effective communication skills takes time and effort, so be persistent and keep practicing.

Statistical analysis

We may not need to be experts in statistics, and we do not need to write statistical formulas, because there are many available tools that will take care of that. However, as BI experts, we are required to know how and when to apply it. Statistical knowledge can be an advantage for BI because it provides a way to analyze data and make informed decisions based on that analysis. Statistics can help identify trends, patterns, and relationships in data that may not be immediately apparent. By using statistical methods, businesses can make predictions, test hypotheses, and assess the impact of decisions. This allows them to make data-driven decisions that are more likely to lead to success, rather than relying on intuition or guesswork. In short, statistical knowledge is a crucial tool to turn data into actionable insights in BI.

Becoming proficient in statistical analysis requires a combination of learning, practice, and experience. Here are some steps you can take to improve your skills:

- **Learn the fundamentals**: Study basic statistics concepts such as probability, descriptive statistics, inferential statistics, hypothesis testing, and regression analysis. There are many resources available, including online courses, textbooks, and educational websites.

- **Practice with real data**: Gain hands-on experience by working with real datasets and applying statistical methods to answer questions and make predictions.

- **Use software**: Familiarize yourself with statistical software such as R or Python, which can automate many calculations and help you visualize your results.

- **Collaborate with others**: Join a study group, or seek out a mentor who can help you deepen your understanding and provide feedback on your work.

- **Stay up-to-date**: Keep learning and reading about recent developments in the field of statistics and its applications. Attend workshops and conferences, or take online courses to stay up to date with the latest techniques and tools.

It's also important to note that proficiency in statistical analysis takes time and consistent effort, but with dedication and practice, you can become a skilled statistical analyst.

Technical knowledge

As the fishermen and explorers of the New World found out through various trials and tribulations, you cannot traverse the ocean without a proper boat and knowing how to navigate choppy waters. Similarly, when dealing with treacherous, murky oceans of data, the use of dependable tools is encouraged and *critical* to quickly turn around business problems. In this context, dependable tools are the ones that facilitate and speed up the process of analyzing data, since computers are faster at processing data than humans. This book will mention *some* (both authors agree that it is in the best interest of our readers to be as tool-agnostic as possible) of the tools and the basics to use them; however, we want to reiterate the importance of taking time to research and find which tool is right for your organization's needs.

At the time of writing this book, these are examples of tools used in BI:

- To move and transform data based on data modeling rules and designs, these are recommended:

  - DataStage
  - Informatica

- Fivetran

- Data Factory

- Database Migration Service

- Apache Airflow

- Stitch

- Talend

- dbt

- There are many tools available for modeling data and governance. Here are a few:

  - ER Studio

  - Erwin

  - Enterprise Architect

  - Paradigm

  - IDA

  - PowerDesigner

  - Terraform

  - DBeaver

  - Lucidchart

  - DbSchema Pro

- Some of the main vendors of data visualizations and enterprise solutions for BI are as follows:

  - Tableau

  - Power BI

  - Looker Studio

  - Superset

  - QuickSight

  - Qlik

  - ThoughtSpot

  - MicroStrategy

  - Sisense

- Oracle Analytics
- SAP Analytics
- Yellowfin
- Business Objects
- Cognos

As you can see, there are numerous tools, software, and options to start your journey in BI; for any one of these examples, a programming language such as SQL, Python, or R will complement your technical expertise by a considerable margin. Another thing to keep in mind is that many of these tools (especially any software that is open source) offer a free version you can play with. It is important to learn them and be able to use them properly. Take time to train on your preferred tool, as only practice can help you become proficient and pave the way to start working on real-life projects.

Business acumen

Business acumen refers to a person's understanding and knowledge of how businesses operate and the factors that contribute to their success. This includes an understanding of finance, strategy, market trends, and the competitive landscape.

Business acumen is important for BI because it allows individuals to put data into context and make informed decisions that are aligned with the overall goals of an organization. With a strong understanding of business operations and trends, individuals can better understand what data is relevant, what questions to ask, and how to interpret the results of their analysis.

Moreover, business acumen helps individuals to use data in a way that supports a business strategy, rather than just generating reports and visualizations. They can also understand how their insights can be leveraged to improve business performance and drive growth.

Business acumen is a crucial component of successful BI, as it enables individuals to turn data into actionable insights that support the success of an organization.

Keep up with innovation

Always innovate, research, and keep up to date with the latest technology, and get trained in it. Find out what the main issues in your BI world are and find tech that solves them. Automate and learn how to be lazy while productive. Don't implement new technologies just for the sake of innovation but because they really solve an existing problem, and always monitor their return on investment.

Potential entrances to the BI world

Now that you have some idea of what skills and technologies are important, you might still be asking yourself, how do I enter the BI world? We're ready to examine some plausible scenarios and find possible entrances to that skyscraper we described at the beginning of the chapter. Please keep in mind these are some ideas on how you could potentially approach starting a BI career given different situations.

Let's say you're an undergraduate student studying computer science, getting exposure to operating systems, database theory, and artificial intelligence for the first time. As someone just learning how to navigate the environment, you may be torn between the different disciplines and systems (i.e., networks, servers, programming languages, and **relational database management systems (RDBMSs)**). In this scenario, you might think that a good first step would be to get an internship within a BI department at a large multinational corporation to start getting a feel for how computer science is used in day-to-day operations. However, competing for a coveted internship at a highly sought-out company is sometimes a difficult and risky proposition without a guarantee of success. With that in mind, we surmise that a good starting point would be to learn how to extract, transform, and play around with data using a service such as Kaggle, or start with a simple approach, gather data around your life, make sense of the data, and keep looking for patterns. That being said, if you do manage to get an internship that might be non-BI related, you can still follow a similar process of collecting and analyzing statistics about the process taking place in that area. You could try doing it at a frequency of time that makes sense – that is, taking monthly snapshots of KPIs to measure a business unit's performance. Chart your results and keep track of trends.

Now, let's imagine that, instead, you are a business school graduate with several years of experience and an intermediate level of proficiency as a financial analyst, but your *technical* knowledge and skill set still needs some refinement. If you already have the ability and know-how to produce reports, then start gathering information on the critical KPIs for your business unit while keeping a monthly snapshot of these results (and, if possible, compare year over year). By creating these metrics on your own, you are able to showcase your data analysis capabilities and then potentially start working on your own BI projects. If there's not much chance to get hold of data, think about indicators of the actual work your team does – for example, how many activities each one of your team performs, or what the usual duration it takes for your team to finalize a project is. Find out more about your customers, internal or external, and engage with them to obtain some of this information.

If you are an IT professional, with a computer science background, you may find yourself programming an interface; you may need to understand how an application will store the data, or see whether there are any database rules or constraints your interface needs to enforce on the user. In cases like these, you learn the schematics of the data model, how the data flows, and how to better present it to the user. This is a great window for you to enter into the BI world. If real data is restricted to you, think about usage monitoring; you may want to track how much CPU, memory, or storage your application consumes and then enhance it accordingly. Along with that, tracking your users' peak hours and click activity could be a great source material for amazing analysis. This example applies to database administrators, database developers, server administrators, backend programmers, and so on. As long as you have the desire to measure performance, you will be able to find a window to enter into BI.

You may be a nurse, a teacher, a logistic coordinator, or a salesperson; you can always start your BI journey by measuring events and keeping track of those measures by any given frequency. What are the most critical times in the day, week, and month of patient traffic in a year? What subjects are students more proficient in? Which cost centers are slower to process input? Who are your most responsive customers? Understanding what the different processes involved in a BI project are can help you find out not only how to implement them in your current organization but also which ones align more with your skills, and which ones you will have to train yourself on.

BI roadmap

During a BI project, you will find a list of activities ordered almost in a sequential way, representing the flow of data throughout a pipeline. At the same time, these activities may belong to specific roles of their own; they are highly technical, and the use of modern tools is almost mandatory. Use this section of the book as a guide to position yourself and your skills along this roadmap. However, as with any other roadmap, you may want to go through all of the steps, but depending on your preferences, some of these may not be appealing to you. Skipping them is always an option, as the objective of this book is for you to find your path in the BI world.

The reason it is possible to skip some of these steps is due to the nature of the purpose. Some are a means to an end, meaning they are a necessary evil; if we could, we would avoid them altogether but, there are many impediments – computing power, memory, storage, even the laws of physics. Let's examine them one by one.

In general, the data we work with in BI comes from different sources, and transactional systems are the most common ones in an organization. A company may have an **enterprise resource planning (ERP)** system on which all transactions are created, involving internal cost centers and several business processes. All these transactions translate into computing costs in a database. The database can only handle so much when trying to input every single transaction happening across a company. Depending on the size of the company, this can scale up to unmeasurable amounts. Imagine for a second that while you try to read all that information and create reports and dashboards, thousands of employees enter information in the same database. The servers holding the database would collapse, and you may cause a lock on the database, halting all activity until the database administrators take care of it. It would be like trying to read a book at the same time the author is writing it. Because computers struggle to handle both writing and reading data simultaneously, ETL was born.

ETL developers

ETL, which stands for **extract, transform, and load**, is a data integration process that combines data from multiple sources into one data store, which typically gets loaded into a data warehouse. With the wide-scale adoption of cloud technologies, companies are taking advantage of the increased processing power, which is shifting towards ELT. However, either process has the same basic flow – a scheduled task/job will execute and *extract* a desired portion of data, then the data is *transformed* based on some logic (business requirements) that has been defined beforehand, and finally, it is *loaded* into a database, where the sole purpose is to allow analysts and developers to produce reports and dashboards. Generally speaking, this database is called a data warehouse, and it is typically large enough to hold all of a company's analytics sources. In the BI world, the responsibility for building these data pipelines may fall upon an ETL developer or data engineer, depending on the company.

Usually, an ETL developer would have to master SQL or, sometimes, a procedural SQL-based language such PL/SQL, T-SQL, or a programming language such as Python, Scala, or Java. The ETL developer may use tools such Talend, Informatica, or Fivetran. The ETL developer gathers requirements from business customers or data modelers and, after assessing the source of the data, analyzes the desired output and builds an algorithm or a process that will extract the data, performs the proper transformations, and then loads it to where the data will be consumed. Sometimes, this data may reach its final destination further down subsequent pipelines, depending on the needs of the projects and the architecture of the platforms.

Data architects

One part of working with tools is having an infrastructure that can hold and scale a workload derived from processing data. The main role of a data architect is to design and oversee the overall data strategy and architecture of an organization. This includes defining data structures and systems, ensuring data security and integrity, and ensuring the efficient and effective use of data to support business objectives. Data architects also work to align an organization's data strategy with its overall business strategy, and they collaborate with stakeholders from various departments to understand their data needs and requirements.

Data modelers

Gathering data needs and requirements is the art of translating business needs into computational parameters. Sometimes, this role is played by data modelers or even data analysts; they produce the necessary steps that developers need to take in order to generate the desired output the business requires, and they are responsible for the schematics and blueprints of data structures and the relationships between them. A data modeler is responsible for creating, maintaining, and managing conceptual, logical, and physical data models for an organization. This involves analyzing the data requirements of various business processes, defining data elements and relationships, and creating visual representations of the data structure.

The data modeler works closely with data architects, business analysts, and stakeholders to ensure that the data models accurately reflect the business requirements and align with the overall data strategy. The ultimate goal of a data modeler is to create a clear and efficient data architecture that supports an organization's data management and decision-making processes.

BI developers

When it comes to decision-making processes, reports and dashboards are the main tools used to help in this goal. Building a good tabular report and the use of techniques in data visualization help us find accurate answers to important business questions. A BI developer is responsible for designing, developing, and maintaining a company's BI systems and reporting tools. Their main objective is to help organizations make informed decisions by transforming raw data into meaningful and actionable information.

The role of a BI developer involves working closely with business stakeholders to understand their data needs and requirements and then creating and implementing appropriate data models, data warehouses, and reporting systems. They also design, develop, and deploy BI reports, dashboards, and data visualizations to meet an organization's reporting needs.

In addition, the BI developer is responsible for ensuring the accuracy, completeness, and reliability of the data and reports, as well as testing and maintaining the BI systems to ensure they work optimally. The ultimate goal of a BI developer is to provide stakeholders with the information they need to make informed business decisions and improve organizational performance.

A BI developer may work with report developers that usually are business analysts, and they are the ones producing reports and making use of data visualization techniques. Data visualization is the graphical representation of data and information in a visual format. It's used to present complex and large amounts of data in a way that is easy to understand and interpret. The goal of data visualization is to help people see patterns, trends, and insights in data that would be difficult or impossible to detect in raw data form. Data visualization can take many forms, including charts, graphs, maps, and infographics, and is often used not only in BI and data analysis but also in scientific research. By effectively visualizing data, organizations can make better informed decisions and communicate information more effectively.

Data scientists

In analytics, there's a ladder that dictates how an organization should progress in the use of data. Analytics and BI take care of the past and present state of a business process, but **machine learning** (**ML**) or **artificial intelligence** (**AI**) take care of the analysis of the future. For this reason, BI has become the foundation on which data science can thrive successfully in an organization; although it is out of the scope of this book, it is important to understand how BI fits into data science, and vice versa. The progression that connects them is illustrated in the following figure:

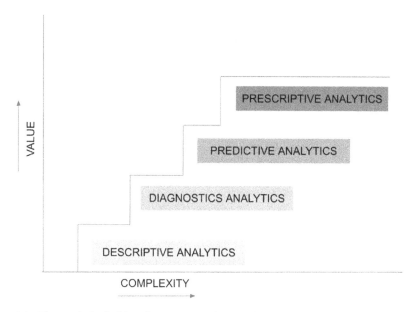

Figure 1.1 – The analytics ladder allows us to understand the value generated from interloping from traditional BI to data science, as well as the complexity it requires to achieve it

Data scientists exist to turn data into insights and action. They are responsible for using data to answer complex business questions, make predictions, and identify opportunities for improvement. Data scientists use a combination of mathematical, statistical, and computational techniques to process, analyze, and interpret large and complex datasets.

The role of data scientists has become increasingly important as organizations collect more and more data from a variety of sources. Data scientists use their skills to extract valuable insights from this data and present them in a way that is easy for others to understand and use. They help organizations make better informed decisions and drive improvements in areas such as marketing, product development, and customer experience.

Data scientists also play a key role in developing and implementing machine learning models, which can be used to automate decision-making processes, improve prediction's and enhance operational efficiency. The existence of data scientists is critical to the success of organizations that look to leverage data and analytics to drive business growth and competitiveness.

BI and data science are related fields that share the goal of using data to improve business performance and decision making. However, they differ in terms of the methods, techniques, and tools they use to achieve this goal.

BI focuses on providing information and insights through reporting, dashboards, and data visualization tools. The main objective of BI is to support informed decision-making by providing stakeholders with access to accurate, relevant, and timely information.

Data science, on the other hand, is a more advanced and in-depth field that uses advanced mathematical and statistical methods to analyze and understand data. The goal of data science is to extract valuable insights and knowledge from data, make predictions, and identify patterns and trends that can be used to improve business outcomes. Data scientists use a range of techniques such as machine learning, data mining, and predictive analytics to achieve this goal.

In summary, BI provides the information that stakeholders need to make informed decisions, while data science provides the deeper insights and understanding needed to drive innovation and improvement. Both fields are complementary and work together to support effective data-driven decision-making in organizations, and it is critical that both are built over robust and stable processes to avoid data conflicts.

This is the reason why we find many roles in the BI space; every role is derived from the notion that data follows different paths and makes many stops. Most of these are projects of their own and represent milestones for entire organizations. The larger the company, the larger the teams, so you can have a huge conglomerate with an army of data engineers just for the purpose of building data pipelines of a certain number of tables, or a start-up with a one-man army doing ETL development, data modeling, report development, and more. In your BI career, you may want to pick a path or a specific role, depending on what you like the most.

Technology solutions stack

Technology is the vessel of our projects, and navigating the ocean of data requires mastering the right tools and skills. A typical technology stack consists of the following components:

- **Data warehousing**: A centralized repository that stores large amounts of data from various sources.

  Becoming proficient in designing data warehouses requires a combination of theoretical knowledge and practical experience. Here is some guidance you can follow to improve your skills:

  - **Gain a strong understanding of data warehousing concepts and methodologies**: This includes understanding the differences between transactional and analytical systems, the basics of dimensional modeling, and the differences between star and snowflake schemas. There are many philosophies out there on how to properly design a data warehouse; researching them will improve your understanding and provide use cases for each of them. Examples include Ralph Kimball, Bill Inmon, and Dan Linstedt.

  - **Study the architecture and design of data warehouses**: Learn about the different components of data warehouse architecture, such as the data store, ETL process, **online analytical processing (OLAP)** cube, and data marts, and how they interact with each other.

  - **Get hands-on experience with designing data warehouses**: This can involve working on real-world projects or working through example scenarios and exercises. You can also use tools such as Microsoft SQL Server, Oracle, or Amazon Redshift to build and experiment with different design choices.

- **Keep up to date with the latest technologies and industry trends**: Data warehousing technology is constantly evolving, so it's important to stay informed about new tools and techniques. Read industry blogs, attend conferences and webinars, and participate in online forums to stay up to date.

- **Network with others in the field**: Connect with other data warehousing professionals through online communities and meetups, and consider seeking out a mentor who can provide guidance and feedback.

By following these steps, you can develop the theoretical knowledge and practical skills you need to become an expert in designing data warehouses.

- **ETL tools**: These tools are used to extract data from multiple sources, cleanse and transform it, and load it into a data warehouse.

ETL Tools require a variety of skills from developers:

- **Database skills**: ETL developers should have a strong understanding of relational databases and SQL. They should be able to write complex queries to extract data from databases and be familiar with database design and normalization concepts.

- **Data integration and transformation**: ETL developers should be skilled at transforming data from one format to another, including mapping data from source systems to target data models. They should be familiar with various data integration techniques, such as batch processing, real-time integration, and incremental updates.

- **ETL tools and technologies**: ETL developers should be familiar with the most common ETL tools, such as Talend, Informatica, and Microsoft **SQL Server Integration Services (SSIS)**. They should understand how to use these tools to extract, transform, and load data.

- **Data warehousing**: ETL developers should have a good understanding of data warehousing concepts, including dimensional modeling, star and snowflake schemas, and OLAP cubes.

- **BI and reporting**: ETL developers should have an understanding of BI and reporting concepts, such as data visualization, report writing, and dashboard creation.

- **Problem solving and critical thinking**: ETL developers should be able to identify and solve problems related to data integration and transformation. They should be able to critically analyze data to identify trends, patterns, and anomalies.

- **Communication and collaboration**: ETL developers should be able to work closely with other members of the IT team, as well as with business stakeholders, to understand their data needs and requirements. They should be able to communicate complex technical concepts to non-technical stakeholders.

- **Project management**: ETL developers should be familiar with project management methodologies, such as agile and waterfall, and be able to manage their own time and workload effectively.

By developing these skills, you can position yourself to be a successful ETL developer and play an important role in designing and implementing effective data integration and warehousing solutions.

- **Data visualization tools**: These tools are used to create interactive charts, dashboards, and reports to visualize data clearly and concisely. Examples include Tableau, Power BI, and QlikView.

Building good data visualizations requires a combination of technical skills, design skills, and storytelling abilities. Here are some key skills that are important for this role:

  - **Data analysis and statistics**: A good understanding of data analysis and statistics is essential to create effective data visualizations. This includes the ability to aggregate, summarize, and analyze data, and to identify trends, patterns, and outliers.

  - **Visualization software**: Familiarity with visualization software, such as Tableau, Power BI, and QlikView, is critical to building high-quality visualizations. A good understanding of the capabilities of these tools, and how to use them effectively, is essential.

  - **Design skills**: A good eye for design is important to create aesthetically pleasing and effective visualizations. Knowledge of color theory, typography, and composition is important to create visualizations that are easy to understand and memorable.

  - **Storytelling**: Data visualizations are often used to tell a story about data. Good data visualizers should be able to identify the key insights in the data and communicate them effectively through the use of visualizations.

  - **Technical skills**: Familiarity with programming languages such as Python and R is important for data visualization, as these languages can be used to automate the process of creating visualizations and integrate visualizations into other applications.

  - **Domain knowledge**: A good understanding of the business domain and the context in which the data was collected is important for creating visualizations that are relevant and meaningful.

  - **Communication skills**: The ability to communicate the insights gained from the data visualizations to both technical and non-technical stakeholders is critical. Good data visualizers should be able to explain the results of their analysis in a clear, concise, and accessible manner.

By developing these skills, you can position yourself to be a successful data visualizer and play an important role in making data accessible, understandable, and actionable.

- **Reporting tools**: These tools are used to generate reports from the data stored in a data warehouse. Examples include Crystal Reports, SAP Lumira, and IBM Cognos. To build good reports in a typical tool, you need to know your business and have knowledge of your domain. Good communication can be beneficial if you don't possess the previous attributes but work closely with a subject matter expert.

- **Analytics tools**: These are tools used for data analysis and modeling. Examples include R, Python, and SAS. Mathematical and statistical knowledge is a must and cannot be compromised, as are good analysis skills and an eye for spotting patterns and trends.

- **Collaboration tools**: These are tools used to share data and insights with others, such as chat and document collaboration tools. Examples include Slack, Microsoft Teams, and Google Drive.

- **Database management systems**: Relational databases such as Oracle, MySQL, and PostgreSQL, and NoSQL databases such as MongoDB and Cassandra, are used to store and manage data. This skill is straight out a technical requirement that can be complemented with good organization and time management skills, especially when it comes to planning for risk and implementing data loss prevention mechanisms.

This technology stack can vary, depending on the specific requirements and needs of a business, but these components form the foundation of a typical BI solution. A whole BI organization may be in charge of the aforementioned architecture components, but, depending on the company, it may be supported by more than one cost center. A team of data engineers will build ETL pipelines, and a team of **Database Administrators** (**DBAs**) will administer the databases. The synergy between all these teams or team members is critical to ensure success in the delivery of projects and maintenance. Typical data architecture refers to the overall design and organization of a company's data assets, including data sources, data storage, and data processing. It provides a blueprint for how data should flow through an organization, from its creation to its final use. The following are the key components of a typical data architecture:

- **Data sources**: This includes all the systems, applications, and databases that generate data, such as CRMs, ERP systems, and web logs

- **Data storage**: This includes data warehouses, data marts, and data lakes where data is stored in a centralized location

- **Data processing**: This includes ETL tools, data pipelines, and data processing engines used to manipulate and cleanse data before it is stored

- **Data analytics**: This includes data modeling, statistical analysis, and data visualization tools used to extract insights from data

- **Data governance**: This includes policies, processes, and tools used to manage data quality, data security, and data privacy

- **Data access**: This includes the tools and systems used to access, retrieve, and share data within an organization

Architecture should be flexible and scalable, allowing an organization to grow and evolve over time while still being able to effectively manage its data assets. The exact components of a typical data architecture may, vary depending on the specific requirements and needs of a company, but these components form the foundation of a comprehensive data architecture solution. While the aforementioned is a great outline of enterprise BI solutions, as a non-technical reader, you might wonder what approach you should take. A better way to answer this is to go through non-technical analysis cases from different industries and implement the same steps according to your needs.

Non-technical data analysis

The path into BI is filled with data analysis, and it's a path we all walk every day. To say that BI is a private field is to disregard the very nature of human intuition. In this book, we say no to gatekeepers, as it closes the opportunity for non-technical fields to experiment and create a sandbox of new ideas where analysis mechanisms emerge from within. There are many examples in which a scientist of a specific field invents their own visualization technique that then is distributed and taught everywhere. You don't have to create anything from scratch, as we all walk on the shoulders of giants. This book encourages anyone from any field to make use of BI techniques, such as data analysis, to explore more about their work or industry.

Case 1

A nurse can use data to perform better in many ways. For example, consider a nurse working in a hospital who is responsible for administering medication to patients. The nurse can use data to improve the medication administration process in the following way:

- **Collecting data**: The nurse can use **electronic health records** (EHRs) to collect data on each patient's medication history, including the type of medication, dosage, frequency, and any adverse reactions.

- **Analyzing data**: The nurse can analyze data to identify patterns and trends in medication administration. For example, they may notice that a particular medication is frequently associated with adverse reactions and can adjust the administration process accordingly.

- **Improving processes**: Based on the analysis of the data, the nurse can make improvements to the medication administration process to ensure that patients receive the right medication at the right time, in the right dose, and with minimal adverse reactions.

- **Monitoring outcomes**: The nurse can also use data to monitor the outcomes of the improved medication administration process. For example, they can track the number of adverse reactions and compare it to the previous period to assess the impact of the improvements.

A nurse can improve the safety and quality of care for patients, reduce errors and adverse reactions, and provide more effective treatment thanks to the use of data analysis.

Case 2

A UPS delivery driver can use data to perform better in many ways, such as the following:

- **Route optimization**: The delivery driver can use data from GPS tracking and their delivery history to optimize their route and minimize the distance they need to travel, saving time and fuel

- **Package tracking**: The driver can use data from the UPS package tracking system to monitor the status of packages and know when they need to be delivered

- **Customer preferences**: The driver can use data from customer preferences, such as the preferred delivery time or location, to ensure that deliveries are made according to the customer's preferences, improving their satisfaction

- **Time management**: The driver can use data from their delivery history and GPS tracking to monitor their delivery time and make adjustments to their schedule as needed

- **Safety and efficiency**: The driver can also use data from the vehicle's onboard computer, such as fuel consumption and speed, to monitor their driving habits and make adjustments to improve safety and efficiency

By using data in these ways, the UPS delivery driver can improve the efficiency and accuracy of their deliveries, increase customer satisfaction, and operate more safely on the road.

Case 3

A biology professor can use data to perform better in many ways, such as the following:

- **Research**: The professor can use data from experiments and observations to analyze and interpret the results of their research. By using statistical analysis and visualization tools, the professor can gain deeper insights into their research questions and make more informed conclusions.

- **Teaching**: The professor can use data to improve their teaching methods and better engage students. For example, they can use data from student performance and feedback to identify areas where students struggle and adjust their teaching methods accordingly.

- **Collaboration**: The professor can use data to collaborate with other researchers and institutions. For example, they can use data from shared databases to identify common research interests and opportunities for collaboration.

- **Grant proposals**: The professor can use data to demonstrate the impact and significance of their research in grant proposals. By presenting data that supports the importance of their research, the professor can increase their chances of securing funding.

- **Outreach**: The professor can use data to communicate the results of their research to a wider audience. By visualizing data in an accessible and engaging way, the professor can make their research more accessible and understandable to the general public.

There are many ways in which the biology professor can improve their research, teaching, collaboration, grant proposals, and outreach and have a greater impact in their field with the help of data analysis.

Case 4

A store manager can use data to perform better in many ways, such as the following:

- **Sales analysis**: The manager can use data from sales records to analyze the performance of the store, including which products are selling well and which are not. This information can help the manager make informed decisions about inventory management, pricing, and promotions.

- **Customer behavior**: The manager can use data from customer tracking systems, such as loyalty card information or website analytics, to better understand their customers and their buying habits. This information can help the manager improve the customer experience and increase sales.

- **Employee performance**: The manager can use data from time and attendance systems, as well as customer feedback, to monitor and evaluate the performance of their employees. This information can help the manager identify areas for improvement and provide more effective training and coaching.

- **Inventory management**: The manager can use data from inventory systems to monitor stock levels and sales patterns. This information can help the manager make informed decisions about when to reorder products, reducing the risk of stockouts and overstocking.

- **Loss prevention**: The manager can use data from security systems, such as cameras and loss prevention systems, to monitor a store for theft and other security issues. By analyzing the data, the manager can identify patterns and trends, taking steps to prevent losses.

Data analysis can help the store manager to improve sales, customer satisfaction, employee performance, inventory management, and loss prevention, ultimately increasing the overall efficiency and profitability of the store.

Case 5

A firefighter can use data to perform better in many ways, such as the following:

- **Fire behavior analysis**: The firefighter can use data from simulating building and forest fires, thermal imaging cameras, and other sources to better understand the behavior of fires (i.e., how fuel, weather, and topography interact) to make more informed decisions about potential life-saving firefighting strategies.

- **Risk assessment**: The firefighter can use data from building plans, fire code violations, and other sources to assess the risk of fires and develop pre-incident plans. This information can help the firefighter respond more effectively in emergency situations.

- **Equipment management**: The firefighter can use data from equipment maintenance records to track the condition and readiness of firefighting equipment. This information can help the firefighter ensure that their equipment is in good working order and ready for use in an emergency.

- **Training**: The firefighter can use data from training records and performance evaluations to monitor their skills and training progress. This information can help the firefighter identify areas for improvement and receive targeted training to increase their effectiveness on the job.

- **Incident response**: The firefighter can use data from incident reports and fire department communications to respond more effectively to fire incidents. By analyzing the data, the firefighter can identify trends and patterns and take steps to improve their response and mitigate the impact of fires.

Even though the firefighter has no technical skills, through the use of data analysis, they can improve their understanding of fire behavior, risk assessment, equipment management, training, and incident response, providing more effective and efficient fire protection.

As you can see, there are many examples in which you are exposed to data and presented with the opportunity to enter one of the side doors that leads into the building of BI. Being able to identify these opportunities is key for you to understand which of your skills match the requirements and which you need to gain and train for.

Finding a job if you are not experienced can be challenging, but with offline practice, personal projects, and training material, you could identify a position that leads you to BI as a career. Find jobs that have a gentle introduction to data analysis or report development; entry-level jobs may be the first ones to consider, depending on your level of confidence. The more no-code tools and the fewer raw languages you require, the easier it is for you to grasp how the different data-handling mechanisms work.

No-code (or a no-code tool, to be more practical) is a method and a movement of programming that does not necessarily involve writing code but, instead, works with **graphic user interface (GUI)** tools.

Summary

The best advice on how to enter the BI world is to enter it by any means – through personal projects, through work or a "side quest" in your organization, or through a problem you identified in either your life or at work. Data can always help, as data is the language used in the BI world.

To wrap things up – in a typical BI project, we can find several steps, and each one is handled by a BI role, and each BI role requires the development of certain skills to be successful.

At the same time, a BI project is part of a larger picture we call a BI roadmap, and it is driven by the organic inclination of companies to generate value. A traditional BI roadmap, which every organization should have in place, should attempt to interpolate from basic analytics, including BI reports, dashboards, and ETL development, all the way to data science projects to predict internal and external factors in the operation of your organization.

Each role and BI component has specific technical complexity that will help you assess your skill and determine where you fit best. Once you understand what your capabilities are, it's time to find out how to leverage them and work on improving them. This is the starting point; the next step is to become proficient.

2

How to Become Proficient in Analyzing Data

At this point, you might be working for an organization or are about to start a project, and you are wondering what to do first and how to keep improving your skills. Like everything in life, we have to take it step by step. This chapter will focus on a methodical approach to navigate through the ocean of data. Remember that it is easy to get lost in the different analysis techniques and methodologies, but it is imperative that you develop your own discipline and rhythm. In this book, we will give you some advice and examples on how to tackle a data project, the minimum sequential steps you can take, and a routine if you do that will serve as the basis for your future projects.

This is not a final recipe, nor is it supposed to be the norm, but it will help you create, as quickly as possible, a picture of the roadmap your data journey will take you through, thus helping you navigate it. These are minimal common-sense steps that will spark your creativity. Most of your work is not quantifiable and is not an algorithm; it takes deviations, branches out and comes back to the original point, and moves far away to a different path. This is supposed to give a sense of order to a chaotic enterprise.

Building a taxonomy of your data sources

The initial and imperative step is to construct a comprehensive taxonomy of your data sources. Without any delay, dedicate yourself to gathering all the relevant data sources, and meticulously sketch out a well-structured diagram that depicts the interdependencies and relationships within the data flow, across the various repositories it encounters. By creating a clear visual representation of this data ecosystem, you will gain valuable insights into the origins, transformations, and destinations of your data, facilitating a more organized and systematic approach to data management.

Building a taxonomy of your data sources involves organizing your data into a hierarchical structure that reflects its relationships and dependencies:

- **Identify the scope and purpose of your taxonomy**: Determine the purpose of the taxonomy and what it will be used for. Decide on the level of detail and granularity you need for your taxonomy.

- **Collect information about your data sources**: Gather information about all your data sources, including databases, files, applications, and systems. Identify the attributes that describe each data source, such as type, format, subject matter, and frequency of updates.

- **Categorize your data sources**: Identify the categories and subcategories that your data sources belong to. Create a hierarchy that reflects the relationships between the categories and subcategories.

- **Define the relationships between the categories**: Determine how the categories and subcategories are related to each other. For example, a database of customer information might be related to a sales system and a marketing system.

- **Create a classification scheme**: Develop a set of rules and guidelines to classify data sources. This will ensure that new data sources can be easily categorized and added to the taxonomy.

- **Test and refine the taxonomy**: Test the taxonomy with a small sample of data sources to ensure that it reflects the flow as expected. Refine the taxonomy as needed to ensure that it accurately reflects the relationships between your data sources. Find leaks and adjust for possible branches that data hangs from.

Technically speaking, this translates into finding logs and monitoring data pipelines. However, this might be complicated, as you may not have access to these resources. In a worst-case scenario, your data sources consist of a simple file in your possession that some data engineer lands in your inbox, so what would we do next in this scenario?

- Ask where it comes from.

- Ask with what frequency it gets generated.

- Ask how long it takes to generate.

- Find out what other processes or data sources are involved in its creation.

- Find out whether the source is larger or smaller. Is it an aggregate?

- Start mapping and demanding information to map out and reach other levels in your taxonomy.

At the end of this exercise, you will have a sort of sequence that is missing lots of steps and levels, but it is like a candle; the more you navigate, the more you light up with your inquiries. The whole map of data sources often is a convoluted one and is designed to please specific situations, rather than a holistic solution that prioritizes data flow efficiency. There are many reasons why this happens, but that's what makes this exercise even more important. It will encourage you to ask more questions. Having a whole image of the map in mind (as shown in the following figure) will help you find the paths where data flows, improving the gaps in your knowledge.

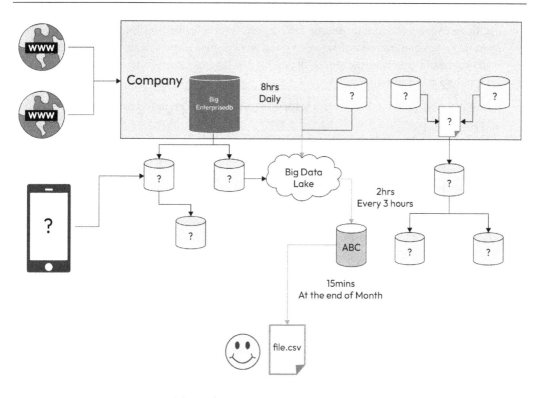

Figure 2.1 – A typical data infrastructure showing the unknown paths data takes

Gather all the facts at your disposal, and like a detective, put them in sequence. Once you hit a wall, like a rat in a maze, find your way around by asking the teams involved in those unknown systems. In the scenario portrayed in the preceding diagram, this is what we know so far as a new data analyst at Big Corp X:

- You now have a data.csv file
- It comes from database ABC as an aggregate table called agg_data
- This table pulls from a data lake called Big Data Lake
- This data lake also gets data from a transactional system called Big Enterprise System

Building a taxonomy of your data sources is important in a data project for several reasons, as listed here:

- **Improved data management**: A taxonomy can help you better organize and manage your data sources. It can help you identify data redundancies, data quality issues, and gaps in data coverage. By having a clear understanding of your data sources, you can make more informed decisions about how to collect, store, and analyze your data.

- **Enhanced data analysis**: With a taxonomy in place, you can more easily perform data analysis across multiple data sources. A taxonomy can help you identify relationships and dependencies between data sources and select the most appropriate data sources for your analysis.

- **Facilitate collaboration**: A taxonomy can help facilitate collaboration among team members. By having a standardized way of organizing and labeling data sources, team members can more easily share and communicate about data. This can lead to more efficient and effective data analysis and decision-making.

- **Better decision-making**: By having a taxonomy in place, you can more easily identify patterns and trends in your data and make more informed decisions based on this information. A taxonomy can help you identify which data sources are most relevant to a particular business question and can help you ensure that you use the most accurate and complete data available.

Building a taxonomy of your data sources is important in a data project because it can improve data management, enhance data analysis, facilitate collaboration, and lead to better decision-making. At the end of this exercise, you will have a clear idea of where to go and who to ask for any data-related questions. It is not about knowing everything in terms of data but, instead, knowing where you need to get information from in order to make your analysis better.

Here are the steps on how to build an effective data model of your data sources:

1. **Define your business needs**: What are you trying to accomplish with your data model? What data do you need to collect and store? What questions do you need to answer?

2. **Identify your data sources**: Where is your data coming from? What format is it in?

3. **Understand your data**: What are the different types of data you have? What are the relationships between the data?

4. **Design your data model**: Create a diagram that shows how your data is related.

5. **Implement your data model**: Create the tables and columns in your database.

6. **Test your data model**: Make sure that you can access and use your data.

7. **Maintain your data model**: As your data changes, you need to update your data model accordingly.

Now that you have created a map and have an idea of where data is located at every step of the pipeline, it is time for you to explore it. Doing it manually would be a waste of energy when we have modern BI tools that excel beyond our capabilities. The question here is not only how to pick the best one but also a more general one – what features you should use in order to allow you a thorough exploration of the data.

How to use a BI tool to explore data

There are many BI tools and programming languages that will help you along the way to visualize and explore data in many ways. In *Chapter 5*, we will discuss some of the tools out there in the market. In this section, we will discuss how to use them. Regardless of the tool type, there are data manipulation techniques that every data tool should do as a minimum.

As we define each of these, we will discuss the tool-less alternative and find the cost-benefit of using a BI tool to perform each of these. There are two basic concepts we need to understand before moving on – **metrics** and **attributes**. These can also be unveiled by asking *What do we want to measure?* and *How do we want to describe such a measurement?*

For example, if we measure *sales by region*, what are we measuring? Sales. What describes such measurements? Regions. This basic statement, although simplistic, is the basis of every analysis and exploration. Many complex analyses will derive from asking such questions. With additions, filters, and other types of calculations, you can make a more robust report.

Another basic term we need to understand is **granularity**. Granularity in **Business Intelligence (BI)** refers to the level of detail or the degree of aggregation of the data that is analyzed. It refers to the size of the individual units of data that are examined.

For example, if you analyze sales data, the granularity can be at the level of individual transactions or a higher level of aggregation, such as monthly sales, quarterly sales, or annual sales. The level of granularity can have a significant impact on the insights that can be derived from the data. Granularity may be accompanied by a temporal dimension. It is important to notice the difference because repeating a record over time doesn't mean the granularity changes if the analysis is made using different measures of time (i.e., year, month, or day).

Here's a mental exercise on granularity.

If we have a dataset that describes employees' performance, each record could represent how many sales we had in a department by month. Each row has a sales amount, a department ID, and the number of employees.

Granularity level: department

Month	Department ID	Number of Employees	Sales Amount
January 2023	C24	14	57,324
January 2023	C25	19	25,888
February 2023	C24	15	62,108
February 2023	C25	19	27,305

Figure 2.2 – A table depicting the granularity at the department level by month. In this table, granularity shows when a row is unique, and there are no two rows with the same department ID in a given month

The temporal unit of measurement here is month, so we can expect departments to repeat or not every month. Different model techniques may repeat a department with zero sales in a given month, but this will totally depend on the preferences of the design. Zero sales could mean no sales, but on some occasions, this may represent sales that add up to zero for many reasons (discounts, gifts, promotions, or devolutions).

Now, if we want to analyze on a more detailed level, we could change the level of granularity to the employee; every record would have the following: **Employee ID**, **Department ID**, **Sales Amount**, and **Date**.

Granularity level: employee

Employee ID	Department ID	Sales Amount	Date
11401	C24	1,502	01/01/2023
11402	C24	899	01/15/2023
11403	C25	902	02/07/2023
11404	C25	7,205	02/24/2023

Figure 2.3 – A table depicting granularity at the employee level. In this table, granularity shows when a row is unique. There are no two rows with the same employee ID on a given date, and sales are added up and stored daily

The temporal unit now is Date, a day in the life of a salesperson. Again, many experts in *dimensional modeling* may offer different ways to represent this; some may require each individual sale during a day, and some would show the summary of sales by an employee during that day.

Can we go one level further down? Certainly – let's imagine now records storing sales of every product by every employee on a given date. This is exactly the kind of analysis we could find in **master-detail modeling**. This is where the header of the sale may have a summary of what was sold and the detail level contains each individual product, itemized with the proper measurements of such sale – for example, quantity, **stock-keeping unit (SKU)**, and unit of measurement.

In BI, master-detail modeling is a data modeling technique used to represent the hierarchical relationships between data entities. It involves creating a relationship between two tables or datasets, where one table is the master and the other is the detail.

The master table contains the main data elements, while the detail table contains the related data elements that are associated with the main data elements. For example, in a sales analysis, the master table may contain information about sales transactions, while the detail table may contain information about the products sold in each transaction.

The master-detail relationship is typically created by defining a primary key in the master table and a foreign key in the detail table. The foreign key is used to link the detailed data to the corresponding master data.

Master-detail relationships are often used in reporting and analysis to drill down from summary information to more detailed information. For example, a report may show total sales by product category, with the ability to drill down to see the sales by individual products within each category.

Master-detail relationships are also used in data visualization tools to create interactive dashboards and reports. By using the master-detail relationship, a user can interactively explore the data, filter it, and drill down to view more detailed information as needed.

Master-detail relationships are an important data modeling technique in BI, allowing for the flexible and powerful analysis and reporting of hierarchical data structures.

As you can see, granularity can go up and aggregate detailed data, but it definitely can go down to levels that you can find deep inside an **online transactional processing** (**OLTP**) when your customers require it. A high level of granularity means that data is analyzed at a more detailed level, which can provide more specific insights but may require more time and effort to analyze. On the other hand, a lower level of granularity means that the data is analyzed at a more summarized level, which can provide a broader view of the data but may miss out on important details.

The choice of granularity depends on the specific business problem and the goals of the analysis. Generally, the level of granularity should be chosen based on the level of detail required to support the business decisions that need to be made. Data modelers and architects may decide to specify a low granularity level even though reports and dashboards are shown at the department, organization, or even company level. Part of their job involves building future-proof data structures; hence, they may find it advantageous to define a fine granularity level so that other analyses become supportable when the business requires it. However, modeling techniques are out of the scope of this book.

By understanding metrics, attributes or dimensions, and granularity, we can extrapolate to other concepts that follow these three, as they represent the lowest level in terms of "data hierarchy." Now, we go up, and **aggregations** are at the next level. In BI, aggregations refer to the process of summarizing or grouping data into higher-level units, such as totals, averages, counts, or percentages. The purpose of aggregation is to make data more manageable, understandable, and actionable.

Aggregations are used to reduce the volume of data to be analyzed so that it can be processed more efficiently and effectively. By summarizing data into higher-level units, it becomes easier to identify patterns, trends, and outliers in the data.

For example, in a sales analysis, aggregating data by month or by product category can help identify which products are selling well and which ones are not. Aggregations can also be used to compare performance over time or across different regions or customer segments.

Aggregations can be performed at different levels of detail, depending on the business needs and the data available. Aggregations can be pre-calculated and stored in a data warehouse, or they can be calculated on the fly using BI tools and technologies.

A BI tool should be able to create aggregations with little to no performance issues, as a good data model is based on the premise that users can take advantage of the aggregation engine behind a BI tool. An example of aggregations in different technologies is shown here:

For SQL, you can have aggregation at the following levels:

- **Aggregation at a departmental level**:

```
Select region, organization, department, sum(amount) as sales_
amount
From sales_table
Group by region, organization, department
```

- **Aggregation at an organization level:**

```
Select region, organization, sum(amount) as sales_amount
From sales_table
Group by region, organization
```

- **Aggregation at a regional level:**

```
Select region, sum(amount) as sales_amount
From sales_table
Group by region
```

Consider doing the same operation in Excel, as shown in the following screenshot. You can use the interface to aggregate at different levels and obtain the same result:

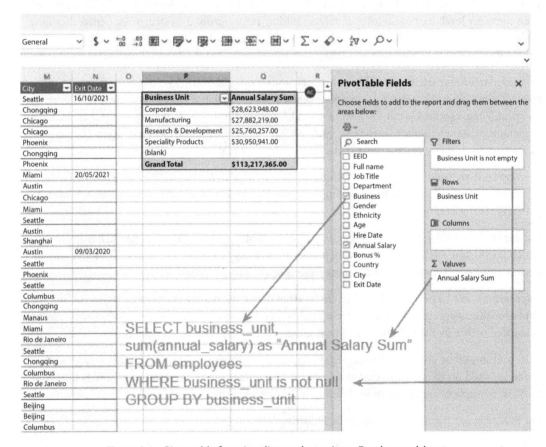

Figure 2.4 – Pivot table functionality, as shown in an Excel spreadsheet

If you want to make large and complex datasets more manageable and meaningful, thus enabling better decision-making based on actionable insights, aggregations are the BI technology that will achieve it.

When picking the right tool, you have to make sure you can perform these basic activities:

- Creating metrics or calculations
- Analyzing them by dimensions
- Exploring granularity
- Aggregating data to different levels

Now that we know we can create a report with aggregations, calculations, and attributes from a certain granularity, the report itself should have some level of interaction with a user. This interaction sometimes allows the user to navigate the data in an easier way and, at the same time, get every metric to recalculate for the different scenarios required. We call this **drilling down** and **rolling up**.

In BI, drilling down and rolling up are techniques used to navigate through hierarchical data structures and analyze data at different levels of detail.

Drilling down refers to the process of moving from a higher-level summary of data to a lower-level detail. For example, starting with a report that shows total sales by region, drilling down would involve clicking on a specific region to see the sales by country, and then clicking on a specific country to see the sales by city.

Rolling up, on the other hand, refers to the process of moving from a lower-level detail to a higher-level summary. For example, starting with a report that shows sales by city, rolling up would involve aggregating the data to show the sales by region, and then by country.

Drilling down and rolling up are often used together to analyze data at multiple levels of detail. By drilling down to lower levels of detail, analysts can gain insights into the factors that drive overall trends. By rolling up to higher levels of summary, analysts can identify patterns and trends across different regions or segments.

Drilling down and rolling up can be performed manually by analysts using BI tools, or they can be automated through the use of drill-down and roll-up functionality in reporting and analysis tools.

Overall, drilling down and rolling up are important techniques in BI that enable analysts to explore data at different levels of detail, gaining insights that can inform decision-making and drive business performance.

A successful tool should allow us to navigate these data structures up (the aggregation levels) and down (the granularity) with different dimensions and the recalculation of metrics, helped by modeling techniques. One modeling technique a BI tool should allow us to create is known as **hierarchies**. In BI, a hierarchy is a way of organizing data elements into a logical structure that reflects their relationships and dependencies. Hierarchies are used to represent complex data relationships in a simplified and intuitive way, making it easier for users to navigate and analyze the data.

A hierarchy consists of a series of levels, with each level representing a different category or dimension of data. For example, in a sales analysis, a hierarchy may be defined as follows:

- **Level 1**: **Year**
- **Level 2**: **Quarter**
- **Level 3**: **Month**
- **Level 4**: **Week**
- **Level 5**: **Day**

Each level in the hierarchy contains a set of members, which represent the values for that level. For example, the members for the month level might include January, February, and March.

Hierarchies can be used to organize data for reporting and analysis and to facilitate drilling down and rolling up through different levels of detail. For example, a user might start by looking at total sales for the year, and then drill down to see the sales by quarter, month, week, and day.

Hierarchies can also be used to define relationships between different data elements. For example, a hierarchy might be defined that relates products to product categories, which in turn are related to product departments.

Hierarchies are really an important concept in BI that enable users to navigate and analyze complex data structures intuitively and efficiently.

As we learn about hierarchies, dimensions, calculations, aggregations, and the act of drilling down and rolling up the granularity level, we can now conclude what things we should be able to do at a minimum with a BI tool. The act of putting all of these together in an ad hoc report is called **slicing and dicing**. In BI, slice and dice is a technique used to analyze data by selecting a subset of data (slicing) and then examining it from different perspectives (dicing). It allows users to break down data into smaller, more manageable parts and analyze them from different angles to gain deeper insights.

Slicing involves selecting a subset of data based on a specific dimension or category. For example, slicing by time might involve selecting data for a specific month, quarter, or year. Slicing by location might involve selecting data for a specific region, country, or city.

Dicing involves examining the sliced data from different perspectives or dimensions. For example, dicing by product might involve analyzing sales data by product category, brand, or SKU. Dicing by the customer might involve analyzing sales data by demographic, loyalty level, or purchase history.

Together, slicing and dicing allow users to drill down into specific areas of interest and then analyze them in more detail from different perspectives. For example, a user might start by slicing the data by time to look at sales for a specific quarter, and then dice the data by product to look at sales by category, brand, and SKU.

Slice and dice functionality is often built into BI tools and software, allowing users to easily select and analyze data based on different dimensions and categories. It enables users to quickly identify trends, patterns, and outliers in data and make informed decisions, based on the insights gained from the analysis.

This is it – these are the basis for any robust analysis and charts. Trend analysis, forecasting, time series, bar charts, pie charts, scatter plots, correlations, and so on – it all derives from being able to perform such basic operations on top of your dataset. If you are in search of a good BI tool, performing such activities will guarantee you find your BI career path, as they will show you not the end of your roadmap but, instead, spark new ideas and help you understand your data gaps and needs.

Understanding your data needs

In retrospect, every single task or operation we do on top of our data is an iterative process that sends us on the path of understanding what needs we have in terms of data. While analyzing sales, let's imagine that you find out that an organization, department, or region draws an imperfect picture, and numbers don't match with official financial revenue systems. A storm is coming, and it is going to make the data ocean wild and turbulent… numbers won't match.

We could start a drama here and show you the many meetings it took, the teams that collaborated, the back and forth, directors contacting directors, developers messaging developers, databases being queried, and hours and hours of investigation, but instead, let's forward to months into the future. It is now known that the ERP system was patched with a customized interface that allows the sales department in Japan to do cross-department sales. Yes, there's now new knowledge in the business process that throws light on the root cause, and a complex calculation has been implemented to allocate sales percentages to departments if a given department participated in a demo of a product for a different department.

The nightmare is finally over; tables called `sales_ratio`, `sales`, `foreign_rate`, and many more, are now part of the equation. You have to put all of them together in order to come up with an accurate calculation of sales. This is your job – create a full tracking of your data needs and gaps you have in order to make your analysis more complete. This is an iterative and sometimes recursive operation that you need to perform every day when trying to assess your data needs:

- You find your data, and you perform an analysis.

    A. You test and find out that something is missing.

    - You find the stakeholders.

        - You ask.

        - You gather.

- You perform analysis.
- You test again.

We can actually see these steps and organize them sequentially, resulting in better project management. If you visualize them, then you can plan better and specify deadlines that adjust according to the complexity of each step. Such a flow should be close to the following:

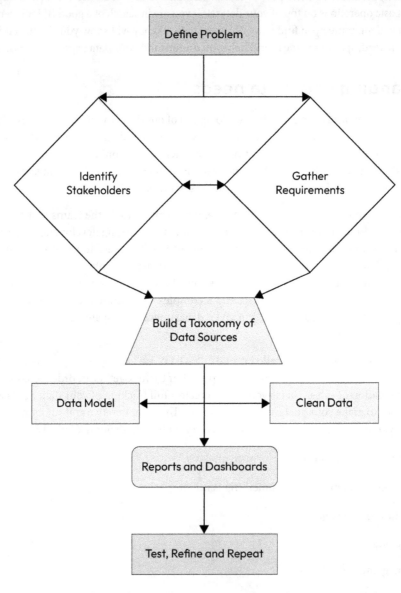

Figure 2.5 – A process flow to follow when trying to understand your customer's data needs

Undoubtedly, it may seem challenging to emphasize this enough, but adhering to established guidelines is remarkably crucial when engaging in the inherently subjective and creative exercise of analyzing and exploring data. While this may appear contradictory, following a structured approach based on established principles adds objectivity to the process. By employing standardized methods and techniques, you can ensure a more consistent and unbiased analysis, allowing for meaningful insights to emerge from the data. Ultimately, by playing by the book, you foster a solid foundation for your data exploration endeavors, enabling a more rigorous and reliable interpretation of the information at hand:

- **Define the business problem**: Start by identifying the business problem or question that needs to be answered. This will help to determine what data is required and how it should be analyzed.

- **Identify the stakeholders**: Identify the stakeholders who will use the data and the insights generated from the analysis. This will help to understand their specific data needs and preferences.

- **Conduct a requirements gathering**: Conduct a requirement gathering process to collect information about the data needed for analysis. This process may involve interviews, surveys, focus groups, or other methods of gathering information from stakeholders. If this is difficult, create mock-ups, do not wait for your customers, find similar reports done by other analysts in the company or investigate common sales reports in the industry, study the domain, study sales if this is the subject of your investigation, and use common sense when creating basic reports. Go back to the stakeholders and go back and forth, iterating new improved versions of such mock-ups, in the hope that these spark some creativity in their minds. Any feedback will help you improve your prototypes. Prototyping is key; we'll discuss more of this in *Chapter 4*.

If you don't have any specific business requirements for a dashboard, you can still prototype a mock-up by following these steps:

1. **Define the purpose of the dashboard**: Even without specific business requirements, you can define the general purpose of the dashboard. For example, is it intended to provide an overview of key metrics, or to allow users to drill down into specific data?

2. **Identify the target audience**: Consider who the dashboard is intended for and what their needs might be. For example, do they need to see real-time data or historical trends? What level of detail is required?

3. **Choose the right visualization types**: Select the visualization types that are best suited for the purpose and audience of the dashboard. For example, use pie charts to show proportions, bar charts to show comparisons, or maps to show geographic data.

4. **Create a wireframe**: Use a tool such as Balsamiq or Sketch to create a wireframe of the dashboard. A wireframe is a basic mock-up that shows the layout and content of the dashboard without going into too much detail.

5. **Refine the design**: Once you have a basic wireframe, you can start to refine the design by adding more detail, choosing colors and fonts, and adding real data where possible. You may also want to get feedback from stakeholders to help refine the design further.

By following these steps, you can prototype a mock-up dashboard even without specific business requirements. While the dashboard may not be fully optimized for the needs of the business, it can still provide a starting point for further development and refinement as requirements become clearer. The following are examples of actions you can take to refine and formalize data prototypes:

- **Identify the data sources**: Identify the data sources that contain the required data. This may include internal data sources such as databases or spreadsheets, as well as external data sources such as third-party data providers.

- **Assess the quality of the data**: Assess the quality of the data to ensure that it is accurate, complete, and relevant to the analysis. This may involve data cleansing, data validation, or other data quality assurance processes.

- **Develop a data model**: Develop a data model that defines the relationships between the different data elements. This will help to ensure that the data is organized in a way that is suitable for analysis.

- **Create reports and dashboards**: Create reports and dashboards that visualize data in a way that is easy to understand and analyze. This may involve creating charts, graphs, tables, or other visualizations.

- **Test and refine the analysis**: Test the analysis and refine it based on feedback from stakeholders. This may involve making changes to the data model, modifying the reports and dashboards, or adjusting the analysis approach. By following these steps, an analyst can understand the data needs of a business and develop a BI solution that meets those needs. This will help to ensure that the analysis is accurate, relevant, and actionable and that it provides insights that drive business performance.

This process is quite subjective, and depending on your company, the output could be different. By setting your expectations correctly and continuously improving your mapping of your data architecture, you will become proficient when trying to identify new data needs in your organization.

Summary

In this chapter, you gained valuable insights and practical advice on how to enhance your proficiency in data analysis. We emphasized the significance of thoroughly mapping out each data source and adopting a systematic process to gain a deeper understanding of your organization's data requirements. It is important to acknowledge that while this chapter serves as a valuable resource, it is not an exhaustive guide. Rather, it aims to inspire you to explore new avenues and bridge any knowledge gaps you may have in your data architecture. It is your responsibility to adapt and refine these techniques to gather the necessary information effectively. As you accomplish this, your path forward becomes clearer – having identified your sources and obtained the required data, it is now time to derive meaning from it and effectively present it to your intended audience. Preparing to share your data story necessitates honing your skills in data visualization and analysis, empowering you to effectively communicate insights derived from your data.

3
How to Talk Data

Data visualization is a vital aspect of data analysis and decision-making. It involves presenting data in a visual format, such as charts, graphs, and maps, to make complex information more accessible and easier to understand. Data visualization plays a crucial role in understanding trends, patterns, and relationships in large datasets. In today's world of big data, knowing how to present data effectively is essential for businesses, governments, researchers, and individuals to make informed decisions.

By presenting data in a visual format, it allows us to see patterns and relationships that may not be apparent in a raw data format. Effective data visualization can also provide a competitive advantage to businesses. In today's data-driven world, companies that can analyze and interpret data quickly and accurately can make better-informed decisions. Effective data visualization can help businesses identify trends, patterns, and relationships, which can lead to new business opportunities or cost savings. It can also help businesses communicate their performance metrics to stakeholders effectively, including investors, employees, and customers.

Finally, knowing how to present data effectively is essential to avoid misinterpretation or misunderstanding. When data is presented poorly, it can lead to confusion, misinterpretation, and even incorrect conclusions. By presenting data visually, it makes it easier to spot errors or anomalies and ensure that the insights are accurate and reliable. It is essential to consider the audience and the context of the data to select the appropriate visualization tool.

This chapter will focus on data visualization as an essential aspect of data analysis and decision-making. The purpose of this chapter is not to teach you about data visualization per se but to guide you on the components you need to master to become a better **Business Intelligence** (**BI**) professional. As you learn more about data visualization, you'll realize how it allows you to understand complex data quickly and accurately, communicate insights effectively, and gain a competitive advantage in business. By knowing how to present data effectively, we can avoid misinterpretation and misunderstanding and make informed decisions based on reliable and accurate insights.

Presenting data

Effective data presentation is essential to ensure that the message being conveyed is clear, accurate, and easy to understand. You have to learn the techniques to make data spit out answers by just looking at it. On some occasions, it will be a difficult endeavor, but you have to make it as smooth as possible, and when the complexity increases, you should guide your audience along an easy-to-follow path.

Poorly designed data visualizations can lead to misinterpretation of the data, also leading to a waste of time, effort, and resources by doing further analysis and investigation of data that could have been avoided if the data had been presented correctly. There are some warnings you should consider before starting to plot charts without a proper understanding:

- **Poor use of color**: Using too many colors or colors that do not contrast well can make visualizations difficult to read and interpret. For example, using too many shades of the same color can make it challenging to distinguish between different data points.

- **Inconsistent scaling**: Using inconsistent scaling can misrepresent the data being presented. For example, if the y axis of a line chart is not scaled proportionally, the trend being presented may be exaggerated or downplayed.

- **Misleading axis labeling**: Misleading axis labeling can skew the interpretation of the data being presented. For example, starting the y axis of a line chart at a value greater than zero can make the trend look more significant than it actually is.

- **Overcomplicated visualizations**: Overcomplicated visualizations can be overwhelming and difficult to interpret. For example, a 3D pie chart with multiple segments and angles can be challenging to read and may not accurately represent the data.

- **Lack of context**: Lack of context can make it difficult to understand the significance of the data being presented. For example, presenting sales figures without comparing them to previous periods or industry benchmarks can make it challenging to interpret the trends.

By avoiding these common mistakes, it is possible to avoid losing your audience when trying to present data effectively. Now let us analyze what minimal steps you should take to excel at presenting data.

Know your audience

Understanding your audience's knowledge level, interests, and preferences can help you select the appropriate type of visualization, tone, and level of detail. For example, presenting data to a technical audience may require a more detailed and complex visualization, while presenting data to a non-technical audience may require a more straightforward and intuitive visualization.

If you know your audience, you'll be able to tailor your communication style, choose appropriate data visualization techniques, and ensure that your message is clear and relevant. Later, in the *Talking to stakeholders* section of this chapter, we will explore how to approach communication for a particular type of audience and stakeholders.

Do some research about your audience before the presentation. Find out their background, their level of technical expertise, and their expectations of the presentation. Consider their knowledge level about the topic you are presenting. If they are experts in the field, you can use technical terms and data visualization techniques that are more complex. However, if they are not familiar with the topic, you may need to use simpler language and more straightforward visualizations. Raise or lower your technical language. A more technical audience allows you to drill down into numbers and possibly code, but a domain-savvy individual would require more to become effective with such abstractions; hence, data visualization techniques will help you here.

Try to identify the needs of your audience. What questions do they have? What concerns do they want to be addressed? By understanding their needs, you can tailor your message to address their specific concerns. Use examples that your audience can relate to. This can help to make your message more relevant and relatable to your audience. Practice active listening during the presentation. Watch for non-verbal cues and feedback from your audience. This can help you adjust your message or approach if needed.

Understanding your audience is crucial when presenting data. By researching your audience, identifying their needs, and using appropriate language and data visualization techniques, you can ensure that your message is clear, relevant, and effective.

Choose the right visualization

There are many types of data visualizations, including line graphs, bar charts, scatter plots, heat maps, and more. Selecting the right type of visualization depends on the type of data you have and the message you want to convey. For example, a line graph may be best suited for showing trends over time, while a scatter plot is useful for showing the relationship between two variables. A map with different colors representing the concentration of a particular variable can convey the message of spatial patterns effectively. Some data visualization techniques are more appropriate for your audience. Later, in the *Advanced data visualizations* section, we will explore different visualizations and use cases that are more effective.

Understand the data. Before choosing a visualization technique, it is essential to understand the data you have. You need to know what the data represents and what insights you want to communicate. Know the purpose and the path it follows, how it drills down, and the root of the information it contains. Based on this, set an order that makes sense – it could be sequential, hierarchical, or narrative. Later, in the *Storytelling* section, we will talk about storytelling. The most critical part of choosing the right visualization is to find out what the data's main entity is and what levels this entity gets analyzed at.

For example, take an HR analytics dashboard. You have a dataset that contains employee turnover information, and you have employee names and attributes that describe their path through their time in the company. The main entity in this data is always the employee, and the levels are the department they worked in, organization, profit center, and so on. Attributes of this employee that could be analyzed are manager, salary, the number of departments they've been in, tenure, age, gender, number of years of experience, education level, the number of projects they are working on, and so on.

Identify the message you want to communicate with the data. This will help you choose the most appropriate visualization technique that can effectively communicate the insights. Again, this will also depend on your research of the audience. If your audience is not technically savvy, you may want to choose a simpler visualization technique that is easy to understand. Different types of data are best presented using different types of visualizations. If you want to compare different data points, a bar chart or a line chart may be the best option. If you want to show how a data point changes over time, a line chart may be the best option. If you want to show the distribution of data, a histogram may be the best option.

Keep an eye on the use of best practices to ensure that the visualization is easy to read and understand. For example, use appropriate colors, choose the right font size, and ensure that the data is clearly labeled. Finally, testing is always necessary. Before presenting the data visualization to your audience, test it to ensure that it is easy to read and understand. This can be done by showing it to a colleague or running a pilot test with a small group of people. Selecting the right data visualization technique is essential to ensure that your message is clear and easily understood. By understanding the data, identifying the message, considering the audience, choosing the right type of visualization, using best practices, and testing the visualization, you can ensure that your data visualization is effective in communicating insights.

Keep it simple

Too much information or a cluttered visualization can be overwhelming and confusing. Keep your visualization simple, with only the necessary information that is required to convey the message. Use clear, concise labels and titles to help your audience understand the key takeaways from the data.

Use color and formatting effectively

Color can be used to highlight important data points or to distinguish between different categories. Use color and formatting consistently throughout the visualization to avoid confusion. Avoid using too many colors, which can be distracting and difficult to interpret.

Provide context

Providing context can help your audience understand the significance of the data being presented. For example, including historical data or benchmarks can help your audience understand how the current data compares to previous trends or industry standards.

Tell a story

Presenting data in the form of a story can be a powerful way to engage your audience and help them understand the significance of the data. Use a narrative structure to guide your audience through the data, highlighting key insights and trends along the way.

Presenting data effectively is a critical aspect of data analysis and decision-making. By understanding your audience, choosing the right visualization, keeping it simple, using color and formatting effectively, providing context, and telling a story, you can create compelling and informative visualizations that communicate your message effectively.

High-level dashboards

Following our previous advice, the intended audience for these dashboards are decision-makers, top executives, or business analysts. Here's a mock-up of things we consider in a high-level dashboard:

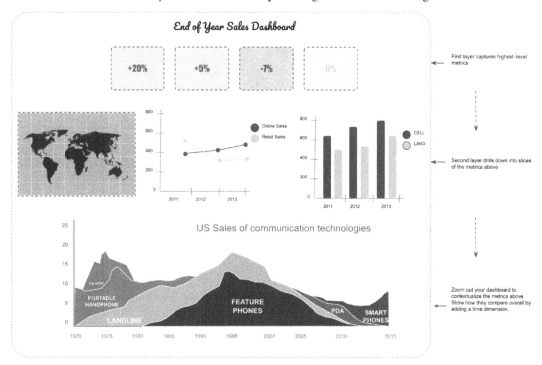

Figure 3.1 – Example of a typical dashboard

The annotations on the right show the natural order an avid analyst tends to study. Keeping this format allows the flow to be more effective

Operational reports

Operational reports focus on details, raw numbers, or aggregated data that allow you to investigate and ascertain behavior around a business process. Operational reports are also part of your expertise and require many processes to produce them. As previously discussed, operational reports are the result of heavy ETL development, data modeling, database design, and semantic layers. Along with data quality assurance, unit testing, and governance, operational reports need to be exact and accurate. The main audience for these is business analysts and subject matter experts, who will then convey answers found in these to a higher-level audience.

Here's an example of an operational report. Notice the heavy use of numbers and much lower granularity, with zero use of visualizations. Notice how some key elements are uniformity, cleanliness, and accuracy:

		January 2021	January 2022	January 2023
Revenue				
	Delivery	$25,000	$24,300	$25,677
	Retail	$53,788	$56,790	$59,880
	Online purchases	$3,440	$3,576	$3,698
	B2B	$44,007	$50,350	$50,228
	Subscription	$973	$990	$954
	Professional services	$528	$550	$589
	Total Revenue	**$127,736**	**$136,556**	**$141,026**
Cost of Sales				
	Licenses	$1,500	$1,500	$1,750
	Support	$250	$100	$3,500
	Transportation	$34,056	$35,098	$30,200
	Storage	$15,700	$17,344	$15,653
	Total Cost of Sales	**$51,506**	**$54,042**	**$51,103**
Operating Expenses				
	General and Administrative	$25,933	$23,550	$25,980
	Sales and Marketing	$14,739	$14,288	$14,233
	Research and Development	$5,708	$5,316	$7,899
	Total Operating Expenses	$46,380	$43,154	$48,112
Loss		$277	$475	$320
Net Profit		**$29,850**	**$39,360**	**$41,811**

Figure 3.2 – A traditional profit and loss report for a hypothetical retail business

There is no one correct way to present data; it will depend on the type of report, how the data is shaped, and your target audience. By following the basic principles and experimenting with different ways to present your data, you will be able to find the right formula to use, and once you are ready, it will be time for you to address your audience. Let's examine the role of a BI professional when talking to stakeholders.

Talking to stakeholders

Although learning public speaking is out of the scope of this book, we can't avoid making a case for learning the skill of talking to stakeholders, not only for data presentation but also for gathering data requirements. Stakeholders are the ones that will dictate the business process we will follow to produce meaningful data pipelines and reports. Failing to do this will lead to improper technical requirement translation, thus missing the target and producing unmeaningful answers. Stakeholders may have a different understanding of data, but they have a clear understanding of its purpose – reducing costs, increasing revenue, and becoming efficient at making decisions.

As a BI professional, it is your job to be able to establish a relationship with them and know how to talk to them and how to extract the information you need to perform your duties. Stakeholders may not know anything about databases, enterprise systems, or any programming language or technical process. You have to ask the right questions and understand what they are trying to get from the data.

Identify all the stakeholders who are involved in the project. This may include project managers, team members, subject matter experts, and end users. Schedule meetings with the stakeholders to gather requirements. These meetings can be held in person or online, depending on the location of the stakeholders.

Ask the right questions. Ask open-ended questions to the stakeholders to understand their requirements. Questions should focus on the purpose of the data visualization, the type of data, the target audience, and the desired outcome. Use prototypes to gather requirements from stakeholders. This can be done by creating mock-ups of data visualizations and showing them to the stakeholders to gather feedback.

Analyze the feedback from stakeholders to identify common themes and patterns. This can help to identify the key requirements that need to be addressed in the project. Document the requirements of stakeholders in a clear and concise manner. This can be done using a requirements document, which outlines the requirements, priorities, and deadlines. Review the requirements with stakeholders to ensure that they are accurate and complete. This can help to avoid misunderstandings and ensure that everyone is on the same page. Finally, prioritize the requirements based on their importance and impact on the project. This can help to ensure that the most critical requirements are addressed first.

Gathering requirements from stakeholders is a critical step in any data visualization project. By identifying stakeholders, asking the right questions, using prototypes, analyzing feedback, documenting requirements, reviewing requirements, and prioritizing requirements, you can ensure that the data visualization project meets the needs of all stakeholders and is successful.

When talking to stakeholders, there are several things to consider to ensure effective communication and a successful project outcome. It is essential to listen actively to stakeholders to understand their needs, expectations, and concerns. This involves being present and engaged during conversations, asking clarifying questions, and taking notes to ensure that you capture all the relevant information.

Another helpful tip: avoid using technical jargon or complex terms that your business stakeholders may not easily comprehend or understand. Instead, use plain, simple language to communicate in a way that is easy to understand (*try to imagine explaining the analysis to a five-year-old*). This can help to ensure that stakeholders are fully informed and can provide feedback that is valuable and relevant.

Try to understand the stakeholders' perspective and consider their priorities, values, and goals. This can help to build trust and rapport and ensure that the project meets their needs and expectations. Thus it is also important to be transparent. Be transparent about the project's objectives, timelines, budget, and any potential risks or challenges. This can help to build trust and ensure that stakeholders are fully informed about the project's status and progress.

When you provide the status and details about your progress, it is imperative that you manage stakeholders' expectations by being clear about what is achievable and what is not. This can help to avoid misunderstandings and ensure that stakeholders understand the project's limitations and constraints. This can also give you some buffer time to take a break and a deep breath whenever required.

Keep stakeholders informed of the project's progress by providing regular updates. This can be done through meetings, reports, or other communication channels. Regular updates can help to build trust and ensure that stakeholders are aware of any changes or challenges that may arise and address their concerns. Be responsive to stakeholder concerns and address them in a timely and appropriate manner. This can help to build trust and ensure that stakeholders feel heard and valued.

When talking to stakeholders, it is important to listen actively, use plain language, understand their perspective, be transparent, manage expectations, provide regular updates, and address concerns. By considering these factors, you can build effective relationships with stakeholders, ensure successful communication, and achieve project success.

Finally, there's no final guide you can use to gather requirements. Just bear in mind that no matter what process you follow, by the end of your stakeholder meetings, you should document the answers to the following questions to the best of your knowledge:

- What is the purpose of this data visualization?
- Who is the intended audience for this data visualization?
- What type of data will be included in this visualization?
- What is the source of the data?
- What are the key insights or information that stakeholders are looking for in the data visualization?
- What are the current pain points in data analysis or reporting?

- What are the current data visualization methods used?

- What are the desired outcomes or goals of this data visualization?

- How often will the data visualization be updated or refreshed?

- What are the **key performance indicators** (**KPIs**) or metrics to be tracked in the data visualization?

- Are there any specific data visualization styles or techniques that stakeholders prefer or have used before?

- Are there any specific data visualization platforms or software that stakeholders prefer or have used before?

- What are the accessibility requirements for the data visualization?

- Are there any specific design or branding requirements for the data visualization?

- Are there any specific technical or data integration requirements that need to be considered?

By answering these questions, you can gather requirements effectively and ensure that the data visualization meets the needs and expectations of stakeholders.

Data visualization taxonomy

There are numerous data visualization charts available that are used for displaying different types of data in a clear and effective manner. Here are some of the most common types of data visualization charts and their use cases. It is important that you analyze them and find parallelism with the data you work on. By doing so, you will be able to pick the right visualization at any time.

Bar charts

Bar charts are used to compare categorical data across different groups. They are typically used to show the frequency or proportion of data within each category, such as the following:

- A bar chart can be used to compare the sales of different products

- A bar chart can be used to display the number of employees in different departments of a company

- They can display the revenue generated by different product lines

- They can be used to display the number of students in each grade level at a school

Here's an example of what a bar chart looks like:

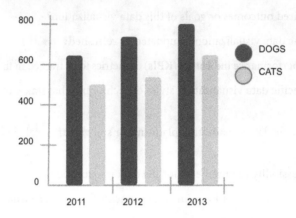

Figure 3.3 – A simple bar chart displaying comparing dog versus cat food sales

To create such a chart, the underlying data may be represented either at a detailed granularity or aggregated at a certain level.

For example, at a detailed level, the data should be represented as follows:

Breed	Species	Quantity	Date
French Poodle	Dog	3	01/07/2011
Egyptian Mau	Cat	2	02/05/2012
Burmese	Cat	5	08/15/2012

The same information is displayed in the following table but aggregated at the year and category levels:

Category	Sum of Sales	Year
Dogs	3	2011
Cats	7	2012

Line charts

Line charts are used to display data trends over time. Examples of places where it would be apt to use a line chart are to represent the following:

- Stock prices
- Website traffic
- The trend of daily temperatures over a month

Here is an example of a line chart:

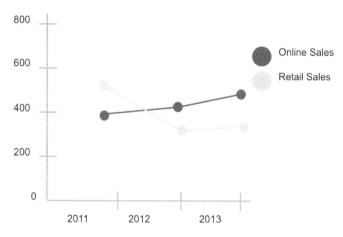

Figure 3.4 – Line chart comparing online versus retail sales over time

Pie charts

Pie charts are used to show the proportion of data in different categories. They are typically used to display percentages of a whole. They work better when the categories are few and the percentages are visible. Here are some example use cases:

- The percentage of the population that has a certain education level
- The percentage of votes received by each candidate in an election
- The percentage of the population in different age groups
- The percentage of a company's expenses that are spent on different departments

Scatter plots

Scatter plots are used to display the relationship between two variables. They are often used to show correlations between data, such as the relationship between two variables. Some examples are as follows:

- Height and weight
- The relationship between the hours spent studying and the grades achieved by students
- The correlation between the number of hours worked and the amount earned by employees
- The relationship between the number of years of experience and the salary of employees

Here is an example of a scatter plot:

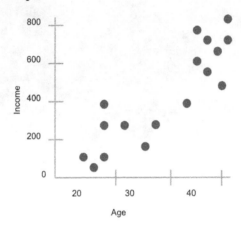

Figure 3.5 – A scatter plot displaying the relationship between age and income

Area charts

Area charts are used to display the cumulative total of data over time. They are often used to show trends in data, such as the following:

- The growth of a company's revenue over time

- The cumulative number of COVID-19 cases over time

- The growth of a company's revenue over a year

- The change in the number of customers over time

Here is an example of an area chart:

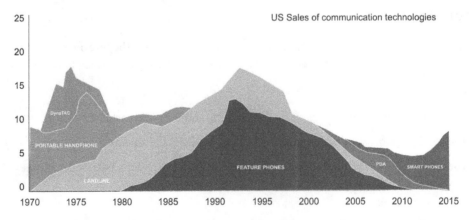

Figure 3.6 – An area chart showing a size comparison between elements across time

Heat maps

Heat maps are used to display data density in two dimensions. They are often used to show the frequency of events in a certain area, such as the following:

- The number of people living in different parts of a city
- The frequency of crimes in different areas of a city
- The number of people living in different zip codes
- The number of students enrolled in different courses

Here is an example of a heat map:

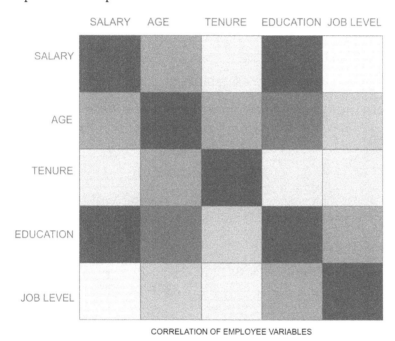

Figure 3.7 – A heat map being used to display the correlation between different variables

Bubble charts

Bubble charts are used to display three dimensions of data. They are often used to show the relationship between variables, such as the following:

- The relationship between the size of a company, its revenue, and the number of employees
- The relationship between the price of a product, the number of units sold, and the profit generated

Here is an example of a bubble chart:

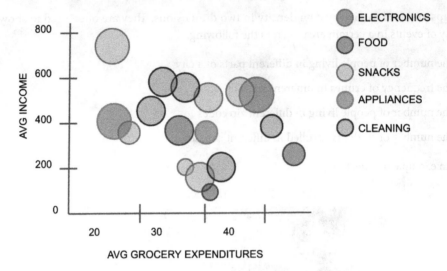

Figure 3.8 – A bubble chart can display different dimensions – color, size, and position – which allows you to fit more information on a single chart

Gauge charts

Gauge charts are used to show progress toward a goal. They are often used to show how close a project is to completion or how much progress has been made toward a certain goal, such as the following:

- The progress of a fundraising campaign
- The progress of a construction project
- The progress of a product development process

Here is an example of a gauge chart:

Figure 3.9 – A gauge chart showing the progress of a project. Usually, these charts are used to show real-time or current data

Tree maps

Tree maps are used to display hierarchical data in a way that is easy to understand. Here are some examples:

- They are often used to show the breakdown of a company's expenses by department
- They can be used to show the distribution of different types of land use in a city
- They can be used to show the number of books sold by different authors

Here is an example of a tree map:

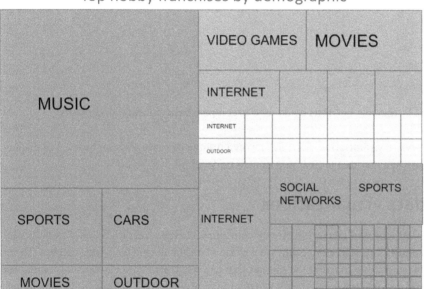

Figure 3.10 – A tree map can be used to compare the size of several data points. If interaction
is possible, it could have zoom-through capabilities to enlarge small squares

Box plots

Box plots are used to display the distribution of data. They are often used to show the range, median, and quartiles of a dataset. These are some examples:

- A box plot can be used to show the distribution of test scores among students in a class
- They can be used to show the distribution of salaries among employees in a company
- They can be used to show the distribution of the prices of products sold by a retailer

Here is an example of a box plot:

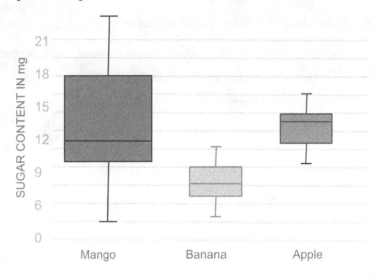

Figure 3.11 – Multiple box plots being used to compare basic statistical data points

Overall, each type of data visualization chart has its own unique use case and can be used to display different types of data in a way that is clear and easy to understand.

Advanced data visualizations

While conventional graphs and charts effectively communicate data narratives, occasionally, the intricacies of data points necessitate an additional dimension for unveiling novel insights. There exists a spectrum of innovative charting techniques that can transform data exploration, taking on varied and complex forms. Nevertheless, their construction may prove to be significantly challenging. Moreover, their application might not always be suitable for every context, thereby emphasizing the critical role of discernment in selecting the appropriate data visualization. Always bear in mind the powerful axiom that, sometimes, simplicity trumps complexity.

Sankey diagrams

A **Sankey diagram** is a type of data visualization chart that displays flows of data, information, or resources through a system or process. It is named after Captain Matthew Henry Phineas Riall Sankey, an Irish engineer who created a flow diagram in 1898 to illustrate the flow of energy in a steam engine.

Sankey diagrams use a series of connected arrows or lines of varying widths to show the flow of data or resources through different stages or levels of a process. The width of each arrow or line represents the quantity or volume of data or resources being transferred at each stage, making it easy to see where the most data or resources are being used or lost.

Sankey diagrams are particularly useful for visualizing complex systems or processes and can help to identify inefficiencies or bottlenecks in a system, as well as opportunities for improvement or optimization. Sankey diagrams can also be used to compare different scenarios or outcomes, such as the flow of resources in different policy or investment scenarios.

Here is an example of a Sankey diagram:

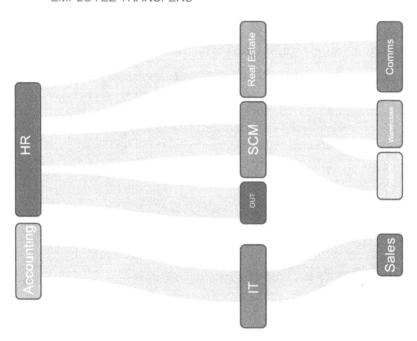

Figure 3.12 – A Sankey diagram can effectively show the flow of metrics between data points, and the size of the flow can show the amount it represents

Some common use cases of Sankey diagrams include the following:

- **Energy flows**: Sankey diagrams can be used to visualize the flow of energy through different sources, such as fossil fuels, renewable energy, or nuclear power
- **Water usage**: Sankey diagrams can be used to show the flow of water through different stages of a process, such as irrigation, treatment, and distribution
- **Supply chains**: Sankey diagrams can be used to visualize the flow of goods and materials through different stages of a supply chain, such as manufacturing, transportation, and distribution
- **Financial flows**: Sankey diagrams can be used to show the flow of money through different channels, such as investment portfolios, banking systems, or government budgets

Bullet charts

A **bullet chart** is a type of data visualization chart that is used to display performance data against a goal or target. It was developed by Stephen Few, a data visualization expert, as an improvement over the traditional bar chart.

Bullet charts typically consist of a single horizontal bar that represents the performance data, with a vertical line or marker that indicates the goal or target. The length of the bar shows the actual performance data, while the color or shading of the bar can be used to indicate different levels of performance (e.g., green for good, yellow for average, and red for poor). Additional markers or labels can be added to show the current status or trend of the data.

Bullet charts are particularly useful for visualizing performance data in a compact and easy-to-read format. They allow viewers to quickly compare actual performance against a goal or target and to see how well they are doing relative to different levels of performance. They are also versatile and can be used for a wide range of performance metrics, including sales revenue, customer satisfaction, employee performance, and website traffic. Here's an example of a bullet chart:

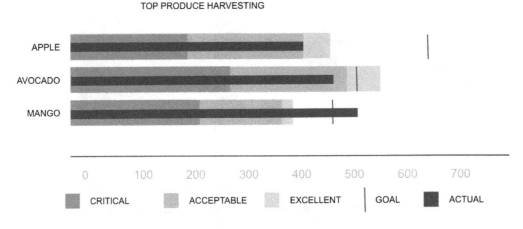

Figure 3.13 – A bullet chart is a multi-metric visualization by fitting several metrics and references to measure performance at a given time

Some common use cases of bullet charts include the following:

- **Sales performance**: Bullet charts can be used to show the sales revenue for different products or services and to compare actual revenue against a target or goal

- **Customer satisfaction**: Bullet charts can be used to display customer satisfaction ratings and to compare the actual ratings against a desired rating or benchmark

- **Employee performance**: Bullet charts can be used to show employee performance ratings or scores and to compare the actual ratings against a desired rating or benchmark

- **Website analytics**: Bullet charts can be used to display website traffic data, such as the number of page views or conversions, and to compare the actual data against a target or goal

Taxonomy diagrams

A **taxonomy diagram** is a type of data visualization chart that is used to organize and categorize different elements or concepts according to their relationships and attributes. It is commonly used in fields such as biology, information science, and education to classify and organize complex systems or concepts.

Taxonomy diagrams typically consist of a hierarchical tree structure, with each branch representing a different level of classification or category. The nodes or leaves of the tree represent individual elements or concepts and are connected by lines or arrows to show their relationships and attributes. Additional labels or annotations can be added to provide more information about each element or category.

Taxonomy diagrams are particularly useful for visualizing complex systems or concepts and for organizing information in a structured and systematic way. They can help to identify patterns and relationships among different elements and to provide a framework for further analysis or exploration. They can also be used to communicate complex ideas or concepts in a clear and concise manner. A taxonomy diagram looks like the following figure:

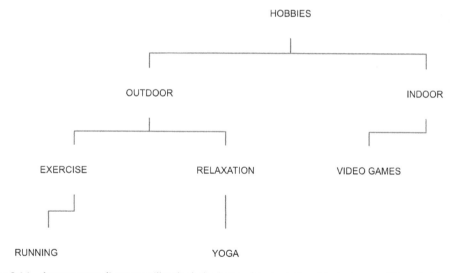

Figure 3.14 – A taxonomy diagram will unlock the hierarchical relationship between different data points

Some common use cases of taxonomy diagrams include the following:

- **Biological classification**: Taxonomy diagrams are commonly used in biology to classify and organize different species of animals, plants, and microorganisms according to their characteristics and relationships

- **Information architecture**: Taxonomy diagrams are often used in information science to organize and classify digital content, such as websites, databases, or knowledge management systems

- **Education**: Taxonomy diagrams can be used in education to classify and organize different types of learning objectives, such as Bloom's taxonomy of cognitive skills

- **User experience design**: Taxonomy diagrams can be used in user experience design to organize and classify different user needs or behaviors and to inform the design of user interfaces or interactions

Overall, taxonomy diagrams are a powerful tool for organizing and categorizing complex systems or concepts and can help to provide structure and clarity to information and ideas.

Pareto diagrams

A **Pareto diagram**, also known as a Pareto chart or Pareto analysis, is a type of data visualization chart used to identify the most significant factors contributing to a particular problem or issue. It is named after Vilfredo Pareto, an Italian economist who developed the concept of the Pareto principle, also known as the 80/20 rule.

Pareto diagrams typically consist of a bar chart with bars ordered in descending order of frequency or size. The bars are accompanied by a line graph that represents the cumulative percentage of the total. The bars on the chart are used to represent the frequency or size of each factor or category, while the line graph shows the cumulative percentage of the total.

The Pareto diagram is used to identify the most significant factors contributing to a particular problem or issue. The idea behind the Pareto diagram is that a relatively small number of factors will contribute to a large majority of the problem. By focusing on the most significant factors, it is possible to identify the root causes of the problem and take appropriate action. A Pareto diagram looks like this:

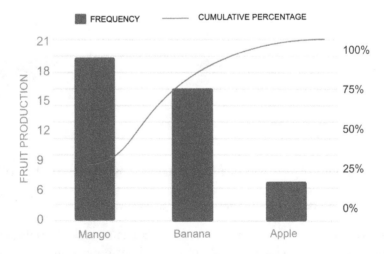

Figure 3.15 – A Pareto diagram displaying fruit sales with their characteristic cumulative percentage line

Some common use cases of Pareto diagrams include the following:

- **Quality control**: Pareto diagrams are commonly used in quality control to identify the most common causes of defects or quality issues
- **Customer complaints**: Pareto diagrams are used to identify the most common reasons for customer complaints, allowing businesses to address the most significant issues first
- **Manufacturing efficiency**: Pareto diagrams are used to identify the most common causes of inefficiencies in a manufacturing process, allowing businesses to take action to improve efficiency
- **Sales performance**: Pareto diagrams can be used to identify the products or services that are contributing the most to a business's sales revenue, allowing businesses to focus their resources on those products or services

Overall, Pareto diagrams are a powerful tool for identifying the most significant factors contributing to a particular problem or issue. They allow businesses to focus their resources on the most important areas, leading to more effective problem-solving and decision-making.

There are many advanced visualization techniques worth exploring, but it is more important to analyze which one is correct. To do so, you have to follow a decision process that will lead you to find the pros and cons of each visualization type. This process is not written in stone, and the steps followed here are just meant to be a guide in the creative process that will help you talk more about your data in front of your audience.

Decision tree for picking a visualization

When presenting a data story, it is important to learn how to pick the right visualization. It will vary case by case, but here is a guide you can use to make such decisions:

- **Bar charts**: Bar charts are good for showing comparisons between different groups or categories
- **Line charts**: Line charts are good for showing trends over time
- **Pie charts**: Pie charts are good for showing the relative size of different parts of a whole
- **Scatter plots**: Scatter plots are good for showing the relationship between two variables
- **Maps**: Maps are good for showing geographic data
- **Tables**: Tables are good for presenting large amounts of data in a clear and concise way

Remember to always be mindful of the shape your data has. Your storytelling may only work once, at a given time, or under certain circumstances. In the future, the same visualizations may not work as the data constantly changes. There may be new values added, new categories created, or even outlier events that skew the values, making it difficult to display them side by side. Exploring your data is not a one-time task and is meant to be constant and iterative to mitigate this issue, making sure your storytelling is always up to date.

Storytelling

Data storytelling is the process of using data and visualization techniques to communicate a narrative or a story to an audience. It involves taking complex datasets and presenting them in a way that is easy to understand and compelling for the viewer.

Data stories can be used to inform decisions, solve problems, and create change.

There are many different ways to tell a data story. The most important thing is to choose a format that is right for your audience and your data. Some common formats include the following:

- **Presentations**: Presentations are a great way to tell a data story to a large group of people. You can use slides, videos, and other visuals to help your audience understand the data.

- **Reports**: Reports are a more detailed way to share data. They can be used to share data with decision-makers or to provide more context for a data story.

- **Interactive dashboards**: Interactive dashboards are a great way to let your audience explore the data for themselves. They can be used to share data with a large group of people or to provide more context for a data story.

To become good at data storytelling, here are some steps you can follow:

1. **Start with a question**: You can approach the process of discovery for your research project in two different ways. You can either start with a question and then try to find the data that will help you answer it, or you can start with the data and then try to find a question that it can help you answer. If you start with a question, you're more likely to end up with a story that is interesting and relevant to your audience.

2. **Tell data stories that others want to share**: If you want your data story to have an impact, you need to make sure that it's something that people will want to share with others. This means making sure that it's interesting, relevant, and easy to understand.

3. **Provide the right kind of evidence**: When you're telling a data story, you need to provide evidence to support your claims. This evidence can come in the form of data, statistics, quotes from experts, or anything else that will help your audience understand and believe your story.

4. **Pick the right tool for the job**: There are many different tools that you can use to tell data stories. The right tool for you will depend on the type of story you're trying to tell, the audience you're trying to reach, and your own personal preferences.

5. **Understand your audience**: Knowing who your audience is and what they care about is key to creating a story that resonates with them. Consider their expectations. What do they already know about the topic? What are they interested in learning? How can you present the data in a way that will be most helpful and engaging for them?

6. **Identify the key message**: Start with a clear and concise message you want to convey through your data story. This message should be the focal point of your story and guide the visuals and supporting data you use.

7. **Gather and analyze the data**: Collect relevant data and analyze it to extract insights that support your key message. Use data visualization tools to create charts, graphs, and other visual aids that help convey the story.

8. **Structure the narrative**: Plan the structure of your story by organizing the data and visuals in a logical sequence that supports the key message. Use storytelling techniques such as plot, character, and conflict to create a compelling narrative.

9. **Use visuals effectively**: Choose visuals that are easy to understand and align with your message. Use color, typography, and other design elements to create a consistent and visually appealing story.

10. **Practice and refine**: Practice presenting your story and get feedback from others. Refine your story based on their feedback and continue to iterate until you have a compelling and engaging data story. Practice, practice, practice. The best way to become a great data storyteller is to practice. The more you tell data stories, the better you'll get at it. So don't be afraid to experiment and try new things.

By following these steps and continuously refining your skills, you can become an effective data storyteller and use data to communicate insights and inspire action.

There are many examples we encourage you to take a look at to obtain inspiration in your data storytelling process:

- **The New York Times**: The New York Times frequently uses data visualization to tell stories. One example is their piece on the geography of America's opioid epidemic, where they used interactive maps to show how the epidemic has affected different regions of the country.

- **Hans Rosling's "The Joy of Stats" TED Talk**: In this TED Talk, Hans Rosling uses data visualization to tell the story of global economic development over the last 200 years. He uses interactive charts and graphs to engage the audience and convey complex data in a simple and compelling way.

- **FiveThirtyEight**: FiveThirtyEight is a website that uses data to tell stories about politics, sports, and other topics. One example is their analysis of which NFL teams were most likely to win the Super Bowl, which used data modeling to predict the outcomes of each game.

- **The COVID Tracking Project**: During the COVID-19 pandemic, the COVID Tracking Project used data visualization to tell the story of the pandemic's impact on the United States. They created a dashboard that showed the number of cases, deaths, and hospitalizations in each state, along with other key metrics.

- **Gapminder**: Gapminder is a nonprofit organization that uses data visualization to promote global development. One of their projects is the Dollar Street website, which uses photographs and data to tell the story of how people around the world live at different income levels.

Summary

When presenting data, you want to communicate the message the data conveys. That is the number one priority – that, at least, your audience is able to interpret the output of your research. In this chapter, we analyzed how to achieve this by implementing critical steps in your project:

- Know your audience. What are their interests? What do they need to know? What level of detail do they want?

- Tell a story. Data is more than just numbers and charts. It's a story about your business, your customers, and your results.

- Make it actionable. What do you want your stakeholders to do with the information you're presenting? Give them clear next steps.

- Keep it simple. Use visuals and clear language to make your data easy to understand.

- Practice. The more you practice, the more confident you'll be when you present your data.

Communication skills will always give you a boost, so think about starting with a strong introduction. Grab your audience's attention and tell them what they can expect from your presentation. Use visuals effectively because data visualizations can help you tell your story in a more engaging way. Don't forget to be clear and concise. Avoid jargon and technical language that your audience may not understand. Also, encourage questions. Answer any questions your audience may have about your data. End with a call to action. Tell your audience what you want them to do with the information you've presented.

By following these tips, you can give a data presentation that is informative, engaging, and persuasive. Having mastered entry into the BI domain, honed your data analysis skills, and learned the art of effective visualization techniques, you are now prepared to integrate these competencies and pursue your dream job in the data industry.

4
How To Crack the
BI Interview Process

Thus far, we've navigated through entering the world of business intelligence, what the various BI roles (i.e., architect, developer, analyst, etc.) are, how to become more proficient at analyzing and talking about data, and the basics of data visualization. Now, we'll turn our focus away from the foundational concepts of BI and move toward more practical applications and solutions. For many, much of the consternation and stress from BI comes from one of the most challenging parts of getting hired for any job: the (dreaded) interview process.

The business intelligence interview process can be challenging for a number of reasons. First, business intelligence professionals are in high demand (with very little on the horizon to suggest that this won't be the case for many decades to come), and there are *many* qualified candidates for each position. This means that companies can be very selective in their hiring decisions, and they often look for candidates with strong technical skills and experience.

Second, business intelligence as a discipline is constantly evolving, and companies are looking for candidates who are up to date on the latest technologies and trends. This means that candidates need to be able to learn quickly and adapt to new situations while being able to demonstrate a track record of successful projects and implementations.

Finally, business intelligence analysts often work with sensitive data, and companies need to be confident that they can trust their employees. This means that candidates need to be able to demonstrate strong ethical standards and a commitment to confidentiality.

Before we dive in, here are some general tips for preparing for a business intelligence interview:

- Research the company and the position you are applying for (this applies to any job!)

- Practice answering common business intelligence interview questions

- Discuss your technical skills and experience

- Answer questions about your knowledge of the latest technologies and trends

- Discuss your ethical standards and your commitment to confidentiality

Finding the right interview

There are a few things you can do to find the right business intelligence interview:

- **Network with people in the field**: Attend industry events, connect with people on LinkedIn, and reach out to friends and family who work in business intelligence. The more people you know in the field, the more likely you are to hear about job openings.

- **Search for job openings online**: There are a number of websites that list business intelligence jobs, such as Indeed, LinkedIn, and Dice. You can also search for job openings directly on the websites of companies you're interested in working for.

- **Reach out to recruiters**: Recruiters specialize in finding candidates for open positions. They can help you find job openings that match your skills and experience.

- **Prepare for the interview**: Once you've found a job interview, take some time to prepare. Make sure you know your resume inside and out, and practice answering common interview questions. You should also research the company you're interviewing with so you can ask intelligent questions during the interview.

- **Be specific in your search**: When you're searching for job openings, be as specific as possible about the type of position you're looking for. This will help you narrow down your search and find the most relevant job openings.

- **Be prepared to relocate**: If you're serious about finding a business intelligence job, be prepared to relocate. Many of the best jobs in this field are located in major cities.

- **Be patient**: Finding the right business intelligence interview can take time. Don't get discouraged if you don't find the perfect job right away. Keep searching, and eventually, you'll find the right opportunity.

Here are some tips on how to find the right interview for a data professional:

- **Do your research**: Before you start applying for jobs, take some time to research the different types of data professional roles that are available. This will help you to understand what skills and experience are required for each role.

- **Network with other data professionals**: Attend industry events and connect with other data professionals on LinkedIn. This will help you to learn about different companies that are hiring data professionals and to get referrals for jobs.

- **Tailor your resume and cover letter to each job**: When you apply for a job, make sure to tailor your resume and cover letter to the specific role. This will show the hiring manager that you are interested in the job and that you have the skills and experience that they are looking for.

- **Be prepared to answer questions about your skills and experience**: In your interview, be prepared to answer questions about your skills and experience. The hiring manager will want to know that you have the skills and experience necessary to be successful in the role.

- **Ask questions**: At the end of the interview, be sure to ask questions. This will show the hiring manager that you are interested in the job and that you are engaged in the interview process.

There are a few things you can do to know whether a job is the right fit for your skill set:

- **Read the job description carefully**: Make sure that the job description lists the skills and experience that you have. If the job description lists skills that you don't have, it's probably not the right fit for you.

- **Talk to the hiring manager**: The hiring manager will be able to tell you more about the job and what they are looking for. If you talk to the hiring manager, and they seem to be interested in your skills and experience, it's a good sign that the job might be a good fit for you.

- **Do some research on the company**: Learn more about the company and what it does. If you are interested in the company and its work, it's a good sign that you might be a good fit for the job.

- **Ask questions**: At the end of the interview, ask questions. This will show the hiring manager that you are interested in the job and that you are engaged in the interview process. You can ask questions about the job, the company, or the culture.

The following figure shows how different topics are broken down during BI analyst interviews:

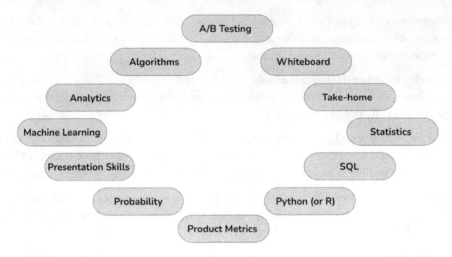

Figure 4.1 – A breakdown of frequently asked topics in BI analyst interviews

The most challenging part of a business intelligence interview is often the technical portion, where you will be asked to demonstrate your ability to use data analysis tools and techniques. This can be a daunting task, especially if you are not familiar with the specific tools or techniques that the interviewer is expecting you to use. However, there are a few things you can do to prepare for this part of the interview and increase your chances of success.

First, make sure you have a good understanding of the basics of data analysis. This includes topics such as data mining, statistics, and machine learning. We covered a lot of this material in *Chapters 2 and 3*. There are many resources available online and in libraries that can help you go further when researching these topics.

Secondly, make an effort to practice using the specific tools and techniques that the interviewer may want you to be familiar with based on the job's technical requirements. However, keep in mind that you might not always have prior knowledge of these tools, as it varies from one job to another. In such cases, try to capitalize on your existing experience with your current set of tools during the interview process.

Finally, be prepared to answer questions about your experience with data analysis. The interviewer will want to know about your previous projects, what tools and techniques you used, and what results you achieved. Be prepared to talk about your work in a clear and concise way.

We have covered some general tips about the BI interview process and what topics are typically covered during interviews. As we continue the chapter, we'll go into specifics on what techniques can be used for different parts of interviews and go through a mock interview process in depth to give you a more comprehensive view of what is asked and how to approach answering the interviewer's prompts. To begin, we will start with what we call a *business problem and data solutions matrix*.

Building a business problem and data solutions matrix

During BI interviews, you will often be presented with a business problem or scenario that the interviewer would like you to solve using a technology solution. Presenting a solution to a business problem allows you to showcase your technical proficiency in BI tools, data manipulation, and data visualization. It provides an opportunity to discuss the specific techniques, methodologies, and technologies you used to address the problem effectively. Discussing a business problem and solution helps you showcase your ability to identify and understand the needs of different stakeholders. You can discuss how you align your analysis with their requirements, tailor your solution to address their concerns, and deliver valuable insights that drive business value.

The best approach for dissecting a business problem is to follow a systematic and methodical process. This will help you identify the root cause of the problem and develop an effective and efficient solution.

Here are the steps involved in dissecting a business problem:

1. **Identify the problem**: The first step is to clearly define the problem that you are trying to solve. This may involve gathering information from customers, employees, and other stakeholders.

2. **Analyze the problem**: Once you have a clear understanding of the problem, you need to analyze it to identify the root cause. This may involve looking at data, conducting research, or brainstorming solutions.

3. **Develop a solution**: Once you have identified the root cause of the problem, you can develop a solution. This may involve implementing a new process, developing a new product, or changing the way that you do business.

4. **Implement the solution**: The next step is to implement the solution that you have developed. This may involve training employees, changing the way that you do business, or launching a new product.

5. **Evaluate the solution**: The final step is to evaluate the solution to see whether it has resolved the problem. This may involve collecting data, conducting surveys, or interviewing customers.

For each business problem, try to find a data solution that matches the requirements. In the interview process (and in real-life implementations), you should always consider following our method for problem resolution to align your organization's needs and limitations with industry solutions and methodologies. Consider the following as a guide to uncovering the limitations of your business solutions:

- **Delivery times**: What is the time frame for your project? Data warehouses may take *years* to be developed and mature, while on the other hand, data mashups can be created in a matter of hours:

  - Data lakes: longer time frame

  - Data warehouses: medium time frame

  - Data mashups: short time frame

- **Costs**: Consider the cost of licenses, server consumption, processing, and storage costs.

- **Organization size**: Team size and the number of stakeholders may play an important role in how much bureaucracy you will have to contend with when gathering requirements and solving problems. As stated previously, in *Chapter 1*, it is important to know the roles of key individuals and subject matter experts in order to speed up the delivery process.

- **Human resources**: The learning curve of a project can be affected by the tenure and skills of the employees involved.

- **Data volume**: As we discussed in the first two points, data volume may push you to optimize for a rushed or more robust solution. Large datasets may not require a data warehouse precisely, but a long list of medium-sized tables could, and the number of joins could make computation expensive and explode the number of records considerably.

- **Company prioritization**: Every company has its own distinct set of priorities at the time of project implementation, so it's important to try to align your project with the company goals by making a strong case for it. We recommend thinking in terms of potential **return on investment (ROI)** and adoption usage.

- **Technology**: Your current technology stack is also relevant when picking the right solution, especially in instances where your organization's entire transaction ecosystem is based on a specific vendor (e.g., Oracle, SAP). In these instances, you can suggest two paths: a tech-agnostic solution to help your organization bridge the gap of vendor independence or opt for a vendor solution that integrates better with your needs (and possibly obtain a reasonable deal or package).

- **Know-how**: Whether you are able to provide your own solutions or you outsource them will be very important to assess during the BI project planning; costs and time to delivery will likely depend on this criteria.

As discussed, we implore you to identify the data solution that best meets the needs of each business problem. This means understanding the problem, the data that is available, and the tools and techniques that can be used to solve the problem. It is also important to consider the resources that are available, such as time, money, and people.

We also encourage you to not be afraid to think outside the box and come up with new and innovative solutions. It is important to be realistic about what can be achieved with the data that is available. Be willing to adapt your solution as needed and work with others to find the best possible solution.

Potential business cases and solutions

Now that we've covered an approach for building a business problem and data solutions matrix, we'll turn our attention to one of the most challenging components of any interview process – behavioral or situational questions.

Behavioral interview questions are a type of question that asks candidates to share examples of situations they have been in (typically at work but sometimes in daily life) where they had to use certain skills or are asked to demonstrate how they navigated certain types of scenarios. You have likely heard these via a prompt that starts with *"...tell me about a time when you..."*. The reason for the popularity of these questions is that it gives interviewers a better sense of how potential employees would handle situations that they will inevitably encounter while working at the organization.

While behavioral-type questions can cause a lot of stress for potential interviewees, there's no reason to be fearful. You might be asking why you should feel confident to take these types of questions head on. Because behavioral interview questions are non-technical, something you can prepare for in advance, and crucially, completely focused on you and your relevant work experience and skill set. It is very likely that you have the answers already and simply need to find the right stories relevant to the question and polish them a bit.

As much as we wish we could tell you exactly which behavioral questions you'll get in an interview, there are simply too many to try to cover in this book. Our hope is that this list will give you a general sense of the types of questions you might be asked in an interview process. As you read through them, take the time to think of stories you can share in response to each question (write them in a separate document if you find that helpful!). You will find that, oftentimes, your answers can be tweaked on the spot to cover any variation an interviewer might present.

Teamwork

As companies and businesses become infinitely more complex, most jobs will require you to work with others to be able to manage that complexity. BI professionals will need to be able to demonstrate they can work as part of a larger team. This is because teamwork is an essential skill for any BI professional. To be successful, BI professionals need to be able to work effectively with others, both inside and outside of their department. They need to be able to communicate their ideas clearly, collaborate with others, and resolve conflicts.

One way to prepare for questions about teamwork is to think about specific examples of times when you have worked successfully with others. What were the challenges you faced? How did you overcome them? What were the results of your collaboration? Here are some examples of teamwork-related questions:

- "Give us an example of a time you had conflict with a coworker and how you handled the situation."
- "Describe a time when you needed to get some additional requirements from a stakeholder who wasn't being responsive. What did you do?"

- "Tell me about a time you had a challenging manager and how you handled the situation."
- "Describe a time when you had to collaborate with someone who had a different working style than you."
- "Give me an example of a time when you had to take charge and show leadership skills."

Customer service

For most business and data analysts, a large part of your workflow is interacting with clients, customers, or other external stakeholders to gather requirements and produce analyses. However, BI professionals working in more technical roles aren't off the hook; it behooves you as a professional to be ready for one or more of these responsibilities. Think through scenarios where you went above and beyond to meet a customer's needs. The interviewer will be interested in hearing about how you were able to exceed the customer's expectations and how you were able to build a positive relationship with the customer. Here are some examples of customer service-related questions:

- "Give an example of a time when you represented your company or team well in a customer interaction."
- "Highlight a time when you built a positive relationship with a customer."
- "How do you prioritize your customers' needs when working with multiple stakeholders?"
- "Recall a time when you handled a customer complaint in a professional and satisfying manner."
- "Share a story about a time when you went above and beyond to make a customer happy."

Adaptability

Adaptability is a key attribute of any successful BI professional, as we have discussed and will discuss several times in this book. While times of turmoil can be challenging, it isn't all bad – we often learn the most when we overcome challenging problems or environments. For these questions, think through any recent work crisis you successfully navigated. In those instances where the outcome wasn't ideal, find a lesson learned you took from the situation. This demonstrates to the interviewer your level of maturity and ability to grow. Here are some examples of adaptability-related questions:

- "Tell me about a time when you were under a lot of stress and how you handled it."
- "Share a time when you fell short of your own or your manager's expectations and how you handled it."
- "Tell me about a time when your team went through a major change or reorganization and how it directly affected you. What did you do to manage the situation?"
- "Describe a time when you had to find a solution to a challenging problem without having much time to assess the problem."

- "Tell us about a time you had to adjust to a new role. How did you get up to speed and acclimate yourself to a new environment?"

Time management

Time is not infinite, and oftentimes time constraints are a huge factor in the success or failure of a project. BI professionals will often have to juggle multiple projects and deadlines, so it is important for them to be able to manage their time effectively (recall that earlier in the chapter, we talked about the importance of delivery times when designing a solution for a business problem). Therefore, it is very likely that interviewers will ask about your time management skills and what steps you typically take to prioritize, schedule, organize, and complete projects before their deadlines. Here are some examples of time management-related questions:

- "Tell us about a time you felt overwhelmed by your responsibilities. What did you do to manage your time and stress?"

- "Share with us a time when an unexpected issue caused you to miss a deadline. What did you do to recover and ensure your deliverables would be met?"

- "Describe a time when you had a lot of competing responsibilities and how you were able to manage them successfully."

- "Tell me about a time when you were assigned a year-long assignment and how you broke it down into smaller steps to achieve it."

- "Describe a project that almost got derailed because of your teammates' time mismanagement. How did you get it back on track?"

Communication

Communication is an extremely critical component of any BI role and has become even more important with the wide-scale adoption of remote work (video calls, emails, Slack, etc.). As a BI professional, communication skills are used so regularly that it'll be important to tell stories that demonstrate your ability to communicate with coworkers, managers, and business stakeholders. Your interviewers will want evidence that you are able to communicate effectively with your team, managers, and stakeholders to ensure that your insights are understood and acted upon. Here are some examples of communication-related questions:

- "Tell us about a time when you were the most knowledgeable person in your organization about a particular technology or business subject. How did you communicate your expertise in a way that was understandable to others?"

- "Share a time when you gave a technical presentation that was well-received by your audience. What do you think made it successful?"

- "Tell me about a time when you had to communicate your ideas solely through writing (email, Slack messages, documentation). What were the challenges you faced getting your point across, and how did you overcome them?"

- "Describe a situation when you were able to successfully convince someone at work to implement a new way of doing a daily task. What was the situation, and how did you approach it?"

- "Describe a time when you had to deal with a difficult customer or colleague. How did you make sure they knew their concerns were being heard?"

Motivation and values

As with many things in life, motivation can be very fleeting. Being able to convey to your interviewers what motivates you is extremely important in determining whether you are going to be a good fit for the team and organization. But why? By understanding your motivations, interviewers can get a better sense of whether you are a good fit for the company culture and the role. However, motivation by itself is not enough to determine whether you are a fit for the culture. It will be very difficult to be successful in a role if your values don't line up with the company's values. Therefore, it is important to highlight *your* values in interview answers and show how they align with the company's values. Here are some examples of motivation and value-related questions:

- "Share a time when you were able to use your creativity to overcome a technical limitation. What was the challenge, and how did you overcome it?"

- "Describe a time when you saw a problem and took the lead in fixing it. What was the problem, what did you do, and what was the outcome?"

- "Tell me about a time when you wanted to gain more independence in your role. How did you handle having that conversation with your manager?"

- "What is one of your proudest professional or academic achievements?"

- "Tell me about a time you were unhappy with your daily tasks. What did you do to make things better?"

To help our readers prepare for these types of questions, we provided six distinct business problems that demonstrate a potential interview prompt, the project we used to formulate our thinking, and a breakdown of the business problem using the **STAR methodology**.

The STAR method is an interview technique that you can use to tell a story by laying out the Situation, Task, Action, and Result:

- **Situation**: Describe a situation you were in or a task you needed to accomplish, giving the interviewer details to understand the challenge(s) you faced

- **Task**: What goal were you working toward, and what were you ultimately responsible for delivering?

- **Action**: Describe what actions you took to address the situation, making sure to discuss what specific steps you took and how you were able to contribute to achieving the outcome

- **Result**: Describe the outcome of your actions and share how the situation was resolved, what you were able to accomplish, and what you learned from it

By using these four components to shape your story, it makes it easier for you to share a more nuanced answer and provide the interviewer with a simple but informative narrative of how you handled different scenarios. The STAR methodology is a great way to answer behavioral interview questions because it allows you to provide specific examples of your skills and experience. It also helps you to focus on the positive aspects of your experiences, even if they are challenging.

When choosing your own examples to share, be sure to choose ones that are relevant to the role you are applying for. For example, if you are applying for a job as a database administrator, you might share an example of a time when you proactively identified and addressed a potential problem with a database. Or, if you were applying for a job as a data analyst, you might share an example of a time when you communicated your findings to your stakeholders clearly and concisely.

When describing your example, be sure to be specific about what you did, why you did it, and how it turned out. Highlight the positive outcomes of your actions. When answering interview questions, it is important to be confident and enthusiastic. This will show the interviewer that you are someone who is not afraid to take risks and who is always looking for ways to improve.

We hope that you find the following examples informative and useful.

Our first scenario looks at time management and showing initiative. In this example, we are showing the interviewer that we're excited to take on new challenges and responsibilities and that we go above and beyond our stakeholder's expectations.

Interview Prompt	Project Name	STAR Method	Scenario and Outcomes
Initiative Tell me about a time you delivered more than what was requested for a project.	Large Dataset Dashboard	SITUATION	As a business intelligence analyst, I was tasked with developing a new dashboard for a client in the healthcare industry. The dashboard needed to provide insights into patient outcomes, and the project had a tight deadline.
		TASK	My task was to develop a dashboard that could efficiently analyze large sets of data to identify patterns and correlations between patient outcomes and medical interventions.
		ACTION	1. I took the time to understand the client's requirements thoroughly. I collaborated closely with the client to understand their goals, expectations, and pain points. 2. I conducted extensive research to understand the latest trends and technologies in the healthcare industry, which helped me design a dashboard that met the client's needs. 3. I developed a prototype dashboard and presented it to the client for feedback. Following the demo, I incorporated their feedback to ensure the dashboard met their expectations and requirements. 4. I went beyond the initial project scope and included additional features that would add value to the client's operations, such as a data segmentation feature that would help them identify patient cohorts with similar outcomes. 5. I conducted rigorous testing and debugging, ensuring that the dashboard was error-free and that the data presented was accurate. 6. I also developed a user guide that would help the client understand how to use the dashboard, providing step-by-step instructions and best practices.
		RESULT	The client was extremely pleased with the dashboard because it provided them with insights that they did not have access to previously. The dashboard received positive feedback from both the client and patients, who appreciated the increased transparency and ability to see their outcomes over time. The additional features included in the dashboard added significant value to the client's operations, saving them time and improving their decision-making capabilities. The project's success led to new opportunities for our team to work with the client.

Table 4.1: Example scenario 1

Our second scenario looks at teamwork and negotiation skills. In this example, we are showing the interviewer that we're open to feedback and suggestions from others and that we're committed to continuous improvement.

Interview Prompt	Project Name	STAR Method	Scenario and Outcomes
Negotiation Tell me about a time your teammates disagreed with you on a solution and how you convinced them.	Data Visualization	SITUATION	As a business intelligence analyst, my team and I were working on a project for a client in the financial industry that wanted to analyze their customer data to identify patterns and improve their marketing campaigns.
		TASK	My task was to develop a data visualization solution that would help the client gain insights into their customer data and improve their marketing campaigns.
		ACTION	1. As a team, we analyzed the client's requirements and decided to develop a dashboard that would display the data visualization solution. 2. I proposed that we use a specific data visualization tool that I had experience with and was confident would provide the best results. However, some of my teammates were not familiar with the tool and were hesitant to use it because they believed there would be a learning curve to using the tool. 3. I listened to their concerns and feedback, but I felt strongly that what I was proposing would provide the best solution for the client based on their requirements because I had used it for a similar client in a previous project. 4. I created a prototype dashboard using the tool I suggested and presented it to them to help assuage their fears about the tool, highlighting its benefits, including the ability to handle substantial amounts of data, the flexibility, and the different advanced visualizations available. 6. I also addressed their concerns by providing a step-by-step guide on how to use the tool and offered to provide training and support to help them become more comfortable with it.
		RESULT	My teammates were impressed with the prototype dashboard and agreed that the tool I suggested was the best option for the client's needs. We worked together to develop the dashboard using the tool I suggested, and it was a success. The client was pleased with the solution, which provided them with valuable insights into their customer data and helped improve their marketing campaigns. The project's success led our team to work on establishing a long-term partnership with the client.

Table 4.2: Example scenario 2

Our third scenario looks at our commitment to personal development and motivation. In this example, we are showing the interviewer that we're proactive, enthusiastic about our work, and that we're willing to go the extra mile to get the job done.

Interview Prompt	Project Name	STAR Method	Scenario and Outcomes
Personal Development Tell me about your greatest achievement.	Data Warehouse Design	SITUATION	As a senior data engineer, I was tasked with developing a data warehouse for a client in the e-commerce industry. The client had a complex data structure, and they wanted to be able to access and analyze their data efficiently.
		TASK	My task was to design and develop a data warehouse that would allow the client to store and analyze their data efficiently and accurately.
		ACTION	1. I collaborated closely with the client to understand their business needs and requirements, conducting a thorough analysis of their data structure and identifying key areas for improvement. 2. I designed a data warehouse architecture that would meet the client's needs, incorporating data warehouse best practices and the latest technologies. 3. I developed a data extraction, transformation, and loading (ETL) process that would efficiently transfer data from the client's systems to the data warehouse. 4. I conducted rigorous testing and debugging, ensuring that the data in the data warehouse was accurate and could be analyzed efficiently. 5. I developed a set of reports and dashboards that would allow the client to analyze their data effectively, providing insights into their business operations and identifying areas for improvement. 6. I provided training and support to the client, helping them understand how to use the reports and dashboards.
		RESULT	The data warehouse and the reports and dashboards I developed were a tremendous success. The client could access and analyze their data efficiently and accurately, providing valuable insights into their business operations. The project's success led to new opportunities for our team to work with the client, and we were able to establish a long-term partnership with them. I received recognition from both the client and my colleagues for my work, and the project was highlighted as a best practice example within our company.

Table 4.3: Example scenario 3

Our fourth scenario looks at how we learn from failure and showcases our adaptability. In this example, we are showing the interviewer that we're willing to experiment by trying new things, by being open to feedback, and by being comfortable sharing both our successes and failures.

Interview Prompt	Project Name	STAR Method	Scenario and Outcomes
Learning from Failure Give me an example of when you took a risk and failed.		SITUATION	As an HR reporting analyst, I was tasked with investigating why talented faculty and staff were leaving the company, as employee departures are incredibly expensive, requiring onboarding new employees while also losing valuable institutional knowledge when an employee leaves their position. I came up with the idea to build a classification model to try to predict which employees would resign (1) and which would stay (0).
		TASK	My task was to design and develop a machine learning pipeline that would attempt to predict, with a .80 precision-recall score, which employees were more likely to resign based on certain criteria.
	Machine Learning Pipeline	ACTION	1. I did some initial data discovery and requirements gathering while working with the HR team's product owner and subject matter experts to produce the correct business rules for what qualified as a resignation. 2. I developed an ETL process to pull historical employee records from our data warehouse to prepare it for feature engineering. 3. I developed features about our employee population, including how many raises they received, movements across jobs, and many other data points that reflected the employee's job history. 4. I engineered the data using Python and various ML libraries into several hundred unique features that could be loaded into our machine learning models and then developed a few different models for professional staff and faculty. 5. I developed a set of reports that would allow the HR team to analyze the outcomes of the ML predictions, providing insight into what features were important and generating predictions for different sets of employees.
		RESULT	Unfortunately, our models were never able to get above a prediction threshold of .35 (our goal was .80), but the university staff learned a lot about the factors that were driving resignation; two of the biggest drivers were how well the employee was compensated as compared to their peers in similar roles, and what department or college they belonged to (i.e., the dentistry and medical schools had some of the highest levels of turnover due to the intense pressure of being in those fields). The HR leadership was impressed with the results and enjoyed being educated on how machine learning could improve outcomes for the university.

Table 4.4: Example scenario 4

Our fifth scenario looks at our proactiveness and commitment to customer service. In this example, we are showing the interviewer that we're a team player and that we are willing to collaborate with our stakeholders to make sure they get the best possible outcome for their reporting needs.

Interview Prompt	Project Name	STAR Method	Scenario and Outcomes
Proactiveness Tell me about an event when you employed simple and quick strategies and were able to get over of a major hurdle that was keeping your team from moving ahead.	Internal Reporting Redesign	SITUATION	As a data engineer, I was tasked with overhauling our company's internal reporting, a cluttered mess of Data Studio reports with no standard formatting, redundant data sources referencing the same queries, and no centralized location for internal business customers to access them. Any internal business customer who used reporting to help customers or answer operational issues could not trust the data to be trustworthy.
		TASK	My task was to quickly build a reporting solution using our existing data that would give business users the ability to view reports using real-time data as well as to view these reports on demand.
		ACTION	1. I started by collaborating closely with the leaders from each individual business unit to understand their needs and requirements and to design a dashboard that would answer their most immediate questions. 2. I designed data marts for each reporting area to meet each business unit's specific needs and set up new data sources in AWS Redshift that would refresh every 15 minutes. 3. I created five separate Tableau dashboards using the new data sources, demoing each dashboard for each business unit after completion. 4. I went through all the existing reports, decommissioning any that were no longer being used or were no longer required, and merged them all into one of the new dashboards. 5. I conducted rigorous testing and debugging of the dashboards prior to business signoff to confirm they met their needs and captured all relevant data points. 6. I provided training to each business unit, helping them understand how to use the reports and dashboards.
		RESULT	The dashboards were a smashing success; they could be accessed in real time, the data was refreshed frequently, and business customers started to trust the data and the data team's capabilities again. A senior account manager received an account renewal based on data in the operations dashboard showing how many new units had been set up in the last three weeks. I received much appreciation from my colleagues for my work, and the project was highlighted as a best practice example within our company.

Table 4.5: Example scenario 5

Our sixth and final scenario looks at becoming trustworthy to our stakeholders and focuses on our communication skills. In this example, we are showing the interviewer that we are patient, willing to answer questions, and we use visuals effectively to help communicate our findings.

Interview Prompt	Project Name	STAR Method	Scenario and Outcomes
Become Trustworthy Tell me a time when you earned the trust of a group.	Data Analysis	SITUATION	As a data analyst, I was tasked with working with a customer success manager on how to improve the overall experience for their client base, who were small businesses posting their jobs online. The business objective was to identify customer representatives who had low net promoter scores after interactions with customers.
		TASK	My task was to build a comprehensive analysis to determine why customer reps were underperforming and identify the underlying causes (i.e., due to a lack of adequate training or a lack of understanding of the site).
		ACTION	1. I started by working with the customer success manager to understand their requirements and determine the best approach to building an appropriate analysis to answer their questions. 2. I partnered with the BI engineering team to determine where the NPS survey data lived and set up a pipeline to extract the relevant data to a data table for manipulation and analysis. 3. I developed a Python notebook that pulled the raw NPS scores (scaled from 0 to 10, 10 being the highest) and filtered out any of the scores above a neutral/favorable rating. 4. I performed a sentiment analysis to uncover the specific reasons behind the poor ratings and determined that many customers were very traditional brick-and-mortar stores learning to use the internet and were struggling to navigate the site. 5. I set up quite a simple dashboard with the outcomes of the analysis that the marketing manager used to identify customers who had a negative experience to focus more of their resources on additional training and enhancing customer support documentation for representatives.
		RESULT	The results were outstanding, with the customer success team seeing a dramatic improvement in NPS scores, In three months, NPS scores for small business customer representatives went from an average of 6.0 to 8.0, and it improved the overall customer experience for many customers. It demonstrates how a team's customer strategy can benefit from the effective use of BI.

Table 4.6: Example scenario 6

As we discussed earlier in the chapter, the **STAR (Situation, Task, Action, and Result)** methodology is a structured way of answering behavioral interview questions. The STAR methodology is a helpful way to answer behavioral interview questions because it allows you to provide specific examples of your skills and experience while helping you to stay on track and avoid rambling.

To recap:

- Time management is important for BI professionals, who often have to juggle multiple projects and deadlines, so it is essential that they are able to manage their time effectively.

- Teamwork is also an important skill for BI professionals, who will often have to work with other teammates and communicate effectively with teams and collaborate on projects.

- Motivation is key for Bl professionals, who often have to work on complex and challenging projects, so that they stay engaged in their projects and achieve their organization's goals.

- Adaptability is also important for BI professionals because the field of BI is constantly changing and requires adapting to new technologies and new ways of working.

- Customer service is often overlooked by BI professionals, but many will have to interact with customers to gather requirements, explain results, and resolve issues, and they must approach those interactions with an excellent customer service mindset.

- Communication skills are extremely critical for BI professionals because they will have to communicate with technical and non-technical audiences and need to explain complex ideas in a clear and concise way.

By showcasing these skills to interviewers, you can demonstrate how valuable you will be as an employee and increase your chances of success in a BI career.

A hypothetical BI interview process and what to expect

Business intelligence interviews will typically follow a fairly standardized process (with some exceptions based on the company size and industry). In our experience, the process will generally look like and follow these steps:

1. **Phone screening**: The first step is a call with a recruiter or hiring manager. This call is used to see whether your career goals and experience align with the role, whether you have the right skills, and to gauge your overall interest in the position. For the phone screening, we suggest being prepared for questions about your past experience, BI projects you have worked on, and business problems you have been asked to solve.

2. **Technical interview**: The technical screening is used to assess your technical skills. These screens typically focus on SQL and basic statistics (for both analysts and engineers), while engineering interviews usually include a few questions on Python (or a similar programming language). Depending on the company, you may be asked to whiteboard code or write code using a shared IDE.

3. **On-site (or virtual) interviews**: On-site or virtual interviews will vary greatly by company, but most include 3-5 sessions that will dive deeper and focus on SQL, Python, as well as business acumen and culture fit. For example, you might have a set of interviews covering these topics:

    - SQL and basic statistics

    - SQL and scenario-driven behavioral questions

    - A business case study interview

    - A behavioral interview focused on leadership skills

    - A statistics and product sense interview

To help you have more context on what's involved in the interview process, we've created a few example questions that you might see in a typical interview process. *This list is not meant to be exhaustive*, and there are many resources available online to help you prepare for different scenarios. Our hope with this section is to give you a starting point for doing your own research and preparing for the interview process.

While some of the questions may seem silly or too simple, they will likely be asked – so don't overlook them!

General business intelligence interview questions

Here are a few general BI questions that can be asked during an interview:

1. What is OLAP?

    "OLAP, or online analytical processing, is a software tool that you can use to conduct multidimensional analysis on large amounts of data. Where in the past you might have had to pull one record at a time, perform analysis, and then decide on the next dataset you wanted to pull and examine, OLAP allows you to quickly cycle through all the different combinations of datasets and inquiries that are of interest to you."

    "For example, a business's data warehouse typically has data stored in tables (which only contain two dimensions at a time). OLAP allows you to extract data from multiple datasets and then reorganize it into a multidimensional format for faster processing and analysis."

2. What is a pivot table?

    "A pivot table is one of the most commonly used data processing tools. It's a two-dimensional table that is used to summarize large volumes of data. A key benefit of pivot tables is that they allow users to quickly change how data is displayed and can help business intelligence analysts more quickly uncover insights from large datasets."

3. What is the primary key in a database?

    "A primary key is a keyword in a relational database that is unique for each record. Therefore, a primary key is NOT NULL and is also UNIQUE. Examples include records such as driver's license number, customer ID number, telephone number, or patient ID. Relational databases only have one primary key."

4. What are fact and dimension tables?

    "In data warehousing, a fact table consists of the dimension keys and numerical values of a business process. A fact table contains quantitative data that is used for analysis. Dimension tables, on the other hand, are qualitative dictionary tables that provide information about how the data in the fact table can be analyzed."

5. Why is data normalization useful?

    "Data normalization is the process of organizing and formatting data to appear similar across all records and fields. There are many benefits to data normalization. For example, the process helps to remove duplicate data and helps to maintain referential integrity. It also allows analysts to navigate quickly through different datasets, as they are already familiar with how the organization structures their data."

6. What are your favorite business intelligence tools?

    Be sure you are comfortable talking about your favorite tools. Some of the most common include Tableau, Power BI, Looker, and Oracle Business Intelligence Enterprise Edition. This type of question isn't just looking to establish what system you like but also why you like that tool over others. Try to familiarize yourself with the tools cited in the job posting, and give some concrete examples of how you utilized the tools in your previous roles.

7. What makes a good data visualization?

    Data visualization questions are frequently asked in business intelligence interviews. This question assesses your design philosophy and ability to distill business insights into actionable visualizations. A few key things to cover in your response include the following:

    - Color theory and aesthetics

    - Visualization use cases

    - Ease of deployment and development costs

    With your answer, make sure you reiterate that a good visualization is one that makes the data accessible to the target audience. A good visualization tells a story, and that story must be understandable to those to who you are presenting.

8. What are some uses for a data warehouse?

    "Data warehouses are separate databases that are used to store data separately from an operational database (think long-term storage). Warehouses are typically used for analytics tasks such as exploratory data analysis, validation, or tactical reporting. Data warehouses are where all historical data analysis is consolidated."

9. What are some of the benefits of data denormalization?

"Data denormalization, which combines normalized data in a format that can be accessed more quickly, has numerous benefits, including the following:

- Better read/write performance

- It is very useful in data warehouses because fact and dimension tables in warehouses are typically designed without regard to data normalization

- Precomputation and query performance improvements"

Scenario-based BI questions

Here are a few scenario-based BI questions for interview practice:

1. Tell me a time when you presented less than stellar results to leadership.

    You will likely be asked open-ended questions like this. These questions are an opportunity for you to tell the story of your career and how you approach your work. Essentially, the interviewer is trying to get a sense of your experience level and the types of problems you have encountered.

    To answer, first lay out the specifics of the problem you faced and your initial assumptions. Then, help the interviewer understand the steps you took to reach the final solution, including how you may have had to overcome setbacks or failures. This isn't a question designed to have a right or wrong answer; rather, it will show how you deal with complex situations.

2. What would you do if you noticed a decline in revenue?

    Business intelligence analyst interview questions assess your ability to perform analysis. For a question like this, you might be provided with a dataset that includes sales dates, the average percentage and frequency of any discounts, the profit margin per item sold, the total order value, and so on. Then you would walk the interviewer through your approach to discovering the root cause of the decline in sales or patterns you notice in your quantitative analysis that may point to areas of further investigation.

    With those data points, you could determine fairly quickly whether the revenue decline was due to declining sales, rising costs, or a mix of both. Suggest some month-over-month metrics you would be interested in following up on, such as the following:

- Revenue per marketing source

- Internally authorized discount models

- Profit margin per item sold

- Revenue by category

3. You have to develop a new solution for a stakeholder. How do you go about eliciting and designing for their needs?

    Elicitation is a technical term for gathering information from stakeholders and end users. The process changes based on the needs of the project. However, there are some key elicitation tactics you can use, including the following:

    - Interviews

    - Prototyping

    - Brainstorming

    - Workshops and observations

    - Surveys/questionnaires

    - Sentiment analysis

    Go deep into how you approach gathering stakeholder input. You might walk the interviewer through a recent example in which you led a brainstorming session and conducted stakeholder interviews to gain input.

Business case study questions

Here are a few business case study questions for interview practice:

1. How would you calculate the average lifetime value for a subscription-based product?

    To answer this question, you will likely be provided with metrics to use. For example, how would you calculate the lifetime value if provided with the following supplemental information:

    - The product costs $100 per month

    - There is a 10% monthly churn

    - The average customer stays subscribed for 3.5 months

    LTV = Monthly revenue per customer / Monthly churn rate * Average customer lifetime

    In this case, we plug these values into the equation:

    LTV = $100 / 0.10 * 3.5

    LTV = $3500

2. How would you handle duplicate product listings in a database for a large-scale e-commerce business?

    You could follow an approach like this:

    - **Identify duplicates**: Perform a comprehensive analysis of the database to identify duplicate product listings. This can be done by comparing key attributes such as product names,

SKUs (stock-keeping units), UPCs (universal product codes), or unique identifiers specific to your database.

- **Determine criteria for uniqueness**: Define the criteria that determine uniqueness for product listings. This could include attributes such as product name, brand, or a combination of multiple attributes. The goal is to establish a consistent rule to identify and merge duplicates effectively.

- **Merge duplicate listings**: Consolidate the data from duplicate product listings into a single, authoritative listing. This involves updating the relevant fields, such as product descriptions, images, pricing, and inventory information. Additionally, ensure that any linked data, such as customer reviews or historical sales data, are properly associated with the merged listing.

- **Update references**: After merging, update any references or links to the duplicate listings to point to the new, merged listing. This ensures consistency and avoids confusion in the database.

- **Implement data validation checks**: Put in place data validation checks during data entry or import processes to prevent the creation of new duplicate listings. This can include automated checks for matching attributes or integration with external data sources to verify product information.

By following these steps, you can effectively handle duplicate product listings in a database for a large-scale e-commerce business, ensuring data integrity."

SQL business intelligence interview questions

Following are a few SQL questions that you could be asked during a BI interview:

1. What is the difference between DELETE TABLE and TRUNCATE TABLE in SQL?

   "Although they are both used to delete data, a key difference is that DELETE is a **Database Manipulation Language** (**DML**) command, while TRUNCATE is a **Data Definition Language** (**DDL**) command."

   "Therefore, DELETE is used to remove specific data from a table, while TRUNCATE removes all the rows of a table without maintaining the table's structure. Another difference: DELETE can be used with the WHERE clause, but TRUNCATE cannot. In this case, DELETE TABLE would remove all the data from within the table while maintaining the structure. TRUNCATE TABLE would delete the table in its entirety."

2. Write a SQL query to select all records of employees with last names between Herrera and Moncada.

   For this question, assume the table is called Employees, and the last name column is LastName:

   ```
   SELECT * FROM Employees WHERE LastName BETWEEN 'Herrera' AND
   'Moncada';
   ```

   Write a SQL query to find the year from a YYYY-MM-DD date.

EXTRACT allows us to pull temporal data types such as date, time, timestamp, and interval from date and time values. If you wanted to find the year from 1986-12-12, you would write EXTRACT(FROM):

```
SELECT EXTRACT(YEAR FROM DATE '1986-12-12') AS year;
```

3. Write a SQL query to get the current salary for each employee.

    "To start, we need to remove any duplicate entries and keep the most recent salary for each user. We can do this by grouping the Employees table by first and last name. This will give us a unique combination of the two fields, which we can then use to keep the most recent salary for each user."

4. Write a query to return all the duplicate users from the users table:

```
SELECT
    id,
    name,
    created_at
FROM (
    SELECT
        *,
        row_number() OVER
            (PARTITION BY id ORDER BY created_at ASC)
            AS ranking
    FROM
        users) AS u
WHERE
    ranking > 1;
```

Database design business intelligence questions

Here is a list of a few database design questions:

1. What are the primary steps in database design?

    Database design typically includes the following:

    *   Conceptual database design
    *   Logical database design
    *   Physical database design

In the conceptual stage, you would identify entities in the data ecosystem and their relationships and attributes. The conceptual design is transformed into a logical framework during the second stage of logical database design. In the final stage, a physical database model is created. This stage includes making decisions about physically implementing the model, including security, choosing a database management system, storage, and file organization.

2. How would you create a schema to represent client click data on the web?

    "Can we clarify what 'click data on the web' means to you? I am making the assumption that this will constitute any form of button clicks, scrolls, or actions that a customer does via a mobile or web browser on your site."

    "One simple and effective way to design a data schema is to first assign a specific label to each action. For example, you could assign a name or label to each click event that describes the specific action that was taken. Once you have labeled each action, you can then think about how you would structure your data in a way based on your requirements and what type of reporting will be done with this kind of data."

3. How would you design a data warehouse for a new online retailer?

    To solve this, you could sketch a star schema to explain your design.

    You might choose something like this:

    -   Orders – `order_id`, `item_id`, `customer_id`, `price`, `date`, `payment_id`, `promotion_id`
    -   Customer – `customer_id`, `customer_name`, `address`, `city`, `country`, `phone`
    -   Items – `item_id`, `subcategory`, `category`, `brand`, `mrp`
    -   Payment – `payment_id`, `mode`, `amount`
    -   Promotions – `promotion_id`, `category`, `discount`, `start_date`, `end_date`
    -   Date – `date_id`, `date`, `month`, `year`, `day`

Python business intelligence interview questions

1. Write a simple Python function to determine whether a number is prime or not:

```python
a = int(input("enter number"))
if a = 1:
    for x in range(2, a):
if (a % x) == 0:
print("Not a prime number")
    break
    else:
        print("Prime number!")
else:
    print("Not a prime number")
```

2. Write a `minimum_change` function to find the minimum number of coins that make up the given amount of change (in cents). Assume we only have coins with values of 1, 5, 10, and 25 cents (this question is for all the former cashiers who learned how to do this in their head!):

```
def minimum_change(cents):
    count = 0
    while cents != 0:
        if cents >= 25:
            count += 1
            cents -= 25
        elif cents >= 10:
            count += 1
            cents -= 10
        elif cents >= 5:
            count += 1
            cents -= 5
        elif cents >= 1:
            count += 1
            cents -= 1
    return count


Input:
cents = 41
Output:
minimum_change(cents) -> 4
# (25 + 10 + 5 + 1)
```

This set of potential interview questions is not meant to be an exhaustive or definitive list that is typically asked during a business intelligence interview. However, we hope that this gives you some insight into a typical BI interview process and how to assess and break down complex problems into their components.

Summary

In summary, a typical business intelligence interview will start with an introduction from the interviewer and a brief overview of the role. The interviewer will then ask you a series of questions to assess your skills and experience in BI. These questions may cover a variety of topics, including the following:

- Your experience with BI tools and technologies
- Your ability to collect, clean, and analyze data
- Your ability to communicate your findings to stakeholders

- Your problem-solving and analytical skills

- Your creativity and innovation

The interviewer may also ask you behavioral questions to assess your fit for the company culture and the role. These questions may ask about your experience working in a team, your ability to handle stress, and your willingness to learn new things.

At the end of the interview, the interviewer will likely ask you if you have any questions. This is your chance to ask about the company, the role, and the interview process. It is also a good time to reiterate your interest in the role and your qualifications.

By following these tips, you can prepare for a successful BI interview! We wish you luck in your future interviews!

5
Business Intelligence Landscape

The **business intelligence** (**BI**) landscape is constantly evolving, with recent technologies and trends emerging all the time. However, some key components remain essential to any successful BI strategy.

One of the most crucial elements of the BI landscape is data. Data is the fuel that powers BI, and without it, there would be no insights to gain. Businesses need to collect and store data from various sources, including transactional, historical, and customer data.

Once data is collected, it needs to be cleaned and prepared for analysis. This involves removing errors and inconsistencies, and normalizing the data so that it can be used consistently.

Once the data is clean and has been prepared, it can be analyzed using a variety of tools and techniques. BI tools can help businesses identify trends, patterns, and outliers in their data. They can also be used to create interactive dashboards and reports that can be shared with stakeholders.

In addition to data and analysis, BI also requires a strong focus on user experience. BI tools need to be easy to use and navigate, and they need to provide users with the insights they need promptly.

By collecting and storing data, cleaning, and preparing it, analyzing it with BI tools, and focusing on user experience, businesses can gain the insights they need to make better decisions. This blueprint has resisted the passage of time. Innovation in the BI landscape requires technology that accelerates that process or removes steps in between. In other words, for the BI landscape to change drastically, a technology we have not seen yet needs to be created. Buzzwords include blockchain, quantum computing, automated semantic layers, and my personal favorite, **artificial intelligence** (**AI**).

As we wait for those to take off, here are some of the latest trends in the BI landscape:

- **The rise of cloud-based BI**: Cloud-based BI platforms are becoming increasingly popular as they offer many advantages over on-premises solutions. Cloud-based BI platforms are typically more affordable, scalable, and secure than on-premises solutions.

- **The increasing importance of data visualization**: Data visualization is a key component of any BI strategy as it can help businesses communicate their findings concisely. Data visualization tools can help businesses create interactive dashboards, reports, and charts that can be shared with stakeholders.

- **The growing adoption of self-service BI**: Self-service BI platforms let users explore and analyze data without IT or business analysts' help. This can help businesses to get more value from their data and make better decisions.

- **The increasing use of artificial intelligence (AI) and machine learning (ML)**: AI and ML can be used to automate many of the tasks that are currently done by humans in BI. This can help businesses save time and money and improve the accuracy and speed of their analysis. Classifying fields used to be as simple as using an `ALTER` statement in a database table; however, there are cases when we do not know the full list of distinct values it contains or it may contain in the future inside a large table.

Now, let's cut to the chase. Everything you have learned so far needs to be applied and in today's world velocity is in high demand. Manual work is unacceptable and, in most cases, impossible. Humans cannot process data with the same accuracy that machines can. For this, we'll present you with the BI landscape, which will shape your learning process and accelerate your career master plan. Tools, not without restrictions, will be there to capture your knowledge and apply your algorithms for a quicker turnaround of projects.

The current landscape and the most effective technologies to study

Are you ready to dive into the world of BI tools and technologies? Before we continue, let me give you a word of caution: resist the urge to try and learn it all. This will be presented to you after so that you can find the pros and cons of each tool and use them according to your situation. We believe that a *BI Career Master Plan* is not about learning tools but more importantly, about learning which type of tool you should look for by comparing problems to solve and checking and marking matching features.

It is also important to understand how this book does not encourage trendy software but realizes the scenarios different organizations are going through, what budget they have, human capital, technology infrastructure, as well as software dependency. For example, we cannot recommend Fivetran as opposed to SAP Replication Server if your company's ecosystem is already on SAP consisting of on-premises databases; it will depend on many factors, so do not fall for trends just for the sake of being at the front row of innovation.

Remember that many of these companies producing new tools are startups; this means they are subject to going through periods of rapid growth and numerous changes. This means that you are taking a risk implementing their tool because their future may be uncertain, or their software changes rapidly (or not rapidly enough), or they get acquired and their business model changes, or the worst possible outcome, the startup fails. Our main philosophy is *the path of less resistance* and encourages you *not to waste your time* by learning a specific product or learning every product. Learn how to solve problems and how to spot the tool for that problem.

Collecting data

Data collection is at the forefront of any business that wants to use data to improve its decision-making. Businesses collect data from various sources to make informed decisions, improve their operations, and create personalized experiences for their customers. Database replication, batch processing, and data streaming are all important concepts in data collection. Database replication can be used to collect data from a variety of sources, batch processing can be used to process substantial amounts of data, and data streaming can be used to process data in real-time By using a combination of these techniques, businesses can collect and process data more efficiently and effectively. Let's explore each of these concepts in a little more depth.

Database replication

Database replication is the process of copying data from one database to another. This can be done for several reasons, such as to provide a backup of the data, to make it available to multiple users, or to improve the database's performance.

The reason this technology exists as opposed to batch processing or data streaming is to lift an entire set of tables in a database and shift it to a new location. Even though some of these technologies offer near real-time solutions, they are not to be confused with data streaming. Database replication is a synchronous process, while data streaming is an asynchronous process. In database replication, the data is copied from the source database to the destination database before it is available to users. In data streaming, the data is sent from the source system to the destination system as it is generated.

Database replication is a more traditional approach to data duplication, while data streaming is a newer approach that is becoming increasingly popular. Data streaming offers several advantages over database replication, such as the ability to handle large volumes of data and the ability to provide real-time analytics. However, data streaming also has some disadvantages, such as the need for reliable network connections and the need to store the data in a cloud-based storage system.

In this book, the primary use case for data replication is to serve as an excellent choice for applications that require a copy of the data to be available for offline use.

Database replication is essential for BI because it lets businesses keep their data consistent and up to date across all their systems. This is important for BI because BI applications need to be able to access data from multiple sources to generate accurate and timely insights.

Database replication also allows businesses to improve the performance of their BI applications by reducing the amount of time it takes to access data. This is because data is stored in multiple locations, so BI applications can access it from the closest location. Imagine for a second trying to read a book at the same time the author is trying to write it for the first time – you want to turn some pages back to remember what was said before or you may catch up and be at the latest word being written. In either case, the author would have to pause many times for you to go back a few pages, waiting for you to catch up, hence disrupting their writing. This is the same principle behind writing on a database and having applications consuming data in parallel. By replicating the database to a "safe place," any application can now consume it without disrupting any input service.

Finally, database replication can help businesses improve the security of their data by making it more difficult for unauthorized users to access it. This is because data is replicated to multiple locations, so if one location is compromised, the data is still available from the other locations.

Now, let's go through some database replication players in the market:

Product	Features	Comments
Acronis	Automatic. Real-time Flexible options: full, incremental, and differential replication. User-friendly interface. Affordable.	It is not as well known as some other database replication software, can be complex to set up, and can be resource-intensive.
Carbonite	Continuous replication. High availability. Data security. Hybrid cloud.	It is not as well known as some other database replication software, can be complex to set up, and can be resource-intensive.
Dell EMC RecoverPoint	Continuous replication. Point-in-time recovery. Replication to multiple locations. Data compression. Encryption. Disaster recovery. Data protection. Compliance.	Although DELL EMC is sold by a well-known player, the tool itself is not well known and the support may be problematic. It can also be complex to set up and resource-intensive.

Fivetran	Data extraction from over 200+ sources: Fivetran can extract data from over 200+ sources, including databases, SaaS applications, and cloud storage services. Data transformation: Fivetran can transform data into a format that is ready for loading into a data warehouse or data lake. Data loading: Fivetran can load data into a data warehouse or data lake in a variety of formats, including CSV, JSON, and Parquet.	One thing to consider is that Fivetran lacks enterprise data management capabilities. Fivetran lacks broader data management capabilities found in more enterprise-oriented tools such as auto-discovery of data semantics, data virtualization, data governance, and data quality capabilities.
Hevo Data	Data extraction from over 150+ sources. Data transformation. Data loading: Hevo Data can load data into the destination in a variety of formats, including CSV, JSON, and Parquet. Automatic. Real-time. Hybrid cloud.	It is not as well known as some other database replication software, can be complex to set up, and can be resource-intensive.
HVR	Real-time Hybrid replication (both cloud and on-premises). Data compression. Data encryption.	HVR can be complex to set up and resource-intensive.
IBM Spectrum Protect	Continuous replication. Data compression. Data encryption. Hybrid cloud.	Spectrum Protect can be used to replicate data from a variety of database sources, including SQL Server, Oracle, PostgreSQL, MySQL, and IBM DB2 to a variety of backup targets, including disk, tape, and cloud.

Informatica Data Replication	Continuous replication. Data compression. Data encryption. Hybrid cloud.	Expensive licensing model.
Lyftrondata Replication	Real-time, hybrid, compressed, and encrypted replication. Databases: Lyftrondata Replication can replicate data from a variety of databases, including MySQL, PostgreSQL, SQL Server, Oracle, and MongoDB. Data warehouses: Lyftrondata Replication can replicate data from a variety of data warehouses, including Amazon Redshift, Google BigQuery, and Microsoft Azure Synapse Analytics. Cloud applications: Lyftrondata Replication can replicate data from a variety of cloud applications, including Salesforce, Workday, and ServiceNow.	Very versatile.
NAKIVO Backup & Replication	This is a VM data protection solution that can help businesses protect their virtual, physical, and cloud environments with its all-in-one backup, replication, anti-ransomware protection, disaster recovery, and VM monitoring solution.	Some users have reported that it can be difficult to configure, resource-intensive, and expensive.
NetApp SnapMirror	SnapMirror is a feature of Data ONTAP software. Replication of data within the same storage system or with different storage systems. SnapMirror is a feature of NetApp's ONTAP storage operating system. It can be used to replicate data between any two ONTAP systems, at high speeds over LAN or WAN.	Used for applications in Microsoft Exchange, Microsoft SQL Server, and Oracle. Sources include virtual and traditional environments, regardless of the type of storage media or the distance between the two systems.

| Oracle GoldenGate | Real-time data replication.

Transformation across heterogeneous environments means the use of multiple platforms, operating systems, and database technologies.

It is a component of Oracle's Data Integrator product suite.

Real-time BI and stream analytics for improved business insight.

Query offloading to maximize OLTP performance.

Zero-downtime data migration, disaster recovery, and active-active database synchronization for continuous availability.

Auditing to provide you with a complete record of all changes to your data. | Users have reported good reviews about its reliability, which includes no missing items and it having large databases with thousands of tables. This software has shown to be consistent when recreating every object.

However, some users have reported that GoldenGate can sometimes lag in syncing large objects (that is, CLOBs and BLOBs) on tables. Software is quite expensive and complex to implement, and more importantly, its licensing may be tied to other Oracle offerings. |

Here are some other players in the market:

- Quest SharePlex
- Qlik Replicate
- Rubrik Cloud Data Management
- SAP Replication Server
- Veeam Backup & Replication
- Zerto Platform

Batch processing

Data batch processing is the process of collecting and processing large amounts of data in batches, rather than in real-time. This is essential for BI because it allows businesses to collect and analyze data from a variety of sources, including social media, customer transactions, and sensor data.

Batch processing is typically used for tasks such as the following:

- **Data warehousing**: Data warehousing is the process of storing and managing data in a way that makes it easy to access and analyze. Batch processing is often used to load data into data warehouses.

- **Data mining**: Data mining is the process of extracting patterns from data. Batch processing is often used to mine data for insights that can be used to improve business decisions.

- **Data visualization**: Data visualization is the process of presenting data in a way that makes it easy to understand. Batch processing is often used to generate data visualizations that can be used to communicate insights to stakeholders.

Here are a few key platforms that allow batch processing:

- **Apache Hadoop**: This is an open source software framework for storing and processing large amounts of data

- **Apache Spark**: This is another open source cluster computing framework that provides high-performance data processing for both batch and real-time data

The following private cloud-based services can be used to automate the process of collecting, transforming, and loading data into a data warehouse:

- Microsoft Azure and its product, Azure Data Factory

- **Amazon Web Services (AWS)** with its AWS Glue

- **Google Cloud Platform (GCP)** and its product, Dataproc

Data streaming

Data streaming is the process of continuously collecting and processing data from a variety of sources. This is essential for BI because it allows businesses to collect and analyze data in real-time which can help them make better decisions faster.

Data streaming is typically used for tasks such as the following:

- **Fraud detection**: Data streaming can be used to detect fraudulent transactions in real-time This can help businesses prevent fraud and protect their customers.

- **Customer behavior analysis**: Data streaming can be used to analyze customer behavior in real-time. This can help businesses understand their customers better and improve their products and services.

- **Risk management**: Data streaming can be used to monitor risk in real-time. This can help businesses identify potential risks and take steps to mitigate them.

- **Market research**: Data streaming can be used to collect market research data in real-time. This can help businesses understand their market better and make better decisions about their products and services.

Here are some of the benefits of data streaming:

- **Real-time insights**: Data streaming allows businesses to get real-time insights into their data, which can help them make better decisions faster

- **Improved decision-making**: Data streaming can help businesses improve their decision-making by providing them with access to real-time data

- **Increased efficiency**: Data streaming can help businesses increase their efficiency by automating tasks and processes

- **Reduced costs**: Data streaming can help businesses reduce their costs by automating tasks and processes

- **Increased profits**: Data streaming can help businesses increase their profits by providing them with insights into their data, which can help them make better decisions

Here are some use cases of data streaming:

- **Real-time stock market data**: Stock prices are constantly changing, and investors need to be able to access the latest data to make informed decisions. Data streaming allows investors to do this by providing them with a continuous stream of stock prices.

- **Internet of Things (IoT) data**: IoT generates a massive amount of data, and this data needs to be processed in real-time to be useful. Data streaming can be used to process IoT data and extract insights from it.

- **Machine learning data**: **Machine learning** (ML) algorithms need to be trained on large amounts of data to work effectively. Data streaming can be used to train ML algorithms by providing them with a continuous stream of data.

- **Customer behavior data**: Companies need to understand how their customers are behaving to make better decisions about their products and services. Data streaming can be used to track customer behavior and identify trends.

- **Social media data**: Social media platforms generate a massive amount of data, and this data can be used to understand how people interact with each other. Data streaming can be used to collect and analyze social media data.

Apache Kafka, Apache Beam, Apache Storm, and Apache Flink are distributed streaming platforms that can be used to process and store large amounts of data in real-time and have become quite popular in the BI landscape.

Here are some private offerings of real-time platforms:

- **Amazon Kinesis**: Kinesis is a fully managed service that can be used to collect and process real-time data from multiple sources. Kinesis Data Analytics is used to transform and analyze streaming data in real-time while leveraging the open-source framework and engine of Apache Flink.

- **Google Cloud Dataflow**: Dataflow is a fully managed service that can be used to build and run Apache Beam pipelines. Beam pipelines can be used to process and store large amounts of data in real-time.

- **Azure Stream Analytics**: Stream Analytics is a serverless, scalable, complex event processing engine by Microsoft that enables users to develop and run real-time analytics on multiple streams of data from sources such as devices, sensors, websites, social media, and other applications.

When it comes to collecting data, data replication, batch processing, and streaming are there for us in different cases and requirements. It will always depend on basic questions:

- How often is our data going to be consumed?

- How fast is our data being generated?

- Do we have enough off hours to process it?

- Is our computing power enough to process the volume of data?

- Are transformations required?

Imagine a lake that supplies water to a nearby town. The town has water towers and every household has a reservoir. The speed at which water flows from each source to each target is determined by consumption. There might be water trucks that would just extract water from the lake and take it to the farms or the industry, given their requirements for water in bulk. Maybe a pipe that fills up the water towers from the lake is all the village requires, or, in other cases, there is machinery that pumps water faster to be consumed at the same rate as it arrives – for example, the fire department to assist in emergencies.

Storing data

Now that we've collected the data, we need to find somewhere to put it, right? Storing data is the next step in the process, and just like with everything else in BI, there are many ways to store data based on your use cases for the data. For example, blockchain can be used to store data in a secure and tamper-proof way. API consumption can be used to make it easier to access data that is stored in another system. Databases can be used to organize and store data. Object cloud storage can be used to store large objects. Data warehouses can be used to store large amounts of data from different sources. Workflow automation can be used to improve efficiency and reduce errors. By using a combination of these techniques, businesses can store data more efficiently and securely. We'll go into each one in more depth here.

Blockchain

A **blockchain** is a distributed database that allows for secure, transparent, and tamper-proof transactions. It is a type of database that is used to store data in a way that makes it difficult to hack or modify. Blockchains are often used in cryptocurrencies, such as Bitcoin, but they can also be used in other applications, such as supply chain management and financial services.

Blockchains are made up of blocks of data that are linked together. Each block contains a record of transactions, and each new transaction is added to the chain as a new block. The blocks are then verified by a network of computers, and once they are verified, they are added to the blockchain.

Blockchains are secure because they are distributed across multiple computers. This means that even if one computer is hacked, the rest of the network can still verify the transactions. Blockchains are also transparent because they are public. Anyone can view the transactions that are recorded on the blockchain.

Blockchains have been used in databases in a variety of ways. For example, blockchains have been used to create tamper-proof databases of medical records. They have also been used to create databases of customer transactions.

Blockchains are a new technology, and there is still a lot of research being done on how to use them effectively. However, they have the potential to revolutionize the way that data is stored and managed. It is understandable that, being a buzzword, it could be dismissed, but the use cases, although isolated, are real, beyond banking. For example, in genetics, researchers around the world working for the same organization and merging their sequencing could be problematic if it depends on "taking your turn in a queue." You might have users in Germany, the US, South America, and many more countries, with central servers in China. Network latency would make everything more difficult as someone in a closer country may get its turn faster than someone who should be next but it's taking time to get a ping. Blockchains solve this by taking your turn locally and instead of sending your ping or package, the blockchain takes care of merging links in the right order based on their local time.

API consumption

An **application programming interface** (**API**) is a software intermediary that allows two applications to communicate with each other. APIs are used to integrate systems and populate databases by providing a way for one system to access the data in another system. Generally speaking, JSON, XML, and CSV are common output files you could expect from an API. We'll learn more about these and other file formats later in this section.

For example, an API could be used to allow a **customer relationship management** (**CRM**) system to access customer data from a **Salesforce automation** (**SFA**) system. This would allow the CRM system to automatically update the customer records when a sale is made, without it having to manually import the data from the SFA system.

APIs are powerful tools that can be used to automate many tasks and improve the efficiency of systems. They are becoming increasingly popular as businesses look for ways to integrate their systems and improve their data management.

Here are some of the benefits of using APIs:

- **Improved efficiency**: APIs can help automate tasks, which can improve the efficiency of systems
- **Reduced costs**: APIs can help reduce costs by eliminating the need for manual data entry and integration
- **Increased flexibility**: APIs can help increase the flexibility of systems by allowing them to be easily integrated with other systems
- **Improved data quality**: APIs can help improve data quality by ensuring that data is consistent and accurate

Databases

There are many different types of database technology, each with its strengths and weaknesses. Here are some of the most common types of database technology:

- **Relational databases**: Relational databases are the most common type of database. They store data in tables, which are made up of rows and columns. Relational databases are easy to use and can handle large amounts of data.
- **NoSQL databases**: NoSQL databases are a newer type of database that are designed to handle large amounts of data that can't easily be stored in a relational database. NoSQL databases are often used for big data applications. They use a variety of data models, such as document databases, key-value stores, wide-column databases, and graph databases. NoSQL databases are designed to be scalable, efficient, and flexible.

  Some examples of NoSQL databases include the following:

  - **MongoDB**: MongoDB is a document database that is popular for storing data for web applications and mobile applications.
  - **Cassandra**: Cassandra is a distributed database that is designed to be highly scalable and reliable.
  - **Redis**: Redis is a key-value store that is often used to store data for in-memory applications.
  - **Amazon DynamoDB**: Amazon DynamoDB is a fully managed NoSQL database that is designed to be highly scalable and reliable.
  - **Google BigTable**: Bigtable is a key-value store, which means that each piece of data is stored as a pair of keys and values. The keys are unique identifiers for each piece of data, and the values can be any type of data, such as strings, numbers, or objects.

  NoSQL databases are a good choice for applications that need to store large amounts of data, that need to be able to scale quickly, or that need to be able to handle complex data relationships.

- **Object-oriented databases**: Object-oriented databases store data in objects. Object-oriented databases are easy to use and can handle large amounts of data.

- **Graph databases**: Graph databases are designed to store and analyze data that is represented in a graph structure. Graph databases are often used for social media applications. The most famous, Neo4j, is a graph database that is often used to store data for social networks and other applications that require complex relationships between data.

- **Document databases**: Document databases are designed to store and manage documents. Document databases are easy to use and can handle large amounts of data.

Non-relational document databases are sometimes text-based or binary files that require no software. Sometimes, these are used not only for storage but also for exchanging information between systems using an API. Here are some common examples:

File Format	Advantages	Disadvantages
YAML	Easy to read and write, human-readable	Not as widely supported as XML or JSON
XML	Widely supported, can be used to store a variety of data	Can be verbose and difficult to read
CSV	Easy to import and export, can be used to store data in a tabular format	Not as secure as other formats
JSON	Lightweight and easy to read and write	Can be difficult to use for storing large amounts of data
Parquet	Scalable and efficient, can be used to store large amounts of data	Not as widely supported as other formats
Orc	Scalable and efficient, can be used to store large amounts of data	Not as widely supported as other formats
Avro	Scalable and efficient, can be used to store large amounts of data	Not as widely supported as other formats

The best file format for your needs will depend on the specific data you are storing and the applications you are using. If you are not sure which format to use, it is best to consult with a data expert.

Here are some additional details about each file format:

- **YAML** is a data serialization language. It is a human-readable and easy-to-write format. YAML is often used to store configuration files, API data, and other data.

- **XML** is a markup language. It is used to describe data in a hierarchical format. XML is often used to store data about people, places, things, and events.

- **CSV** is a comma-separated value file format. It is a simple and easy-to-use format that is often used to store data in a tabular format. CSV is often used to import and export data from spreadsheets and other applications.

- **JSON** stands for **JavaScript Object Notation**. It is a lightweight and easy-to-read-and-write format. JSON is often used to store data in web applications.

- **Parquet** is a columnar file format. It is designed for storing large amounts of data efficiently. Parquet is often used in big data applications.

- **Orc** is a row-oriented file format. It is designed for storing large amounts of data efficiently. Orc is often used in big data applications.

- **Avro** is a binary file format. It is designed for storing large amounts of data efficiently. Avro is often used in big data applications.

- **In-memory databases** store data in the memory of the computer. In-memory databases are very fast, but they can be expensive.

The best type of database technology for your needs will depend on the specific application you are using. If you are not sure which type of database technology to use, it is best to consult with a database expert. Because of this, we could also find technologies and vendors that offer storage mechanisms based on their business purpose. Examples include cold storage, object cloud storage, and columnar databases.

Cold storage

Cold storage is a type of storage that uses low temperatures to keep data safe. It is often used to store sensitive data, such as financial records or customer data. Cold storage can be used in a variety of ways, including the following:

- **Data backup**: Cold storage can be used to back up data in the event of a disaster

- **Compliance**: Cold storage can be used to comply with regulations that require sensitive data to be stored in a secure location

- **Archiving**: Cold storage can be used to archive data that is no longer needed regularly

Cold storage is a secure way to store data, but it is important to note that it is not a perfect solution. There are a few risks associated with cold storage, as follows:

- **Power outage**: If there is a power outage, the data in cold storage will be lost

- **Hardware failure**: If the hardware that is used to store the data fails, the data will be lost

- **Human error**: If someone makes a mistake, the data in cold storage could be lost or damaged

Despite the risks, cold storage is a secure and effective way to store data. If you are looking for a way to protect your data, cold storage is a good option.

Object Cloud Storage

Google Cloud Storage and AWS S3 are both cloud-based object storage services that offer scalability, high availability, and durability. Its advantage lies in its capability to store multiple formats for different purposes such as the following:

- **Data backup and recovery**: This can be used to back up and recover data from any source, including on-premises data centers, virtual machines, and mobile devices.

- **Data archiving**: This can be used to archive data that is not frequently accessed, such as historical data or data that is required for compliance purposes.

- **Data analytics**: This can be used to store data for big data analytics. This data can be used to create reports, identify trends, and make predictions.

- **Media storage**: This can be used to store media files, such as images, videos, and audio files. These files can be accessed from anywhere in the world, and they can be used to create websites, mobile applications, and other digital content.

Data warehouses and columnar databases

A data warehouse is a centralized repository of information that can be analyzed to make more informed decisions. It is a collection of data from different sources, such as operating systems, customer relationship management systems, and enterprise resource planning systems.

Data warehouses are used by businesses to store and analyze data for a variety of purposes, including the following:

- **Business intelligence (BI)**: Data warehouses are used to store and analyze data for BI applications, which allows businesses to make better decisions by providing them with insights into their data.

- **Data mining**: Data warehouses are also used for data mining, which is the process of extracting patterns from data. Data mining can be used to identify trends, predict customer behavior, and detect fraud.

- **Data visualization**: Data warehouses can also be used for data visualization, which is the process of creating visual representations of data. Data visualization can be used to communicate data insights to business users.

Here are some examples of data warehouses:

- **Google BigQuery**: Google BigQuery is a cloud-based data warehouse that can store and analyze petabytes of data

- **Amazon Redshift**: Amazon Redshift is a cloud-based data warehouse that can store and analyze terabytes of data

- **Microsoft Azure Synapse Analytics**: Microsoft Azure Synapse Analytics is a cloud-based data warehouse that can store and analyze petabytes of data

Data warehouses are an important tool for businesses that need to store and analyze large amounts of data. They can be used for a variety of purposes, including BI, data mining, and data visualization. Modern data warehouses are mounted on columnar databases.

A columnar database is a database that stores data in columns rather than rows. This allows for more efficient storage and retrieval of data as only the columns that are needed for a particular query need to be accessed.

Columnar databases are often used for applications that need to store and analyze large amounts of data, such as data warehouses and BI applications.

Let's look at some of the benefits of columnar databases:

- More efficient storage and retrieval of data
- Better performance for analytical queries
- Scalability to handle large amounts of data
- Data compression

However, there are also some drawbacks to using a columnar database:

- Increased complexity
- Requires more specialized hardware and software
- May not be suitable for all types of applications

Overall, columnar databases are a powerful tool that can be used to store and analyze large amounts of data. However, they are not the best solution for all types of applications.

Orchestration and workflow automation

Orchestration and workflow automation are key parts of the BI landscape because they help processes to be scheduled and monitored while following a sequential logic. These technologies are outside of the scope of this book but we will mention four main products – Docker, Kubernetes, Airflow, and Autosys – because they impact the performance and development speed of any BI project:

- **Docker:** This is a containerization platform that allows you to create, deploy, and run containers. A container is a lightweight, isolated environment that runs on top of a host operating system. Docker containers can be used to run any application, including web applications, databases, and microservices.

- **Kubernetes**: This is an open-source container orchestration system that helps you deploy, manage, and scale containerized applications. Kubernetes provides several features that make it a powerful tool for container orchestration, including the following:

  - **Automatic scaling**: Kubernetes can automatically scale your containers up or down based on demand

  - **Load balancing**: Kubernetes can load balance your containers across multiple hosts

  - **Self-healing**: Kubernetes can automatically restart your containers if they fail

  - **Container networking**: Kubernetes can manage the networking between your containers

  Kubernetes is a powerful tool for container orchestration. It can help you deploy, manage, and scale containerized applications.

- **Airflow**: This is a workflow management system for data engineers. It allows you to author, schedule, and monitor workflows as **Directed Acyclic Graphs** (**DAGs**) of tasks. Airflow is a powerful tool that can be used to automate a variety of data engineering tasks.

  Some of the key features of Airflow include the following:

  - **Scalability**: Airflow can scale to manage thousands of tasks

  - **Flexibility**: Airflow can be used to automate a variety of data engineering tasks

  - **Reliability**: Airflow is designed to be reliable and scalable

  - **Ease of use**: Airflow is easy to use and can be used by both experienced and novice data engineers

  Airflow is a valuable tool for data engineers who need to automate a variety of tasks. It is easy to use, scalable, and reliable.

- **AutoSys**: This is a workload automation tool that helps businesses automate the execution of jobs across multiple systems and applications. It can be used to automate a variety of tasks, including the following:

  - Job scheduling

  - Job monitoring

  - Job reporting

  - Job recovery

  AutoSys is a powerful tool that can help businesses improve their efficiency, reduce costs, and improve the quality of their applications.

  Let's look at some of the key features of AutoSys:

  - **Scalability**: AutoSys can scale to manage thousands of jobs

- **Flexibility**: AutoSys can be used to automate a variety of tasks

- **Reliability**: AutoSys is designed to be reliable and scalable

- **Ease of use**: AutoSys is easy to use and can be used by both experienced and novice users

AutoSys is a valuable tool for businesses that need to automate a variety of tasks. It is easy to use, scalable, and reliable.

Cleaning and preparing data

So far, we've collected and stored our data, but we're far from being done! The next step is to clean and prepare the data for further analysis. ETL, ML, data quality, and metadata management are all important concepts in data cleaning and preparation. ETL is often used as a first step in the data preparation process. ML can be used to identify patterns in data, make predictions, and improve the accuracy of data-cleaning processes. Data quality is important because it ensures that the data is accurate and reliable. Metadata is data about data and can be used to describe the structure of data, the meaning of data, and the relationships between data. Let's describe these in more detail.

ETL

Many ETL tools can take care of cleaning and preparing data. Throughout this book, we have mentioned a few of these, but it is important to understand that in the BI landscape, anyone, from data engineers to data analysts, can participate in cleaning and preparing data in one way or the other. This is sometimes in testing and designing and others when executing the code that cleanses tables. The next section will discuss controversial stands on how the boundaries between every BI-related job are blurry and not as defined as it is believed in certain sectors of the industry. In the BI landscape, regardless of your role, the iterative interaction between the many roles makes it critical to understand the players in the ETL space and their capabilities so that when you are confronted with such scenarios, you know where in the pipeline of a project you should apply cleaning and transformations. There are cases when you would apply some of these at the presentation layer of the pipelines, such as visualization tools, but it will all depend on the scenario, resources, and the speed required to deliver them.

Here are the top players in the ETL space:

- Informatica PowerCenter

- IBM InfoSphere DataStage

- Oracle Data Integrator

- Talend Open Studio

- Pentaho Data Integration

- Microsoft SSIS

- DBT

- CloverDX
- Airflow
- Fivetran
- Stitch

These tools are all designed to help businesses automate the process of extracting, transforming, and loading data from one system to another. They can be used to automate a variety of tasks, including the following:

- Copying data from one system to another
- Integrating data from multiple systems
- Cleaning and transforming data
- Loading data into a data warehouse or data lake
- Help businesses improve efficiency, reduce costs, and improve the quality of their data

Machine learning and artificial intelligence

ML is a branch of AI that allows computers to learn without being explicitly programmed. In other words, ML algorithms can learn from data and improve their performance over time without being explicitly told how to do so. ML algorithms are used to analyze data and identify patterns. For example, an ML algorithm might be used to analyze data from a spam filter to identify which emails are likely to be spam. The algorithm can then use this information to improve its performance over time. ML can be used in ETL in a variety of ways, as follows:

- To identify and extract data from unstructured sources, such as text files or images
- To clean and transform data to make it suitable for ML
- To generate features from data that can be used by ML models
- To evaluate the performance of ML models
- To classify records whose cardinality is unknown and the distinct values that may rise in the future over petabytes of records
- To implement security rules based on the values of columns and identify if a value should be categorized as private information
- To implement row-level security based on past security implementations of similar columns and rows

Data quality

Data quality tools are important in the BI landscape because they ensure that the data used to create BI reports is accurate and reliable. If the data is not accurate, the BI reports will be inaccurate, which can lead to bad decisions. One of the most important tools in recent years is Great Expectations.

Great Expectations is an open source Python library for validating, documenting, and profiling your data. It helps you maintain data quality and improve communication about data between teams.

With Great Expectations, you can do the following:

- Assert what you expect from the data you load and transform, and catch data issues quickly – expectations are unit tests for your data. Not only that, but Great Expectations also creates data documentation and data quality reports from those expectations.

- Data science and data engineering teams use Great Expectations for the following purposes:

  - Test data they ingest from other teams or vendors and ensure its validity

  - Validate data they transform as a step in their data pipeline to ensure the correctness of transformations

  - Prevent data quality issues from slipping into data products

- Great Expectations is a powerful tool that can help you improve the quality of your data and ensure that it is used effectively.

There are several other tools like Great Expectations that can be used to validate, document, and profile your data. Let's look at some of these tools:

- **Anomalo**: Anomalo is a tool that uses ML to detect anomalies in your data. It can be used to identify data quality issues, such as missing values, incorrect values, and duplicate values.

- **Validio**: Validio is a tool that uses data quality rules to validate your data. It can be used to identify data quality issues and ensure that your data meets your business requirements.

- **Data.World**: Data.World is a tool that provides a centralized platform for managing and sharing data. It includes a data quality module that can be used to validate your data and generate data quality reports.

Metadata management

Metadata management is the process of collecting, organizing, and managing data about data. Metadata is data about data, and it helps make data more useful and accessible. Some metadata management solutions allow a project to keep track of data lineage and provide transparency regarding data governance. BI customers are incentivized by having this information available because it promotes trust in the accuracy of the data being used.

Metadata can be used to describe a wide range of things, including the structure of a database, the contents of a file, or the meaning of a word. It can also be used to track changes to data over time and ensure that data is used consistently.

Metadata management is important because it helps make data more useful and accessible. By providing information about data, metadata can help users find the data they need, understand how the data is structured, and make better use of the data.

There are several different ways to manage metadata. Some common methods include the following:

- **Using a metadata repository**: A metadata repository is a central location for storing metadata. This can be a database, a filesystem, or even a cloud-based service.

- **Using metadata standards**: Metadata standards are a set of rules for how metadata should be structured and formatted. This can help ensure that metadata is consistent across different systems and applications.

- **Using metadata tools**: Several different metadata tools are available that can be used to collect, organize, and manage metadata.

Metadata management is an important part of data management. By managing metadata effectively, businesses can make their data more useful and accessible and can improve the quality of their data decisions.

Let's look at some examples:

- SAP PowerDesigner
- OvalEdge
- Oracle Enterprise Metadata Management
- Octopai Platform
- MANTA Platform
- Informatica Metadata Manager
- Infogix Data360 Govern
- IBM InfoSphere Information Server
- erwin EDGE Portfolio
- Collibra Platform
- ASG Enterprise Data Intelligence
- Alex Data Marketplace
- Alation Data Catalog

Analyzing data with BI tools

A BI tool is a software application that helps businesses collect, analyze, and visualize data to make better decisions. BI tools can be used to track sales, monitor customer behavior, and identify trends. There are many BI tools available on the market, and the best one for your business will depend on your specific needs and budget, including self-service and exploratory tools. The main difference between self-service and exploratory BI tools is the level of user control and expertise required. Self-service BI tools are designed to be easy to use by non-technical users, while exploratory BI tools are designed for more experienced users who want to have more control over the analysis process. Let's explore this in a little more depth and talk through what we call the "BI Consumer Spectrum."

Self-service versus exploratory tools

The BI tool is the interface that sits between the final consumer and the databases in such a way that non-technical users can generate answers to common business questions without requiring heavy complex logic. This is the key differentiator of any BI tool; understanding this is critical when you're trying to pick the right tool for your audience. Maybe your audience has high technical expertise, or maybe they want pre-canned reports or wish to build ad hoc reports with the confidence that business rules are pre-configured, or maybe they just want an interface to explore data freely on their own terms. Another scenario is that you may have all of these needs.

Self-service BI tools typically have a drag-and-drop interface that makes it easy to create reports and dashboards. They also typically have a wide range of pre-built reports and dashboards that can be customized to meet the needs of the user. Self-service BI tools are a good choice for users who want to be able to quickly and easily access and analyze data without having to rely on IT support.

Exploratory BI tools, on the other hand, give users more control over the analysis process. They typically have a more complex interface that allows users to write custom queries and create custom visualizations. Exploratory BI tools are a good choice for users who want to have more flexibility and control over the analysis process.

Here is a table that summarizes the key differences between self-service and exploratory BI tools:

Feature	Self-Service BI	Exploratory BI
Level of user control	Low	High
Expertise required	Low	High
Interface	Drag-and-drop	More complex
Capabilities	Pre-built reports and dashboards	Custom queries and visualizations
Best for	Users who want to quickly and easily access and analyze data	Users who want more flexibility and control over the analysis process

BI Consumer Spectrum

The BI Consumer Spectrum classifies the audience by technical capabilities and matches them to the corresponding BI platform's features or applications.

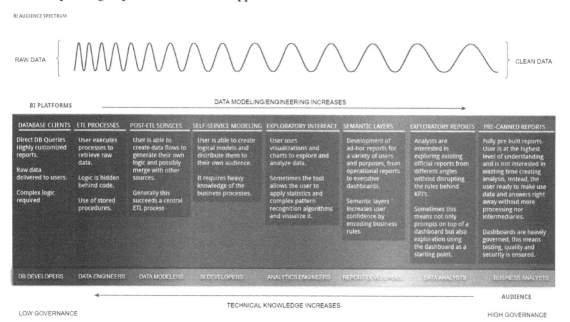

Figure 5.1 - The BI Consumer Spectrum

To the far left, you will find low governance and raw data, which means data that has no presentation layer or that may require certain cleaning to become ready for consumption. By low governance, we refer to the fact that business rules and a security model may be absent. To the far right, you will find high governance – that is, the application is highly monitored, secured, tested, and operationalized, as well as much more cleaned and validated data. Let's go into further details of each:

- Database clients.

  Users: Database developers and Excel users

  Characteristics:

  - Direct database queries

  - Highly customized reports

  - Raw data delivered to users

  - Complex logic required

  Tools: Toad, SQL Developer, Microsoft SSMS, and Azure Data Factory

- ETL on demand.

  Users: Data engineers, ETL developers, and Excel users

  Characteristics:

  - The user executes processes to retrieve raw data

  - Logic is hidden behind code

  - Use of stored procedures

  Tools: Toad, SQL Developer, Microsoft SSMS, Azure Data Factory, and Microsoft Power BI.

- Post-ETL on demand.

  Users: Data modelers.

  Characteristics: Users can create data flows to generate logic and possibly merge with other sources. Generally, this happens after a central ETL process is executed. The final user needs to model the data further or apply transformations that are not required by the general audience.

  Tools: Tableau DataPrep, Oracle Analytics, SAP Analytics, Power BI, and Qlik.

- Modeling on demand.

  Users: BI developers.

  Characteristics: Users can create logical models of their own and distribute them to their audience. This requires heavy knowledge of the business processes. Once the user creates a semantic layer, they can distribute it to their user base and modify the rules as needed or just use it for building reports.

Tools: Oracle Analytics, Looker, Power BI, Cognos, and BI Publisher.

- Exploratory interface.

Users: Analytics engineers, data analysts, data scientists, and more.

Characteristics: The user uses visualizations and charts to explore and analyze data. Sometimes, the tool allows the user to apply statistics and complex pattern recognition algorithms and visualize them.

Tools: Tableau, Power BI, Looker, Superset, Oracle Analytics, SAP Analytics, Sense, Qlik, Domo, and MicroStrategy.

- Ad hoc reports over semantic layers.

Users: Report developers.

Characteristics: The user develops ad hoc reports for a variety of users and purposes, from operational reports to executive dashboards. Semantic layers allow users to trust that their reports have the correct business rules embedded. They can't modify the rules as these were previously vetted by a governing entity or proper data owners.

Tools: Tableau, Power BI, Looker, Superset, Oracle Analytics, SAP Analytics, Sense, Qlik, Domo, and MicroStrategy.

- Exploratory reports.

Users: Data analysts.

Characteristics: Analysts are interested in exploring existing official reports from different angles without disrupting the rules behind KPIs.

Sometimes, this means not only prompts on top of a dashboard but also exploration while using the dashboard as a starting point.

An official report is published, then users interact with the said report by applying filters and adding views to the report. Alternatively, they could use the same report as a base to explore further by adding more slices of data or just rolling up or drilling down on it without modifying the existing business rules that created the report in the first place.

Tools: Tableau, Power BI, Looker, Superset, Oracle Analytics, SAP Analytics, Sense, Qlik, Domo, and MicroStrategy.

- Pre-canned reports.

Users: Business analysts and domain users.

Characteristics: Fully pre-built reports. The user is at the highest level of understanding and is not interested in wasting time creating an analysis; instead, the user is ready to make use of data and answers right away without more processing or intermediaries.

Dashboards are heavily governed, which means testing, quality, and security are ensured.

Tools: Tableau, Power BI, Looker, Superset, Oracle Analytics, SAP Analytics, Sense, Qlik, Domo, and MicroStrategy.

Here's a list of tools and common features for different scenarios:

Tool	Direct DB Queries	Execute Stored Procedures	Create Data Flows	Create Semantic Layers	Create Ad Hoc Reports	Explore Raw Data	Explore Reports	Report Consumption
Microsoft Power BI	X	X	X	X	X	X	X	X
Azure Data Factory	X	X	X					
Qlik				X	X	X		X
Sisense					X	X	X	X
Domo					X	X	X	X
Looker	X			X	X	X	X	X
Cognos	X		X	X	X	X	X	X
MicroStrategy	X				X	X	X	X
Oracle Analytics	X		X	X	X	X	X	X
Business Objects				X	X	X	X	X
Tableau	X		X		X	X	X	X

To identify which scenario fits your needs, let's look at some of the questions you should ask to try and get answers from your audience:

- Are your final users proficient in SQL?

- What is the main use they have for that data?

    A. Systems integration

    B. Report development

    C. Database isolation

    D. Domain analysis

- Is the final user a decision-maker?

- Is your final user trying to transform data?

- What is the frequency at which they need that data delivered to them?

- Are your users planning on creating their own logical models with their own business rules?

Focusing on user experience

Regardless of the tool you pick and the scenario you are fulfilling, there are some basic features that you should look for in a BI tool:

- **Automated monitoring**. Being able to catch discrepancies, data quality issues, or simply radical changes in KPIs is critical for businesses to be able to react to different scenarios on time. A great BI tool should allow you to create dashboards that validate the data you are presenting against safe sources. It may consist of a direct database query compared to a KPI in a report. This would provide certainty that a report developer did not apply any invalid transformation. It should also allow you to expose radical changes in key performance indicators with the use of conditional logic.

  The tool should be able to schedule daily report runs and provide a method for delivery, such as email or Slack. Alerting is also an important feature in a BI tool because it helps reduce the time our business users have to react to changes in the data.

- **Presenting data**. There are many techniques a BI tool uses to display data, tabular reports, dashboards, visualizations, pixel-perfect documents, and more, and recently, some tools have included features that allow users to create slides or presentations, storytelling, and infographic displays. A BI tool should also be able to present data with human-readable names instead of using database names. Voice assistants can also be used in BI. For example, voice assistants can be used to ask questions about data, such as *"What were our sales last month?"* or *"What is our customer satisfaction rate?"* Voice assistants can also be used to generate reports and dashboards.

There are several ways voice assistants can be used in BI. For example, voice assistants can be used to do the following:

- **Ask questions about data**: Voice assistants can be used to ask questions about data, such as *"What were our sales last month?"* or *"What is our customer satisfaction rate?"*

  We can also use them to make straightforward requests in written format:

  - Top 10 customers in the North-East region

  - List today's sales above $500

  - Total sales in the year 2020

  - Products that start with P

- **Generate reports and dashboards**: Voice assistants can be used to generate reports and dashboards.

- **Visualize data**: Voice assistants can be used to visualize data, such as creating charts and graphs.

- **Share insights**: Voice assistants can be used to share insights, such as sending reports or dashboards to colleagues.

- **Automate tasks**: Voice assistants can be used to automate tasks, such as scheduling meetings or sending emails.

Voice assistants can be a valuable tool for BI professionals. They can help automate tasks, generate insights, and share information. However, it is important to note that voice assistants are still in their early stages of development, and several challenges need to be addressed, such as accuracy and privacy. The interaction between humans and machines is becoming more and more seamless.

The use of AI

AI and **large language models** (**LLMs**) are becoming increasingly important tools for BI. AI can be used to automate tasks, such as data collection and analysis, while LLMs can be used to generate insights from large amounts of data.

One of the most common uses of AI in BI is to automate data collection. AI can be used to crawl websites and extract data from documents, which can then be used to populate BI dashboards or reports. This can save BI teams a significant amount of time and effort.

AI can also be used to automate analysis tasks. For example, AI can be used to identify trends in data or classify data into different categories. This can help BI teams quickly and easily identify insights from data.

LLMs can be used to generate insights from large amounts of data. LLMs can be trained on large amounts of text data, such as customer reviews or financial statements. This allows LLMs to generate insights that would be difficult for humans to find on their own.

For example, LLMs can be used to identify patterns in customer behavior or predict future trends. This information can be used by BI teams to make better decisions about their products and services.

The use of AI and LLMs in BI is still in its early stages, but the potential benefits are significant. AI can automate tasks and generate insights that would be difficult for humans to find on their own. This can help BI teams make better decisions and improve their business performance.

However, there are also some challenges associated with the use of AI and LLMs in BI. One challenge is that AI systems can be biased, which can lead to inaccurate or misleading insights. Another challenge is that AI systems can be computationally expensive, which can make it difficult to use them on large amounts of data.

Despite these challenges, the use of AI and LLMs in BI is likely to continue to grow in the future. As AI systems become more accurate and efficient, they will become increasingly valuable tools for BI teams. Some companies are entertaining the idea of dumping raw data into an LLM for it to learn from and test the generation of answers to reduce or even eliminate the data engineer component, but it is too early to try this in a production environment. Moreover, at the time of writing, chatbots highly depend on how the user formulates queries, due to which a new art has emerged: prompting skills.

Prompting skills are important when using GPT chatbots because they allow users to guide the conversation and get the information they need. Without prompting skills, chatbots would simply respond to whatever the user says, which can lead to frustrating and unproductive conversations.

Prompting skills can be used for the following purposes:

- **Get the chatbot to clarify information**: If the user is not sure what the chatbot is saying, they can use a prompt to ask for clarification. For example, the user might say, "Can you please explain that?"

- **Get the chatbot to provide additional information**: If the user is looking for more information on a particular topic, they can use a prompt to ask for it. For example, the user might say, "Tell me more about that."

- **Get the chatbot to perform a specific task**: If the user needs the chatbot to do something, they can use a prompt to ask it to do so. For example, the user might say, "Can you please alert me when sales are hit above the daily average in a day?"

Combining good prompting skills with the proper volume and constant training of clean data may take us closer to removing intermediaries between the user and the database, which would result in the end of data engineering.

Could this happen? It is unlikely in the short term, but it is a possibility, and the rejection of this idea is parallel to the rejection of the rise of other technologies in the past, when cloud computing started, when the concept of big data started to appear, when visualization tools displaced Excel, and so on. There will always be people who oppose change but the reality is that data engineering is just a means to an end. It only exists today due to storage and computing limitations, but in a profit-oriented world, companies move toward a BI landscape in which data engineering disappears and machines process the answers we need in the time we need them. Saving time and reducing expenses will always triumph over hiring data engineer armies.

BI developer versus BI architect versus data engineer versus data modeler versus business analyst

BI developers, architects, data engineers, data modelers, and business analysts all play important roles in the BI process.

BI developers are responsible for building and maintaining BI applications. They use a variety of tools and technologies to extract data from various sources, transform it into a format that can be analyzed, and load it into a BI database. BI developers also create reports and dashboards that allow users to view and analyze the data.

BI architects are responsible for designing and implementing the overall BI architecture. They work with stakeholders to understand their business needs and then design a BI solution that meets those needs. BI architects also work with developers to ensure that the BI solution is implemented correctly and that it meets the needs of the business.

Data engineers are responsible for collecting, storing, and processing data. They use a variety of tools and technologies to build and maintain data warehouses and data lakes. Data engineers also work with BI developers to ensure that the data is in a format that can be analyzed by BI applications.

Data modelers are responsible for designing the data models that are used by BI applications. They work with stakeholders to understand their business needs and then design data models that meet those needs. Data modelers also work with data engineers to ensure that the data models are implemented correctly.

Business analysts are responsible for understanding the business needs of the organization and then translating those needs into technical requirements for BI applications. They work with BI developers, architects, data engineers, and data modelers to ensure that the BI solution meets the needs of the business.

Here's a simple table showcasing the differences between these roles:

Role	Description
BI developer	Creates and maintains the reports, statistical models, and visualizations that are requested by the business to support decision-making
BI architect	Designs and develops BI systems, including data warehouses and ETL processes
Data engineer	Builds and maintains the infrastructure that supports the BI systems, including the data pipelines and data warehouses
Data modeler	Creates and maintains the data models that are used by the BI systems
Business analyst	Works with the business to understand their needs and requirements for BI systems

The BI developer is the most hands-on role and is responsible for creating the actual reports and visualizations that are used by the business. They typically have a background in data analysis and programming.

The BI architect is responsible for designing and developing the BI systems. They typically have a background in data architecture and engineering.

The data engineer is responsible for building and maintaining the infrastructure that supports the BI systems. They typically have a background in software engineering and systems administration.

The data modeler is responsible for creating and maintaining the data models that are used by the BI systems. They typically have a background in data modeling and database administration.

The business analyst works with the business to understand their needs and requirements for BI systems. They typically have a background in business analysis and project management.

The BI developer, BI architect, data engineer, and data modeler roles are often combined into a single role: BI developer. The role of a business analyst is typically separate from the other roles. The industry has no consensus on the definitions of these roles. Regardless, it is your responsibility to read the job description and match it against your career preferences. It is not recommended to accept a position based on the title alone.

However, let's take data engineering as an example. Data engineering is quite ubiquitous along the path of a BI project. Everyone involved in the project will perform a form of data engineering in one way or the other. Everything in BI encompasses data engineering – that is, the act of engineering data – whether you use SQL or create data models or reports, it's up to you to engineer data. Because of this, don't feel you are missing out if you are given an entry role while you are trying to get your "feet wet." Your experience in that BI-related job will allow you to move up or down the ladder of a BI project.

Don't let the gatekeepers stop you from pursuing any activity or task in a BI project. These can be managers, customers, or even co-workers discouraging you from attempting to understand other roles or providing feedback to them. You can always take time to analyze other people's inputs and outputs of data and learn what went in between to acquire new knowledge or simply suggest better procedures for you to open the door to new opportunities in your current job or future ones.

Sometimes, a data engineer ends up just executing steps from a data modeler's design. By building reports and dashboards or semantic layers, you are doing more than just blindly executing SQL or Python code while following a design – you are using your problem-solution skills to come up with a mental image of the data and translate it into a set of steps or algorithms to create the report you need or provide feedback to data modelers/engineers to fulfill gaps in your requests. There's no hierarchy and no link is weaker here; every role in the BI landscape holds the same importance.

So, what is the difference? **Tools.** Tools are a huge part of what companies use to wrongly define what data engineering is. As previously warned, do not focus just on tools. If you consider that data engineering is a different discipline just because of the use of a variety of tools or because employers have blurred the lines between their DBAs, their system, or network administrators and data engineers, then you have lost focus on the purpose of this book, which is to provide guidance on how to solve problems and spot technical solutions by identifying the right set of tools, regardless of your role in the BI landscape. Anyone can make an impact – do not fall for the illusion promoted in the industry. Through abusive corporate practices, a product can be pushed by the marketing efforts of a vendor, or even while looking for support on social networks such as subreddits, including r/dataengineering and r/businessintelligence. Wasting your time in becoming an expert on a single or many tools will not improve your capabilities to solve problems holistically, regardless of the tool an organization uses.

Learning DBT, Snowflake, Fivetran, Superset, Tableau, or any other trendy software does not guarantee that you will be a successful BI problem solver. We want you to be able to arrive at any BI project, assess its needs, and understand what next steps to take. You may not execute those steps, but you will develop literacy in terms of how to work with people in those roles and how to effectively communicate with them.

Business acumen

Business acumen is the ability to understand the complex and ever-changing business environment and make sound decisions that will help your company succeed. It is a combination of knowledge, experience, and judgment that allows you to see the big picture and make decisions that are in the best interests of your company.

Many different factors contribute to business acumen, including the following:

- **Knowledge**: You need to have a deep understanding of the business world and how your company goals are aligned to face this environment and its challenges, including the different industries, markets, and technologies that are involved. You also need to understand the financial aspects of your business, such as accounting, budgeting, and forecasting.

- **Experience**: You need to have experience working in business to develop your business acumen. This experience can come from working in different roles within a company, or from starting your own business.

- **Judgment**: You need to be able to make sound decisions based on the information you have. This requires you to be able to weigh the pros and cons of different options and to make decisions that are in the best interests of your company.

Business acumen is an essential skill for anyone who wants to be successful in business. If you want to be a leader in your company, you need to have strong business acumen. This will allow you to make sound decisions that will help your company grow and succeed.

Here are some tips for developing your business acumen:

- **Read books and articles about the business that interests you**. There are many resources available that can help you learn more about business. Reading books and articles can help you develop your knowledge of the business world.

- **Take courses or workshops**. There are many courses and workshops available that can help you learn more about business. Taking courses or workshops can help you develop your skills and knowledge.

- **Get experience working in the business**. The best way to develop your business acumen is to get experience working in the business. This experience can come from working in different roles within a company, or from starting your own business.

- **Be a good listener**. One of the best ways to learn about business is to listen to others. Talk to people who are successful in business and learn from their experiences.

- **Be inquisitive**. Don't be afraid to ask questions and learn more about business. The more you learn, the better equipped you will be to make sound decisions.

Business acumen allows BI professionals to understand business needs and requirements. BI professionals need to understand the business to develop BI solutions that meet those needs. They need to understand the business goals, the business processes, and the data that is available.

Business acumen allows BI professionals to develop BI solutions that meet business needs. BI solutions need to be aligned with the business goals to be successful. BI professionals need to understand the business needs to develop solutions that meet those needs.

Business acumen allows BI professionals to communicate effectively with business users. BI professionals need to be able to communicate effectively with business users to understand their needs and explain the results of BI analysis in a way that is understandable and actionable.

Business acumen allows BI professionals to explain the results of BI analysis in a way that is understandable and actionable. The results of BI analysis need to be presented in a way that is understandable and actionable to business users. BI professionals need to have business acumen to be able to do this.

Increased productivity

This book offers guidance on how to leave old practices behind – practices that were encouraged at a time when storage and computational power were limited. Nowadays, the price for these has become accessible enough for us to consider new approaches. In the old days, it was convenient to work up the ladder in a BI project, from bottom to top, modeling every single business process in a business area and then publishing the data for report developers to provide answers to stakeholders. That usually meant that stakeholders would not see any finalized report until months into the project.

With the rise of cloud computing technology and concepts such as big data, late-binding data has become the most popular approach for delivering BI projects faster. Late-binding data is data that is not bound to a specific schema or structure at the time it is stored. This allows the data to be more flexible and adaptable to changes.

Late-binding data is often used in data warehouses and data lakes, where the data may come from a variety of sources and may need to be stored in different formats. Late binding allows the data to be stored in such a way that it is compatible with all of these different sources and formats.

There are a few different ways to implement late-binding data. One common way is to use a **data warehouse management system** (**DWMS**). A DWMS can store data in a variety of formats and can provide tools for accessing and analyzing the data.

Another way to implement late-binding data is to use a data lake. A data lake is a repository for storing raw data in its native format. Data lakes can be used to store data from a variety of sources, including social media, sensor data, and ML models.

Late-binding data can be a powerful tool for businesses that need to store and analyze large amounts of data from a variety of sources. However, it is important to note that late-binding data can also be more complex to manage than traditional data.

With this approach, rapid prototyping has emerged as the number one practice to deliver projects faster. Rapid prototyping is a technique that's used in BI projects to quickly create a working model of a data visualization or report. This allows users to test and evaluate the model before it is finalized, and to provide feedback on how it can be improved.

There are several benefits to using rapid prototyping in BI projects:

- It can help reduce the time it takes to develop a BI project
- It can help improve the quality of the final product by allowing users to provide feedback early on
- It can help reduce the risk of costly mistakes by allowing users to test the model before it is finalized

There are several different ways to create a rapid prototype for a BI project. One common approach is to use a tool such as Microsoft Power BI or Tableau. These tools allow users to quickly create interactive visualizations and reports without having to write any code.

Another approach is to use a tool such as RapidMiner or Orange. These tools allow users to create more complex data models and visualizations, but they require more technical expertise.

Once a prototype has been created, it can be shared with users for feedback. This feedback can then be used to improve the model before it is finalized.

Rapid prototyping is a valuable tool for BI projects. It can help reduce the time it takes to develop a project, improve the quality of the final product, and reduce the risk of costly mistakes.

In the old world and even today in some industries, companies have so many handoffs and roles and sub-roles that it makes it quite bureaucratic to deliver a project. Data makes so many stops along the way and the Scrum methodology becomes impossible to implement due to highly heterogeneous skills among the development team:

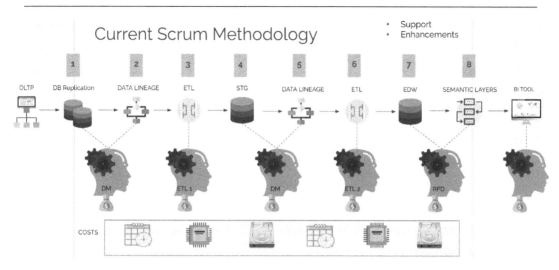

Figure 5.2 – The Scrum methodology

The new approach starts with creating a "primordial SQL" that may or may not hold the data that the user needs to build their main five reports. This may not be sufficient data but iterations can adjust the logic to accommodate for missing requirements. The idea of building five main reports may be simplistic but in reality, it is a pragmatic decision, and it is quite likely that those five reports will result in a data model that covers all the needs a proper bottom-to-top data model would contain. The primordial SQL is then plugged into a semantic layer or directly into your BI tool of choice and then exposed to your final users to test and validate.

Tasks are deposited in a fishbowl and at any point, a developer picks a paper with a random task to deliver. Cross-functional skills are advised; otherwise, a fishbowl per skill would be required. Tasks in the yellow banner happen asynchronously. They are not dependent on each other and can be parallelized. Data testing is locked to a single point (the frontend). Rapid prototyping requires you to quickly analyze the sources and map the initial requirements. A semantic layer connects to the database hosting the source tables and performs quick and dirty dimensional modeling or a SQL prototype is dumped into the BI tool.

This is a great learning opportunity for new data modelers. A quick model is created in a short period in a working session with every member of the team: a BI developer/ETL developer, a data modeler, and a **subject matter expert** (**SME**). As the product gets materialized with backend-supporting objects, instances in the rapid prototype start to get replaced with the final version of the object at the very end. There's an integration task for every handoff.

While every component of the prototype is being replaced by a formal operationalized ETL, the user can continue building and testing reports without disrupting their development in a fully transparent manner. By doing this, the user would never know whether the report is coming from a prototype or a fully-fledged data pipeline:

A Shift in Paradigm

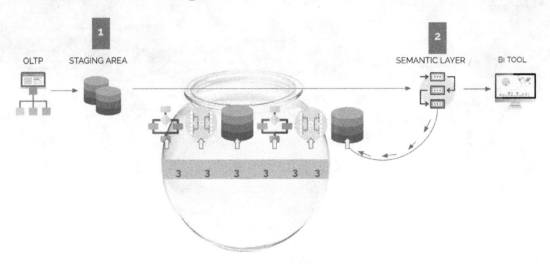

Figure 5.3 – Full Agile rapid prototyping

Let's look at some of the advantages:

- Improve team relationships by removing dependencies and stressful hand-off procedures.

- Time reduction.

- Disk and CPU workload reduction.

- 100% business-oriented. The customer participates and dictates the progress of the development in a working session and finalizes it until there's a go/no-go decision.

- No cross-functional dependencies.

- No overkill.

- Less "lost in translation" requirements. With the old approach, a data modeler designs the flow and hands off the design to ETL developers, BI developers, and report developers. Eventually, it makes it to production, only for them to find out that a report is missing some requirements or can't be built due to an oversight in the design.

- Risk reduction. In the worst-case scenario, we wasted time in developing a semantic layer or a report but we can gain proof that the model will work or not.

- Rework reduction.

Automation

Automation involves using technology to perform tasks that would otherwise be done by humans. In the context of BI, automation can be used to collect, process, and analyze data. This can free up human resources to focus on more strategic tasks, and it can also help improve the accuracy and timeliness of decision-making.

There are several different ways to automate tasks in BI. One common approach is to use data integration tools to automate the process of collecting data from different sources. Another approach is to use data mining tools to automate the process of finding patterns in data. And still, another approach is to use ML tools to automate the process of making predictions. Automation can also be used to create alerts and notifications that can be sent to team members when certain conditions are met.

Automation can be a valuable tool for businesses that want to improve their decision-making. However, it is important to note that automation is not a replacement for human intelligence. Automation can help improve the efficiency of decision-making, but it cannot replace the human judgment that is required to make sound decisions.

Templating

Templating can help ensure that reports and dashboards are consistent and easy to understand. This can be done by using templates that include common elements such as charts, graphs, and tables. Templating can also be used to create custom reports and dashboards that meet the specific needs of a particular business.

Templates are valuable tools for businesses that use BI tools. Templates can help create consistent and visually appealing reports and dashboards, and they can also help save time and effort.

There are several ways to use templates in BI. One common approach is to create templates for specific types of reports or dashboards. For example, you might create a template for a monthly sales report or a template for a customer satisfaction survey.

Another approach is to create templates for specific audiences. For example, you might create a template for internal users or a template for external customers.

Once you have created some templates, you can use them to quickly create new reports and dashboards. This can save you a significant amount of time, especially if you need to create multiple reports or dashboards regularly.

Templates can also help improve the consistency of your reports and dashboards. If you use templates, all your reports and dashboards will have the same look and feel. This can make it easier for users to find the information they need, and it can also help create a professional image for your business.

If you are not already using templates in BI, I encourage you to try them. Templates can be a valuable tool that can help you improve the efficiency and effectiveness of your BI system.

Here are some of the benefits of using templates in BI:

- **Save time and effort**. Templates can help you create new reports and dashboards quickly and easily. This can save you a significant amount of time, especially if you need to create multiple reports or dashboards regularly.

- **Improve consistency**. Templates can help improve the consistency of your reports and dashboards. If you use templates, all your reports and dashboards will have the same look and feel. This can make it easier for users to find the information they need, and it can also help create a professional image for your business.

- **Improve user experience**. Templates can help improve the user experience of your BI system. By making reports and dashboards more visually appealing and easy to use, templates can help encourage users to explore your BI system and find the information they need.

- **Increase productivity**. By helping improve the efficiency and effectiveness of your BI system, templates can help increase productivity. This can lead to better decision-making, improved customer service, and increased sales.

Standardization

Standardization can help ensure that data is collected and processed consistently. This can be done by creating standards for how data is collected, stored, and processed. Standardization can also be used to create common definitions for terms and concepts.

Standards are a vital part of any BI system. They help ensure that data is collected and processed consistently, and they also help make it easier to share data with others.

Several different standards can be used in BI, but some of the most important ones are as follows:

- **Data quality standards**: These standards define how data should be collected and processed to ensure that it is accurate and complete. The use of unit testing techniques can guarantee uniformity in the quality of data. Another way to ensure data quality standards is to implement mechanisms to detect data issues.

- **Data governance standards**: These standards define how data should be managed and controlled. Usually, it consists of a set of decision logs vetted by a steering committee where the rules that have been agreed upon are applied consistently across the BI platform.

- **Metadata standards**: These standards define how data should be described and classified. Auditing techniques applied to data can help meet the metadata standards, including data lineage, and making sure there are no redundant datasets.

- **Data visualization standards**: These standards define how data should be presented visually. Usually, this consists of using human-readable names with consistent naming conventions. Also, it is critical to use the same report distribution and accommodate charts and tabular reports.

By using standards, businesses can ensure that their BI systems are efficient, effective, and easy to use.

Monitoring systems

Monitoring systems can help identify and troubleshoot problems with the BI system. This can be done by monitoring the performance of the BI system, the data's quality, and the user experience. Monitoring systems can also be used to generate reports that can be used to identify trends and patterns in the data. Detecting these as soon as they appear allows our users to save precious time.

Efficient team management

Efficient team management can help ensure that resources are used effectively and that team members are working toward common goals. This can be done by creating a clear hierarchy of responsibilities, setting deadlines, and providing regular feedback. Efficient team management can also be done by using tools such as project management software and collaboration tools.

Summary

The BI landscape is constantly evolving, but these are some of the latest trends that businesses need to be aware of. By staying up to date with the latest trends, businesses can ensure that they are using the most effective BI tools and techniques to gain the insights they need to make better decisions.

You must open your mind and understand what the different tools are, what input they require, how data is shaped, and what output you expect versus the output the tool will produce. Once you understand the difference, you can adjust and retry. Iterate and test. If you expect an aggregated table, make sure you add every element. If the output does not match, your logs and your continuous testing will help you find out what went wrong.

Tools are dumb by nature; as the old saying goes – garbage in, garbage out. But if you learn the art of prototyping, rest assured your logic will scale up with no issues. The art of prototyping consists of being able to mock up the behavior of a larger process by taking the most minuscule sample of its content and applying step-by-step transformations until you get the desired result. From there, you apply the same steps to a larger sample and operationalize and perform user acceptance testing. Once this passes, you can apply it to your complete data repository and make sure you apply testing by creating complex scenarios and testing them against your process. If this passes, you can go to production.

Those principles are going to help you master the use of tools and learn more about the different tools that will help you accelerate each of those steps. You will learn that for every problem, there's a technological solution that, in most cases, will come close to solving your issues and in other cases will fill some gaps. You will learn about the past, but only what remains of it, what the current landscape is, and of course, what comes next: the future. Will our predictions hold true? Is ChatGPT the next big thing in the BI world? Do LLMs even have a role in our landscape? Only time will tell, but if you want quick answers, ask yourself, what problems are you looking to solve today and would you say the upcoming technologies could solve them?

In the next chapter, we'll discuss about data proficiency and subject matter expertise and how you can acquire the necessary skills.

6

Improving Data Proficiency or Subject Matter Expertise

Now that we have explored the vastness of the **business intelligence** (**BI**) landscape and covered the constantly evolving nature of working in BI, let us start talking through how to make yourself indispensable as a BI professional.

In today's rapidly evolving business landscape, the world is becoming more complex and interconnected, driven by advancements in technology, globalization, and the proliferation of data. As a result, organizations are generating vast amounts of data from various sources, such as customer interactions, operational activities, supply chains, marketing campaigns, and many others. Extracting meaningful insights from this data requires the expertise of BI professionals who possess a certain level of *data proficiency* and **subject matter expertise** (**SME**).

Why would BI professionals require data proficiency and SME? This is because data has the potential to be one of the most powerful tools for a business. Data has the potential to provide a comprehensive understanding of various aspects of an organization, including customer behavior, market trends, operational efficiency, and competitive dynamics. By leveraging data, businesses can gain a deeper understanding of their strengths, weaknesses, opportunities, and threats.

BI professionals with elevated levels of data proficiency and SME can help organizations stay ahead of their competitors. By continuously monitoring and analyzing data, BI professionals can identify emerging trends, anticipate market shifts, and proactively adapt business strategies. This enables organizations to be agile, responsive, and innovative in a rapidly changing business landscape. BI professionals can derive actionable insights by using their investigative skills to dig deeper into an organization's data to uncover patterns, correlations, and trends. By leveraging these valuable insights, organizations can make informed and potentially transformational decisions across various parts of their business. These decisions may include refining product development processes, identifying opportunities for market expansion, implementing targeted customer segmentation campaigns, and optimizing resource allocation to maximize efficiency.

Now that we have introduced data proficiency and SME let us explore them a little further and provide some more context on what each of these concepts means.

Data proficiency

Data proficiency is the ability to understand, use, and communicate data effectively. It is a set of skills that lets people collect, analyze, and interpret data to make better decisions. Data proficiency is important for everyone, but it is especially important for people who work in data-driven fields such as marketing, finance, and healthcare. Data proficiency is how you turn numbers into results, and it is a skill that successful data organizations have mastered. There are a few core competencies related to data proficiency, which are listed here:

- **Data literacy**: This is the ability to understand and interpret data. It includes understanding the basics of statistics and data analysis and reading and understanding data visualizations.

- **Data analysis**: This is the ability to collect, clean, and analyze data. It includes understanding several types of data analysis methods and being able to use them.

- **Data visualization**: This is the ability to communicate data effectively using charts, graphs, and other visuals. It includes understanding the principles of good data visualization, as well as being able to use data visualization tools and software.

- **Data storytelling**: This is the ability to use data to tell a story. It includes understanding the principles of good storytelling and using data to support your arguments and conclusions.

Data proficiency plays an increasingly vital role in today's world, empowering organizations to make informed decisions that have far-reaching impacts. Governments and businesses alike are leveraging the power of data to gain valuable insights, enhance their decision-making processes, and drive positive outcomes. For example, many governments today leverage data to inform policymaking, enhance public services, and drive evidence-based decision-making. By analyzing large volumes of data, governments can identify trends, patterns, and correlations that help them address societal challenges, allocate resources efficiently, and improve governance.

In the realm of education, data proficiency enables policymakers to assess the effectiveness of different teaching methods, identify areas of improvement, and allocate resources where they are most needed. By analyzing student performance data, government bodies can identify educational gaps and implement targeted interventions to ensure that students receive the support they require. This data-driven approach helps create more responsive education policies that address the specific needs of learners, leading to improved educational outcomes.

Businesses are also leveraging data proficiency to drive success and gain a competitive edge. Data-driven decision-making has become integral to various business functions, ranging from product development to marketing campaigns. By analyzing customer data, businesses can gain insights into consumer preferences, behaviors, and purchasing patterns. This information allows them to develop products that align with customer needs, optimize pricing strategies, and create personalized marketing campaigns that resonate with their target audience. Data proficiency empowers businesses to make more accurate predictions, identify emerging market trends, and tailor their strategies, leading to better customer satisfaction and increased profitability.

Furthermore, the importance of data proficiency is magnified by the exponential growth in the volume and accessibility of data. In the past, data was scarce, and organizations faced significant challenges in acquiring and accessing relevant information. However, the digital revolution and advancements in technology have ushered in an era where data is abundant and readily available from numerous sources.

The proliferation of interconnected devices, the rise of social media, the **Internet of Things** (**IoT**), and advancements in data collection methods have contributed to an unprecedented surge in data generation. Organizations now have access to vast amounts of structured and unstructured data from diverse channels, including customer interactions, social media platforms, online transactions, sensor networks, and more. This influx of data presents both opportunities and challenges for organizations.

Gaining data proficiency should translate into mastering a variety of reports and data challenges given to you. It requires you to understand how data can be stacked together, updated, and segregated according to business requirements. Data solutions to these challenges can be found in these reports:

- **Point-in-time reports**: Point-in-time reports display data for a specific date or time. These reports are often used to analyze historical trends and identify patterns in data. For example, a point-in-time report could show sales figures for a specific quarter or month.

  To achieve such a mechanism, you can implement two methods:

  - **Daily reports**: Insert daily records, storing the most recent value at that moment, and always retrieve the day you require. This can be costly in terms of storage, but retrieval should be fast.

  - **Effective and expiration date** : This solution requires you to establish a start date when the record begins its existence and an expiration date on which the record ceases to be valid.

- **Current data reports** : Current data reports display the most recent data available in real time. These reports are useful for monitoring ongoing business activities and making real-time decisions. For example, a current data report could show the current inventory levels for a product.

- **Snapshots**: Snapshots are static reports that capture data at a specific point in time. These reports are useful for documenting historical data and trends and comparing data from different time periods. For example, a snapshot report could show sales figures for the first quarter of the current year compared to the same quarter of the previous year.

- **Trend reports**: Trend reports show the direction and magnitude of data over time. These reports are useful for identifying trends and patterns in data that may not be immediately apparent in point-in-time reports. For example, a trend report could show the sales figures for a product over the past year, highlighting any increases or decreases in sales over time.

- **Comparative reports**: Comparative reports compare data across various categories or time periods. These reports are useful for identifying differences and similarities in data and for making comparisons to identify trends or anomalies. For example, a comparative report could show the sales figures for various products, highlighting any differences in sales between them.

- **Exception reports**: Exception reports highlight data that falls outside of predefined parameters. These reports are useful for identifying potential issues or anomalies that require further investigation. For example, an exception report could highlight any sales figures that are significantly lower than expected.

- **Data mining reports**: Data mining reports often require expanding on existing data through various techniques. For instance, in the context of customer intelligence, data mining may involve computing monthly averages for customers shopping for specific products or creating and storing alerts for detecting irregular customer behavior. These techniques rely on fundamental statistical metrics such as standard deviation, mean, and percentile evaluations. In other cases, data mining may involve inferring data in the absence of information.

For instance, when determining which customers did not purchase a particular product each month, we can leverage past customer behavior to fill in data gaps. The absence of data does not mean the data is absent. If a customer bought a product in the past, the existence of that customer gets registered. You can then extract every distinct customer and then extrapolate the existence of such records to every unit of time you require the information on, for example, a specific month. Customers who did buy the product will be followed by the total, while customers who did not will show zero dollars. The use of "Y" and "N" flags is also encouraged to distinguish between hypothetical cases in which sales sum zero from no sales at all.

By acquiring knowledge and understanding of these reports, we can enhance our ability to interpret and analyze data effectively, elevating our professional capabilities and acquiring data proficiency. Developing proficiency in data analysis tools and techniques further enables individuals to extract valuable insights, identify patterns, and make data-driven decisions with confidence. Moreover, honing skills in data visualization and storytelling allows professionals to present complex data in a compelling and understandable manner, facilitating effective communication and driving organizational buy-in.

Concluding thoughts

Organizations that are proficient in handling data can uncover valuable patterns, trends, and correlations within the vast datasets they accumulate. These insights can lead to better market understanding, identification of emerging opportunities, optimization of business processes, and identification of potential risks. Data proficiency enables organizations to make data-driven decisions that are grounded in evidence and have a higher likelihood of success.

In contrast, organizations that fail to develop data proficiency may struggle to keep up with the pace of digital transformation and risk falling behind their competitors. The inability to effectively harness the available data can result in missed opportunities, poor decision-making, and inefficient resource allocation.

As the availability of data continues to expand at an unprecedented rate, organizations must prioritize data proficiency to remain competitive. The ability to collect, analyze, and interpret data effectively is crucial for organizations to unlock their full potential, derive valuable insights, and make informed decisions that drive success in today's data-driven landscape.

Subject matter expertise

SME is an elevated level of knowledge or skill in a particular area or field. It is often gained through years of experience and education in the field. Subject matter experts are often sought out by others to provide their expertise on a specific topic or issue. There are many benefits to having subject matter experts on a team. Subject matter experts can provide valuable insights and guidance, help to solve problems, and develop innovative ideas. They can also help to train and develop others in the field.

If you are looking to develop your own subject matter expertise, there are a few things you can do. First, make sure you have some strong foundational knowledge in the field. There are many ways to gain this knowledge, be it through education, training, or experience. Second, stay up to date on the latest developments in the field by reading industry publications, attending conferences, and networking with other professionals. Finally, be willing to share your knowledge and expertise with others by authoring articles, giving presentations, or mentoring others.

SME is an asset in any field. If you have SME in a particular area, be sure to share it with others; helping others learn and grow from your expertise can make a tangible difference in your team and organization. Subject matter experts play a crucial role in guiding and mentoring less experienced colleagues within their organizations and provide less experienced colleagues with guidance on best practices, industry standards, and effective approaches to problem-solving. Subject matter experts can transfer their knowledge and expertise to others, fostering a culture of continuous learning and development within the organization.

Subject matter experts can be found working in a variety of roles, such as policy advisers, program managers, and researchers. They can also be found serving on advisory boards and commissions. Subject matter experts play a key role in helping governments make informed decisions about a wide range of issues, such as education, healthcare, and environmental issues. Subject matter experts also work as product developers, consultants, and trainers or start their own businesses with the knowledge and expertise gained over their years in an industry. Subject matter experts also play a significant role in helping businesses develop new products and services, improve their operations, and increase their profitability.

SME is essential for BI professionals because it enables them to understand the intricacies and nuances of specific domains or industries. SME allows BI professionals to understand the business context of the data they are analyzing and identify the key drivers of performance and the most relevant metrics to track. SME also gives BI professionals the ability to communicate their findings in a way that is understandable to business stakeholders, which is extremely important since these insights are typically used to make decisions.

Let us explore some of the reasons that SME can be used to improve the effectiveness of BI professionals in more depth:

- **Contextual understanding**: Subject matter expertise allows BI professionals to have a deep understanding of the industry, business domain, and specific challenges and opportunities within an organization. This understanding enables them to ask the right questions, identify relevant data sources, and interpret data in the appropriate context. It helps them grasp the nuances, trends, and dynamics specific to the industry or business sector they are working in.

- **Data interpretation**: Subject matter expertise enhances the ability of BI professionals to effectively interpret data. Subject matter experts have the necessary knowledge to discern meaningful patterns, correlations, and outliers in the data and understand the implications and significance of those findings. By combining their expertise with data analysis techniques, they can extract actionable insights and provide valuable recommendations that align with the specific needs of the business.

- **Data validation and quality assurance**: Subject matter experts can validate and verify the accuracy and reliability of the data being analyzed. They have the knowledge to assess whether the data aligns with the expected patterns and trends within the industry or domain. This validation helps ensure that the insights derived from the data are trustworthy and can be relied upon for decision-making.

- **Business requirements translation**: BI professionals with subject matter expertise can effectively translate business requirements into data analysis processes and methodologies. They can bridge the gap between business stakeholders and technical teams by understanding the specific information needs of the organization and translating them into data-driven solutions. This alignment between business requirements and technical implementation is crucial for successful BI initiatives.

- **Insights communication**: Subject matter expertise enables BI professionals to effectively communicate insights and findings to non-technical stakeholders within the organization. They can explain complex data concepts and analytical results in a language that is easily understandable and relevant to the specific business context. This facilitates better decision-making as stakeholders can fully comprehend and apply the insights to their strategic initiatives.

- **Continuous improvement and innovation**: Subject matter expertise allows BI professionals to stay up to date with industry trends, best practices, and emerging technologies. This knowledge helps them identify opportunities for improvement, propose innovative solutions, and drive continuous innovation within the organization. They can leverage their expertise to identify new data sources, develop advanced analytical models, and explore novel approaches to data visualization and reporting.

Concluding thoughts

SME is critical for BI professionals as it provides them with the necessary industry knowledge, contextual understanding, and data interpretation skills. This expertise enables them to validate data, translate business requirements, communicate insights effectively, and drive continuous improvement and innovation. By combining their subject matter expertise with data analysis capabilities, BI professionals can deliver impactful and meaningful insights that drive informed decision-making and contribute to the success of the organization.

Subject matter experts play a significant role in understanding data in different departments of a company. By delving into the realm of data within different business units, subject matter experts bring a wealth of contextual understanding to the table. They possess a profound grasp of the nuances, intricacies, and idiosyncrasies that shape data behavior within their respective domains. Subject matter experts are intimately familiar with the key metrics, performance indicators, and variables that drive success in their areas of expertise. This domain-specific knowledge empowers them to discern and interpret the patterns, anomalies, and relationships inherent to the data, facilitating a comprehensive understanding of how data behaves within each business unit.

When we shift our focus to exploring the behavior of data within different business units, it becomes apparent that subject matter experts are invaluable assets in comprehending, deciphering, and leveraging the intricate landscape of data within specific domains. Their deep domain knowledge, contextual understanding, and ability to interpret data contribute significantly to optimizing processes, driving informed decision-making, and achieving organizational success within distinct business units.

Data behavior in different business units

Let us turn our attention to how data behaves in different business units. Why would data behave differently in different business units of the same organization? This occurs because the types of data collected, the goals of business units, and the way the data is used vary. Marketing departments might use data to track customer behavior, identify trends, and target marketing campaigns. Sales managers might use data to help their sales reps track leads, close deals, and measure performance. A finance department might use data to track revenue, expenses, and profitability over time. As you can see from these examples, three teams within the same organization have diverse needs and goals with data.

The *way* data is used in different business units also varies. In some cases, data is used to make decisions in real time. A marketing team might use data to decide which ads to show to which customers. In other cases, data is used to make decisions on a more strategic level. For example, a finance team might use data to decide how to allocate resources. The way data behaves in different business units depends on the specific needs of the business unit. By understanding the diverse types of data collected, the goals of the business unit, and the way the data is used, businesses can make better use of their data to improve their performance.

Business data comes in many different varieties, shapes, and sizes. Here are some examples of types of business data:

- Social media activity
- Blog posts
- Inventory data
- Customer satisfaction surveys
- Website traffic
- Interactions with customers

The world of business data is vast and varied, encompassing a multitude of information. From sales figures to complex accounting reports, it can be difficult to discern what data is profoundly important and what can be overlooked. Though this list is not exhaustive, it provides a glimpse into the wide array of business data that exists. Whether it is inventory levels, customer demographics, or employee performance metrics, all of these and many more can be classified as business data. It is important to remember that business data goes beyond just numbers and statistics; it includes qualitative information and other non-numeric data as well.

As savvy BI professionals, we are tasked with managing an ever-increasing amount of data across multiple departments and functions within a company. This can pose a significant challenge in terms of organization and analysis. However, by utilizing a strategic approach, we can effectively manage this broad scope of data. One effective method is to dissect a company's structure into its various business units and identify the **key performance indicators (KPIs)** that are relevant to each unit. By categorizing and locating each type of KPI appropriately, we can streamline data management and ensure that the right information is being analyzed by the right people at the right time. This approach enhances data analysis efficiency and facilitates better decision-making, as stakeholders have access to accurate, relevant data. The success of a BI professional hinges on their ability to navigate the complexities of data management and deliver valuable insights to support the company's objectives.

Let us start by looking at different units at a typical for-profit company. Note that the specific structure and composition of these units may vary depending on the company's size and industry. However, we can categorize a company into six central functional units:

- Production
- Research and development
- Sales
- Marketing
- Human resources
- Accounting and finance

All these functional units have specific goals and deliverables but typically work hand in hand, which will be explored further here:

- **Sales and marketing**: Sales and marketing are two critical components that fuel the success of any business. Without sales, a company cannot sustain itself in the long term, and building strong relationships with customers is essential for repeat business and word-of-mouth referrals. Marketing efforts are crucial in creating awareness of a company's products or services and reaching potential customers. Account management involves maintaining ongoing relationships with customers, ensuring their needs are being met, and identifying opportunities for upselling or cross-selling. In combination, sales, marketing, and account management play a fundamental role in driving revenue growth and sustaining a thriving business.

- **Operations and production**: The operations and production departments are responsible for fulfilling the company's promise or deliverable, which is critical to ensuring customer satisfaction and maintaining brand reputation. While marketing and sales efforts are focused on driving brand awareness and revenue, it is the operations team that ensures the product or service is produced and delivered effectively and efficiently. This involves overseeing the entire production process, from sourcing materials and manufacturing to packaging and shipping. The success of a business relies on the seamless collaboration between the marketing and sales departments to generate revenue and the operations and production team to deliver on the company's promise and ensure customer satisfaction.

- **Finance and administration**: The finance department is responsible for tracking revenue and expenses, producing balance sheets, managing the payroll, and ensuring the timely filing of quarterly financial statements and end-of-year taxes. This financial data provides crucial insights into the financial health of the company and helps inform business decisions. The administration department is responsible for managing the daily operations of the company. This includes overseeing management functions, such as planning, organizing, directing, and controlling resources, and handling the hiring process to ensure a talented and effective workforce. With the help of financial data and effective management practices, businesses can optimize their financial performance and organizational processes to achieve their strategic goals.

Taking it one step further, let us break these business units into the various departments that contribute to the company's overall mission and goals. Common departments include marketing, sales, accounting and finance, operations, human resources, and IT. Let us dive into how data behaves in each department and what challenges come with managing data in those departments (and potential solutions for addressing these challenges!).

Data behavior in marketing

Marketing departments use data to track customer behavior, identify trends, and target marketing campaigns. For example, a marketing team might use data to track which pages on a website are most popular, which products are most frequently purchased, and which demographics are most likely to convert. This data can then be used to create more targeted marketing campaigns that are more likely to be successful.

BI has become an essential tool for marketers as they drive growth for their companies. Data-driven marketing is a top priority for enterprise marketing leaders, and many companies are investing heavily in developing strategies from the analysis of big data. The value of BI in marketing cannot be overstated. By leveraging marketing data and analytics to draw impactful insights, companies can make informed decisions and optimize their marketing efforts to drive business value. BI tools can help identify customer preferences and behaviors, track marketing campaigns, and measure the success of marketing efforts. These insights can lead to increased brand awareness, higher customer engagement, improved conversion rates, and increased revenue. Here is how insights derived from BI can help marketing teams with their short-term and long-term goals:

- **Brand awareness**: By leveraging analytics, companies can gain real-time insights into brand coverage, allowing them to focus their marketing and PR efforts more effectively. This helps companies increase brand awareness and drive growth in their business.

- **Managing costs**: By tracking and analyzing the impact of marketing activities, companies can identify wasteful spending and double down on activities that drive results. This allows them to allocate their marketing budget more effectively and maximize their **return on investment** (**ROI**).

- **Influencing and driving revenue**: By analyzing data on demand generation and campaign ROI, companies can gain insights into the impact of their marketing efforts on revenue. This allows them to make data-driven decisions about future marketing activities and optimize their strategies to drive even greater revenue growth.

By harnessing the power of data to inform their decisions and enhance their marketing strategies, companies can unlock immense potential for driving revenue growth. However, amidst this pursuit, they often encounter a significant marketing data challenge: the need to establish effective KPIs that accurately measure the success and impact of their marketing efforts.

Marketing data challenge – establishing effective KPIs

One significant challenge for marketing teams is the absence of any sort of data-driven approach. Oftentimes, marketing teams rely on simple metrics such as web traffic trends or social media views instead of a comprehensive set of KPIs aligned with specific business goals. This leads to marketing managers not having any sort of roadmap for their data needs or even how to transform the data they *do* have available to them into meaningful insights, never mind any sort of actionable strategies.

Marketing data solution – working with marketing leaders to establish KPIs

Implementing a data-driven marketing strategy can be complex, and many marketing teams struggle with this transition. As a BI professional, you possess the expertise and skills necessary to address this pain point effectively. By leveraging your knowledge of data analysis and interpretation, you can guide marketing teams in adopting a data-driven mindset, establishing relevant KPIs, and deriving valuable insights that drive successful marketing campaigns. How can we go about this?

1. **Understand business objectives**: Work closely with marketing leaders to gain a deep understanding of their business goals, target audience, and marketing strategies. This knowledge will help you align data-driven KPIs with the overall objectives of the marketing department and the organization.

2. **Identify relevant data sources**: Collaborate with marketing leaders to identify the data sources available within the organization that can provide valuable insights. This may include **customer relationship management** (**CRM**) systems, website analytics, social media data, and email marketing platforms, among other things.

3. **Define meaningful KPIs**: Based on the business objectives and available data sources, assist the marketing team in defining KPIs that are relevant, measurable, and aligned with the marketing goals. These KPIs could include metrics such as conversion rates, customer acquisition cost, customer lifetime value, return on ad expenditure, and engagement metrics.

4. **Develop data collection and analysis processes**: Help design and implement systems and processes to collect, organize, and analyze relevant marketing data. This may involve setting up data tracking mechanisms, integrating various data sources, and implementing data visualization tools or dashboards for easy monitoring and reporting.

5. **Provide insights and reporting**: Using advanced data analysis techniques, extract actionable insights from the collected data and present them in a clear and concise manner. This will enable marketing leaders to make data-driven decisions, identify trends, optimize marketing campaigns, and measure the effectiveness of their strategies.

6. **Continuous optimization and guidance**: Support marketing leaders in continuously monitoring and evaluating the performance of data-driven KPIs. This may involve conducting regular reviews, suggesting improvements, and adjusting KPIs as needed to ensure they remain relevant and aligned with evolving business objectives.

Marketing data challenge – the availability and quality of data

Another common data challenge for marketing teams is the availability and quality of data. Marketing teams often deal with vast amounts of data from various sources, such as customer interactions, website analytics, social media metrics, and advertising campaigns. However, this data may be fragmented, incomplete, or inconsistent, making it difficult to derive meaningful insights.

Marketing data solution

A skilled BI analyst can play a crucial role in helping marketing teams deal with fragmented or incomplete data. Here is how you, with your business analyst skills, can help:

1. **Data assessment**: Start with an assessment of the existing data sources and evaluate their completeness and quality. Then, identify gaps in the data and determine the reliability and accuracy of the available information.

2. **Data cleansing and enrichment**: In cases where the data is incomplete or contains errors, collaborate with data experts to clean/validate the data. Through this collaboration, you can develop strategies to fill in missing data points or enrich the existing data by incorporating external data sources.

3. **Data modeling and normalization**: Apply data modeling techniques to structure and normalize the data. By defining consistent data structures and relationships, you ensure that the data is organized and ready for analysis.

4. **Collaboration and training**: Finally, collaborate closely with marketing teams to understand their data needs and provide guidance on how to interpret and utilize the data effectively. You might suggest conducting training sessions to enhance the teams' data literacy and empower them to work independently with data.

Marketing data challenge – meaningful interpretation of data

Data interpretation is another hurdle for marketing teams. While they have access to a wealth of data, it can be overwhelming to make sense of it all. Transforming raw data into actionable insights requires strong analytical skills, the ability to identify patterns and trends, and the expertise to extract meaningful information.

Marketing data solution

Once again, we can put our skills to the test to help our marketers overcome this challenge. We can leverage our data analysis skills to support marketing teams with an interpretation of the data they collect. Here are a few approaches you can take:

1. **Perform exploratory analysis**: Use some basic exploratory data analysis techniques to uncover patterns, trends, and insights within the marketing data. As you dig deeper, employ basic statistical methods, data mining, and machine learning algorithms to identify more meaningful patterns in customer behavior, campaign performance, market trends, and so on.

2. **Tell a story**: After doing some initial exploration, take some of your data insights and communicate them more effectively using storytelling techniques. Translate your technical analysis into a narrative that is easily understandable by highlighting key findings, trends, and actionable recommendations.

3. **Insights and recommendations**: A data analyst can provide valuable insights and recommendations based on their data analysis. They can help marketing teams understand the implications of the data, identify areas for improvement, and suggest actionable strategies to optimize marketing campaigns, target specific customer segments, or allocate resources more effectively.

The implementation of a data-driven marketing strategy often presents complexities, leading many marketing teams to face challenges during the transition. However, as a skilled BI professional, you possess the necessary expertise to effectively address this pain point by leveraging your proficiency in data analysis and interpretation. Your assistance can empower marketing teams to make informed decisions based on data, leading to improved performance and better alignment with overall business objectives.

Data behavior in sales

Sales departments use data to track leads, close deals, and measure performance. For example, a sales team might use data to track how many leads are generated each month, how many deals are closed each quarter, and how much revenue is generated each year. This data can then be used to identify areas where the sales team can improve, such as generating more leads or closing more deals.

In the realm of BI, sales reports hold immense significance to sales teams. They serve as a vital tool for managers to use to consolidate and monitor sales performance, devise effective sales strategies, identify emerging patterns, and adapt the sales cycle accordingly. The accuracy and comprehensiveness of the sales report, coupled with its extensive data sources, significantly enhance the ability of managers to make informed and well-grounded decisions for the department and the entire organization. The integration of BI practices amplifies the value of sales reports, enabling managers to derive precise insights and make data-driven choices that drive sales growth and contribute to the overall success of the company.

Regrettably, numerous organizations encounter time-consuming hurdles within their sales reporting system, which diminishes the accuracy and dulls the insights derived from their reports, reducing their overall value. These challenges manifest in several ways, including sluggish reporting processes that hinder timely access to critical information and potential data loss that compromises the integrity of reports. These impediments not only negatively impact decision-making but also undermine the organization's ability to leverage sales data effectively for strategic planning and performance evaluation. Addressing these challenges and streamlining the sales reporting system is essential to enhance the accuracy, efficiency, and value of sales reports, enabling organizations to make informed decisions and gain valuable insights for driving sales growth and maximizing business success.

Sales data challenge – data integration and accessibility

Sales teams encounter the complexity of managing data from various sources, including CRM systems, spreadsheets, email platforms, and marketing automation tools. Each of these sources captures various aspects of customer interactions, sales activities, and marketing campaigns. However, the challenge lies in integrating and consolidating data from these disparate sources to create a unified and comprehensive view of customer information.

Data integration is crucial to avoid data silos, where information is fragmented and isolated within individual systems. Without proper integration, sales teams may struggle to access a complete picture of customer interactions, which can hinder their ability to understand customer behavior, preferences, and needs.

Sales data solution

By integrating and consolidating data effectively, sales teams can gain a holistic understanding of customers, their interactions, and their journey across various touchpoints. This unified view enables them to identify cross-selling or upselling opportunities, personalize sales interactions, and provide a seamless customer experience. It also empowers sales managers and leaders to analyze performance metrics, track sales pipelines, and make data-driven decisions to optimize sales strategies and drive revenue growth.

So how can we help them avoid data silos? Say you are a data engineer tasked with producing a solution to this problem. You might start integrating data from multiple sources by establishing connections to each data source, followed by creating data pipelines from each source, and then implementing data transformation processes. This integration process enables the synchronization of data across systems, ensuring that updates or changes made in one source are reflected consistently across all connected platforms.

Once that has been set up, you can take the data consolidation one step further by aggregating the data coming from various sources into a central repository or data warehouse. This consolidation allows sales teams to access a unified view of customer information, eliminating the need to navigate between multiple systems or manually compile data from diverse sources.

Sales data challenge – data entry and management

The manual entry and management of data place a substantial burden on sales representatives, consuming a considerable amount of their time and energy, which could be much better spent prospecting new customers, building customer relationships, or closing deals. Engaging in repetitive data entry tasks and managing spreadsheets or CRM systems manually can be monotonous, leading to frustration and decreased job satisfaction among sales professionals.

The manual nature of these processes also opens the door to human errors. Even the most diligent sales representatives can inadvertently make mistakes, such as typos, incorrect data entries, or missing information. These errors can propagate throughout the system, leading to inaccurate and unreliable data. Inaccurate data, in turn, can adversely affect sales forecasting, customer analysis, and decision-making processes; garbage in, garbage out.

Sales data solution

To mitigate these challenges, organizations can leverage automation and technology solutions. Sales representatives can benefit from tools and software that automate data entry, streamline workflows, and eliminate repetitive tasks. Implementing CRM systems that integrate with other data sources, such as marketing automation platforms or inventory management systems, can centralize data and reduce manual data entry requirements. Additionally, utilizing mobile apps or voice-to-text technologies can enhance efficiency and accuracy in capturing and updating data while on the go.

With data engineering expertise, you can play a crucial role in supporting sales teams with data entry and management by leveraging your technical expertise and knowledge of data infrastructure. You might develop some automated processes and scripts to extract data from various sources, transform it into the desired format, and load it into the appropriate systems or databases. By automating data entry tasks, sales representatives can save time and eliminate the need for manual input, reducing the likelihood of errors.

You could also build data pipelines that streamline the movement and transformation of data between different systems. These pipelines can automate data synchronization, ensuring that the sales team has access to the most up-to-date and accurate information. Data engineers can also set up data quality checks and validation processes within the pipelines to maintain data integrity.

Finally, work with your sales team to implement data governance practices that define standards, policies, and processes for data entry and management. Help them to establish data validation rules, data cleansing procedures, and data access controls to maintain data quality and security. These practices help enforce data consistency, improve data accuracy, and ensure compliance with relevant regulations.

Sales data challenge – data visibility and reporting

Sales managers and leaders rely on real-time visibility of sales performance and metrics to effectively monitor and manage their teams. Timely access to accurate and comprehensive sales data is vital for tracking progress, identifying bottlenecks, and making data-driven decisions that drive revenue growth. However, inefficient reporting processes or inadequate reporting tools can significantly impede their ability to obtain the necessary insights quickly.

Inefficient reporting processes can slow down the generation and distribution of sales reports. If the process involves manual data extraction, manipulation, and report creation, it can be time-consuming and prone to errors. Sales managers may face delays in receiving the latest sales data, hindering their ability to assess performance promptly. These delays can result in missed opportunities for intervention or adjustments to sales strategies, impacting overall sales effectiveness.

In addition to inefficient processes, inadequate reporting tools can limit the depth and breadth of insights available to sales managers. If the tools lack robust capabilities for data visualization, analytics, and customization, it becomes challenging to extract meaningful and actionable information from the data. Sales managers may struggle to gain a comprehensive view of key performance indicators, trends, and benchmarks, inhibiting their ability to make informed decisions.

Moreover, outdated or fragmented reporting systems can contribute to a lack of real-time visibility. If data is scattered across multiple systems, databases, or spreadsheets, it becomes cumbersome and time-consuming to consolidate and analyze the information. Sales managers may have to spend significant effort manually aggregating data from various sources, delaying their access to critical sales insights. This fragmented view can hinder their ability to identify emerging patterns, spot opportunities, and address sales challenges promptly.

Sales data solution

To address these challenges, organizations can implement robust sales reporting processes and leverage advanced reporting tools. Automating data extraction, transformation, and report generation can streamline the reporting process, ensuring that sales managers receive up-to-date information in a timely manner. Employing modern reporting tools with interactive dashboards, drill-down capabilities, and customizable reports empowers sales managers to explore sales data intuitively and extract meaningful insights with ease.

Implementing a centralized data repository or data warehouse that consolidates sales data from various sources provides a lone source of truth. This enables sales managers to access real-time, accurate, and comprehensive information on sales performance. By integrating data from CRM systems, marketing platforms, and other relevant sources, organizations can provide a holistic view of sales activities, pipeline status, conversion rates, and revenue figures.

Furthermore, leveraging advanced analytics techniques, such as predictive modeling and sales forecasting, can enhance the depth of the insights available to sales managers. These techniques enable them to anticipate trends, identify potential sales opportunities, and optimize sales strategies based on data-driven predictions.

By improving reporting processes and equipping sales managers with powerful reporting tools, organizations can enhance real-time visibility into sales performance. Sales managers can monitor progress, identify bottlenecks, and make informed decisions promptly, resulting in improved sales outcomes and overall business success.

Data behavior in finance and accounting

Finance departments use data to track revenue, expenses, and profitability. For example, a finance team might use data to track how much money is coming in each month, how much money is going out each month, and how much profit is being made each quarter. This data can then be used to make decisions about how to allocate resources, such as investing in new products or expanding into new markets.

In the realm of finance, the display of data is characterized by its perpetual nature, which is driven by the need for regulations and compliance. Accounting systems, for instance, are designed to operate on a specific fiscal calendar basis. Financial operations are segmented into fiscal periods and quarters within a fiscal year, and this determines the frequency at which data gets updated. Within a month, there may be numerous transactions that occur, with new operations constantly being appended to the existing ones. However, as the month progresses and draws closer to its end, the pace of transactions slows down. This effect is even more pronounced if the month represents the end of a fiscal quarter, and it becomes even clearer when it is the end of the fiscal year. As every company has fiscal obligations, the data it generates will be set in stone once these periods are over.

The perpetuity of financial data displays is an essential aspect of the financial industry, as it facilitates regulatory compliance and accounting. Financial data must be updated regularly to ensure that it remains current and accurate. Companies are required to adhere to specific fiscal periods, which determine the time limit in which they are allowed to update their data. This approach to financial data management ensures that companies can keep track of their financial performance and comply with regulatory requirements. It also helps to create a historical record of the company's financial operations, which can be used for analysis and forecasting purposes.

In addition to the frequency at which data gets updated, the timing of transactions also affects the display of financial data. Typically, there is a surge in financial activity at the beginning of the month, with a slower pace toward the end. This trend becomes more pronounced as the fiscal period ends. At this point, companies are focused on meeting their fiscal obligations and finalizing their financial records. As a result, financial data during this period is often more reliable and accurate, as companies are more meticulous in their reporting.

The perpetuity of financial data displays is a crucial aspect of the financial industry. It ensures that companies comply with regulatory requirements, facilitates accurate accounting, and creates a historical record of financial operations. By understanding the timing and frequency of financial transactions, analysts can gain valuable insights into a company's financial performance, which can be used to inform investment decisions and other financial strategies.

Finance data challenge

Compliance with accounting standards is crucial when managing financial data for several reasons. First, accounting standards provide a consistent framework for recording and reporting financial information. These standards ensure that financial information is recorded and presented in a standardized manner, enhancing financial statements' comparability. This is particularly important when comparing financial statements across companies or time periods.

Secondly, adherence to accounting standards ensures that financial data is accurate and reliable. These standards provide clear guidelines on how financial transactions should be recorded and reported, which helps to minimize errors and ensure that financial statements are presented fairly and accurately. This is important because stakeholders, such as investors and creditors, rely on financial statements to make informed decisions about a company's financial health.

Thirdly, compliance with accounting standards helps to promote transparency and accountability in financial reporting. By following recognized accounting standards, companies demonstrate their commitment to transparency, which can enhance their reputation and build trust with stakeholders. This is particularly important in today's business environment, where companies are under increasing scrutiny to demonstrate their ethical and social responsibility.

Finally, compliance with accounting standards is often a legal requirement. For example, companies in the United States are required to comply with relevant accounting standards and regulations, which are enforced by regulatory bodies such as the **Securities and Exchange Commission (SEC)** and the **Financial Accounting Standards Board (FASB)**. Failure to comply with these standards can result in financial penalties, legal sanctions, and damage to a company's reputation.

Finance data solution

To excel in BI within the field of finance, it is essential to develop an intuition for creating mechanisms that align with the behavior of financial data displays. One way to achieve this is by implementing validation mechanisms that track changes in data that has already been processed and vetted. While past changes could still occur, most financial statements should remain consistent.

Another important strategy is to keep track of monthly metrics by taking regular snapshots and comparing them to point-in-time reports. For instance, at the end of each month, it is wise to take a snapshot of the data and store it in an archive. Then, you can develop a report that compares the monthly metrics with the archived snapshot. This comparison will help identify any discrepancies, and you can track these results over time to identify any trends or patterns.

By creating these validation mechanisms, you can develop a more accurate and reliable understanding of financial data. It can also help you identify any inconsistencies in the data, which can indicate potential errors or fraud. This approach will enable you to analyze and interpret financial data with more confidence and make better-informed business decisions.

Furthermore, it is crucial to stay up to date with changes in accounting standards and regulations, which may impact how financial data is processed, recorded, and displayed. These changes can affect the behavior of financial data displays and require adjustments in your validation mechanisms to ensure that the data remains accurate and reliable.

Data behavior in operations

Operations teams are responsible for the day-to-day running of a business. They need to be able to make decisions quickly and accurately to keep the business running smoothly. Data can be a valuable tool for operations teams, but it can also be a challenge.

Operations departments rely on data to analyze and optimize various business processes. By collecting and analyzing data on KPIs such as production output, cycle times, quality metrics, and resource utilization, operations teams can identify bottlenecks, inefficiencies, and areas for improvement. Data-driven insights help streamline operations, reduce costs, improve productivity, and enhance overall operational efficiency.

Managing inventory is critical for operations departments to ensure smooth production and timely order fulfillment. Data on inventory levels, demand forecasts, lead times, and supplier performance helps operations teams optimize inventory levels, determine reorder points, and plan procurement activities. By leveraging data, operations departments can strike a balance between meeting customer demand and minimizing carrying costs, stockouts, or excess inventory.

Operations departments rely on data to make informed decisions. By analyzing data on various operational aspects, such as production costs, resource allocation, capacity utilization, and performance metrics, operations teams can make data-driven decisions to optimize operations, allocate resources effectively, improve productivity, and drive overall business performance.

Operations teams must be able to rely on accurate and timely data to make informed decisions. Inaccurate or incomplete data can lead to incorrect conclusions, poor decision-making, and negative business outcomes. Data must be properly maintained, validated, and standardized to ensure its quality and integrity.

Operations data challenge – legacy systems and technology constraints

Operations teams often encounter challenges related to outdated legacy systems or technology constraints. Legacy systems may have limitations in terms of data integration, scalability, or data analysis capabilities. Upgrading or integrating modern technologies to address these constraints can be complex and time-consuming, requiring careful planning and implementation.

Operations data solution

To address a data problem related to outdated legacy systems or technology constraints faced by operations teams, a systematic approach is necessary. Begin by conducting a comprehensive assessment of the existing legacy systems and technology infrastructure. Identify the specific limitations, such as data integration issues, scalability constraints, or inadequate data analysis capabilities. This assessment will provide a clear understanding of the problem areas that need to be addressed.

Engage with the operations teams to gather their requirements and understand their pain points. This involves actively listening to their challenges, gathering insights into their data needs, and identifying the desired outcomes. By involving the teams directly impacted by the data problem, a more accurate and tailored solution can be developed.

Conduct thorough research on the available technologies, software solutions, and system upgrades that could address the identified limitations. Evaluate different options based on their compatibility with existing systems, scalability, data integration capabilities, and data analysis functionalities. Consider factors such as cost, implementation complexity, and long-term suitability.

Develop a detailed plan that outlines the steps required to implement the chosen solution. This plan should include a timeline, resource allocation, and dependencies. Ensure that the plan accounts for any potential disruptions to ongoing operations and includes strategies for mitigating risks during the transition.

Execute the planned activities while adhering to best practices and industry standards. This may involve upgrading legacy systems, integrating innovative technologies, or adopting cloud-based solutions.

Collaborate closely with the operations teams to ensure a smooth transition and provide necessary training and support during the implementation phase.

Thoroughly test the newly implemented systems to ensure their functionality, data integrity, and reliability. Conduct comprehensive testing procedures, including integration testing, performance testing, and user acceptance testing. Address any issues or bugs identified during this phase to ensure a robust and efficient solution.

Establish a monitoring and feedback mechanism to track the performance of the new systems and address any emerging issues promptly. Regularly evaluate the effectiveness of the solution and gather feedback from the operations teams to identify areas for further improvement or optimization. Continuously monitor industry trends and emerging technologies to ensure the organization remains up to date and can adapt to evolving data challenges.

By following these steps, organizations can systematically address the data problem associated with outdated legacy systems or technology constraints. This approach enables operations teams to overcome limitations, enhance their data integration and analysis capabilities, and improve overall operational efficiency.

Operations data challenge – real-time data processing

Operations teams often require real-time or near-real-time data to monitor and manage operational processes effectively. For example, in manufacturing environments, real-time data on machine performance, production rates, and quality metrics is critical to ensuring optimal performance. Processing and analyzing real-time data in a timely manner can be complex, as it requires efficient data capture, integration, and processing capabilities.

Operations data solution

To address the data problem of operations teams requiring real-time or near-real-time data for effective monitoring and management of operational processes, a thoughtful and collaborative approach is required.

Collaborate with the operations teams to understand their specific data requirements and the desired outcomes. Determine the KPIs and metrics that need to be monitored in real time to ensure optimal operational performance. This step will help prioritize the data sources and establish the scope of the solution.

Implement efficient data capture mechanisms to collect real-time data from relevant sources. This may involve deploying sensors or IoT devices or integrating with existing systems that generate the required operational data. Ensure seamless integration of data sources into a centralized repository or data management system to facilitate real-time data analysis.

Develop robust data processing capabilities to handle the influx of real-time data. This may involve implementing streaming data processing technologies, such as Apache Kafka or Apache Flink, to handle continuous data streams effectively. Apply appropriate data analytics techniques, such as complex event processing or machine learning algorithms, to derive meaningful insights from the real-time data and identify patterns or anomalies.

Ensure that the underlying infrastructure and systems can handle the data volume and processing requirements of real-time data. Scalable, cloud-based solutions can be considered to accommodate growing data needs and provide flexibility in resource allocation. Regularly monitor the system performance to optimize scalability and address any bottlenecks that may hinder real-time data processing.

Regularly assess the effectiveness of the real-time data solution by gathering feedback from operations teams and stakeholders. Continuously monitor evolving needs and emerging technologies to identify opportunities for improvement and enhancement. Stay up to date with advancements in data processing, analytics, and visualization tools to leverage new capabilities and improve real-time data management.

Operations data challenge – volume and variety of data

Operations teams often deal with a large volume and variety of data. This includes data from various sources such as manufacturing systems, supply chain systems, equipment sensors, quality control systems, and more. Managing and analyzing such diverse and large-scale datasets can be challenging, requiring robust data management and analytics capabilities.

Operations data solution

To address the data problem of operations teams dealing with a large volume and variety of data, start by implementing a comprehensive data integration strategy to bring together data from diverse sources such as manufacturing systems, supply chain systems, equipment sensors, quality control systems, and other relevant sources. This involves identifying the necessary data sources, establishing data connectivity, and developing data pipelines to centralize the data in a unified data repository or data lake.

Set up a scalable and efficient data storage infrastructure capable of handling large volumes of data. Utilize technologies such as cloud storage or distributed filesystems to accommodate the growing datasets. Implement proper data management practices, including data cataloging, metadata management, and data governance, to ensure data quality, accessibility, and security.

Perform data cleansing and preprocessing to address data quality issues and ensure consistency. This involves identifying and resolving data errors, duplication, missing values, and outliers. Standardize data formats, apply transformations, and enrich the data as needed to prepare it for analysis.

Employ advanced analytics techniques such as data mining, statistical analysis, machine learning, and predictive modeling to extract valuable insights from diverse datasets. Develop analytical models and algorithms specific to operational processes to uncover patterns, identify trends, and detect anomalies. Leverage visualization tools to present the analyzed data in a clear and actionable format, enabling operations teams to make informed decisions.

Explore automation and **artificial intelligence (AI)** solutions to streamline data processing and analysis tasks. Implement automated data pipelines, data integration workflows, and data validation processes to reduce manual efforts and enhance efficiency. Leverage AI techniques such as **natural language processing (NLP)** or anomaly detection to automate data anomaly identification or data quality checks.

Ensure that the underlying infrastructure can handle the storage, processing, and analysis requirements of large-scale datasets. Consider cloud-based solutions for distributed computing technologies to scale resources dynamically and optimize performance. Regularly monitor and optimize the infrastructure to accommodate growing data needs and maintain data processing efficiency.

This solution enables streamlined data management, powerful analytics, and data-driven decision-making to optimize operational processes, improve efficiency, and drive business outcomes.

Data behavior in human resources

HR teams can use data in a variety of ways to improve their work. Here are some examples:

- **Recruitment**: HR teams can use data to identify the best candidates for open positions. This can be done by analyzing resumes, social media profiles, and other data sources.

- **Performance management**: HR teams can use data to track employee performance and identify areas for improvement. This data can be used to create development plans and provide feedback to employees.

- **Compensation and benefits**: HR teams can use data to determine fair and competitive compensation and benefits packages. This data can also be used to identify areas where costs could be reduced.

- **Talent management**: HR teams can use data to identify and develop high-potential employees. This data can be used to create succession plans and provide opportunities for growth and development.

- **Employee engagement**: HR teams can use data to measure employee engagement and identify areas where morale is low. This data can be used to create initiatives to improve employee satisfaction and retention.

- **Diversity and inclusion**: HR teams can use data to track diversity and inclusion metrics and identify areas where improvements could be made. This data can be used to create initiatives to create a more inclusive workplace.

These are just a few examples of how HR teams can use data to improve their work. By collecting, analyzing, and using data effectively, HR teams can make better decisions, improve efficiency, and reduce costs. This can lead to a more productive and engaged workforce, which will benefit the organization.

HR data challenge

HR data in business intelligence is always stored in a transactional way. Records are stacked on top of each other, representing every single change an employee registers in a basic HR OLTP system.

Given the number of transactional records, it is difficult to compute the main KPIs that demonstrate essential employee performance throughout their career with the company. An employee not only has a record for relevant employee transactions such as promotions, department transfers, salary increases, and so on but also administrative changes required by the business, such as title changes, new managers, new job codes, department name changes, and so on, making it difficult to compute meaningful KPIs with all those records in the way.

HR data solution

Creating an analytical fact table allows you to crystallize metrics relevant to employee performance and create metrics not explicit in the data. You start by establishing periods for your analysis, for example, every year. Then, you compute the main metrics for every employee in that year:

- Average salary

- Age

- Tenure

- Bonuses

- Commute distance

Then, compute metrics derived from other attributes:

- Number of department transfers

- Number of managers

- Number of employees underneath

- Number of resignations

- Rank of salary within department

- Rank of salary within level

- Rank of salary within job code

- Turnover ratio

- Days since last salary increase

By creating this type of table, you provide a better solution for your customers to use to analyze employee performance and keep track of employee tendencies in your organization.

As we have seen through the exploration of different data challenges across various business units in an organization, the world of business data is an expansive and diverse landscape. It comprises many information types that organizations gather and analyze to gain insights and make informed decisions. This data-rich environment encompasses various sources, including sales figures, customer interactions, operational metrics, marketing campaigns, financial records, and much more. However, amid this abundance of data, organizations often face the challenge of distinguishing what data holds genuine significance and what can be overlooked. By establishing robust data governance practices, leveraging advanced analytics techniques, and aligning data with strategic priorities, organizations can harness the power of data to drive informed decision-making, achieve operational excellence, and thrive in today's data-driven business environment.

However, it is crucial not to overlook our fellow colleagues who may be grappling with data challenges in an academic setting. As researchers, students, and educators, they encounter a unique set of data-related hurdles that require support and guidance. Leaving them to tackle these challenges on their own can hinder their progress and limit their potential for academic success.

Data behavior in academia

In an academic context, data challenges can arise in various forms. Students conducting research projects may struggle with data collection, management, and analysis. They may encounter issues related to data quality, sample size, or statistical techniques. Similarly, educators may face challenges in effectively teaching data-related concepts and methodologies to their students. Navigating through complex datasets, understanding data visualization techniques, or applying appropriate statistical analyses can be overwhelming for those who are new to the field. In the next portion of this section, we will go through some data challenges in the academic world and give our advice on how to address them.

One of the challenges faced in academia is the registration period. To put it simply, it is a chaotic period that consists of students registering and deregistering many times during months, weeks, and sometimes even during a single day. The whole operation of an academic institution depends on this period. Creating schedules and assigning professors and classrooms to classes requires a good registration system, one flexible enough that it can comply with student demands. Students usually enroll in classes they want to take based on many factors – friends, timing, and difficulty, for example. Hence, it is difficult to accommodate all the needs of all the students.

Registration deadlines, even when set, can be overwritten by petition. Administrative personnel, with access to databases, may overwrite records to make the system even more flexible by *backdating* the system dates and making a record valid. There are many situations we cannot even fathom in which this flexibility is required, so institutions allow this alternative to happen. Because of this, BI systems have a lot of difficulty keeping track of the truth. In these scenarios, there are two *truths* being created, one is the **transactional truth**, which is what really happened in the system – the set of steps that happened in the database – and then there is the **business truth**, which is what the business considers should count, regardless of reality. This also happens in any other industry or department. Sometimes, data is entered incorrectly, and those mistakes need to be fixed. Once fixed, the new records become the business truth, despite there being existing records in your data warehouse saying the opposite.

Enter a "point-in-time" solution. While most of the metrics displayed in a registration report are "current" metrics that reflect the most recent state of information available in a data warehouse, some special metrics could be labeled "point-in-time" and allow you to look at data that is no longer current. Point-in-time metrics leverage a data warehouse's incremental data capture to let you "roll back the clock" and approximate the state of information at a particular point in time. These metrics can be tricky to set up correctly and may affect the performance of your reports, so they should be used only when necessary.

To gain a deeper understanding of point-in-time reporting, it helps to take a step back and think a bit about how registration activity data is structured. Let us pretend we have some example students enrolling in an example class. This chart depicts their registration statuses over the course of an example data capture timeline:

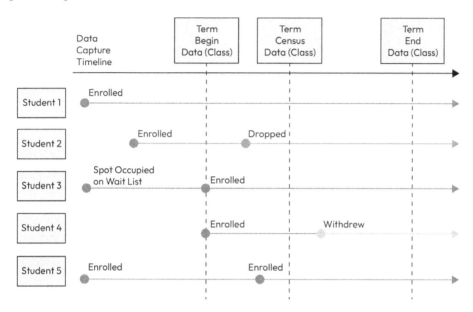

Figure 6.1 – Registration status chart

What is going on with each of these students?

- **Student 1**: This student enrolled on a date near the beginning of the enrollment period and then remained enrolled through to the term's end.

- **Student 2**: This student enrolled prior to the class's term start date but then dropped out shortly after the class began. They dropped out prior to the term census date.

- **Student 3**: This student was put on the class's wait list at the beginning of the enrollment period, but a spot opened, and they were able to enroll from the waitlist on the first day of the term.

- **Student 4**: This student enrolled in the class on the first day of the term, remained enrolled through the census date, but then withdrew from the class after the census date had passed.

- **Student 5**: This student enrolled on a date near the beginning of the enrollment period. They also managed to have their enrollment recorded again for the same class shortly after the term began and then remained enrolled through to the term's end.

> **Note**
>
> This is a rare scenario, but it is an example of the kinds of data anomalies that can show up in student enrollment data, and that makes it important to use "point-in-time" metrics in the registration activity to help correct these kinds of unique cases.

Before using point-in-time metrics in a report, it is important to ask yourself the following:

Do I care about the student registration activity that happened on a certain date?

or

Do I care about the student registration activity that occurred up to a specific date and remained valid on that date?

Here are some example questions that help explain the distinction between the two different point-in-time approaches:

	Happened on	**Valid on**
Example questions	• How many students waited until the last minute to register and ended up registering on the first day of the term? • How many students dropped out of class on the first day of the term? • How many students withdrew on each separate day of the term, starting from the term census date? Are there days in the term on which it is more common than others for students to withdraw?	• How many students were enrolled on the census date for the term (i.e., how many students enrolled at some point prior to the census date and had a status of "enrolled" that remained valid on the term census date for the class?)? • How many students remained on the waitlist on the term's first day? • How many students persisted in the class through to the end and remained enrolled on the term end date?
Solution	Business truth date	Transactional truth date

Figure 6.2 – Distinction between the two different point-in-time approaches

So, using our example timeline illustrated in the preceding figure, let us walk through answering a question on each of these two point-in-time approaches to help understand how point-in-time metrics are calculated:

- **Question 1**: How many students enrolled in this class on the first day of the term?

  Answer 1: This is a "happened on" question. It is asking how many enrollments coincided with the term start date. To answer this question, we need to "slice" the timeline along the term start date and look at how many data points have points of origin that coincide with the term start date. In the visual, this is represented by the dotted line that extends straight down from **Term Begin Date**. Scanning down this line, we need to count the green dots, representing each time we detected that a student's status changed to "enrolled," that fall directly on the line. The answer, then, is that two students – student 3 and student 4 – enrolled in the class on the term start date.

- **Question 2**: How many students were enrolled in this class on the term census date?

  Answer 2: This is a "valid on" question. It is asking how many students had an "enrolled" status that remained valid as of the term census date. To answer this question, we can again "slice" the timeline – this time, along the term census date. Scanning down this line, this time, we need to count not only the dots that fall directly on the line but also any student status line that indicates "Enrolled" (green lines) and that crosses the "slice" line coming down from **Term Census Date**. The answer is that four students – student 1, student 3, student 4, and student 5 – were enrolled on the term census date. The term census date "slice" line intersects with these students' status lines at a segment where their lines are green, indicating that they had a status of enrolled on the term census date.

Point-in-time reports are a complex subject, but if you understand when and how they work, you will open the door to data proficiency because this is a complex requirement across all industries and departments. It is strongly recommended that you spend time understanding the following concepts:

- Slowly changing dimensions (SCD type II)
- Change data capture
- Incremental loading
- Snapshots
- Bitemporal fact tables

By extending support and not leaving our academic colleagues to their own devices, we foster a culture of collaboration, growth, and academic excellence. By nurturing an environment that embraces and addresses data challenges, we enable individuals to unlock their full potential and contribute meaningfully to their academic pursuits. We must recognize the data challenges faced by our colleagues in an academic setting and proactively provide them with the necessary support. Through mentorship, training, collaboration, access to resources, and consultation services, we can empower them to navigate data hurdles effectively, enhance their research capabilities, and contribute to the advancement of knowledge in their respective fields.

Analytical thinking, which involves breaking down complex problems into manageable components and understanding the relationships between them, is an essential skill for effective problem-solving and sound decision-making. Therefore, by empowering individuals to navigate data hurdles effectively, we simultaneously cultivate their analytical thinking abilities, enabling them to approach challenges with a systematic and insightful mindset.

Now, let us delve further into the essence of analytical thinking and problem-solving, exploring why these two skill sets are of utmost importance to BI professionals.

Analytical thinking and problem-solving techniques

Analytical thinking is a cognitive ability that enables individuals to dissect intricate problems into their fundamental components and discern the connections and interdependencies between them. It serves as a foundational skill for solving complex challenges and making informed, sound decisions.

When confronted with a complex problem, analytical thinkers possess the capability to systematically break it down into manageable parts. They analyze the various elements, variables, and factors involved, seeking to understand their individual contributions and how they interact with one another. By deconstructing the problem, they can identify patterns, uncover hidden insights, and gain a comprehensive understanding of the underlying dynamics at play.

Moreover, analytical thinking empowers individuals to identify and evaluate the relationships between the different components of a problem. It involves recognizing cause-and-effect relationships, dependencies, and correlations that exist within the problem space. This holistic perspective allows for a deeper comprehension of how changes in one element can impact the overall system and the potential consequences of various courses of action.

The ability to think analytically is particularly valuable in the context of solving complex problems. Complex problems often involve multiple variables, uncertainties, and interconnected elements. Analytical thinkers excel at navigating these complexities by applying logical reasoning, data analysis, and critical thinking. They are adept at discerning relevant information from irrelevant noise, discerning patterns from chaos, and arriving at well-founded conclusions.

Analytical thinkers can do the following:

- Identify the key elements of a problem.
- Gather and organize the relevant information.
- Identify patterns and trends.
- Develop and test hypotheses.
- Draw logical conclusions.
- Communicate their findings effectively.

BI professionals with strong analytical skills can manage challenging issues by drawing on their own experience and calling on other resources as needed. For example, using strong analytical skills allows them to think of different causes of a particular problem and then also anticipate the potential consequences of implementing solutions to that problem. Strong analytical skills also allow BI professionals to break down complex tasks into manageable deliverables; instead of trying to "boil the ocean," they can focus on solving small problems first, which then lead to tackling the overall problem. This process involves several key steps.

Firstly, analytical thinkers will approach problem-solving with a mindset geared toward exploration and creativity. They understand that there are often multiple ways to tackle a problem and actively seek out alternative strategies. By considering a diverse range of possibilities, they broaden the scope of potential solutions and increase the likelihood of finding an effective one.

Next, analytical thinkers engage in a systematic analysis of each alternative. They carefully assess the feasibility, advantages, and disadvantages of each solution. This evaluation process involves considering several factors, such as cost, time constraints, the resources required, and the potential risks or drawbacks associated with each option.

During the evaluation phase, analytical thinkers also consider the potential outcomes and consequences of each alternative. They consider both short-term and long-term effects, as well as the impact on various stakeholders involved. By considering the pros and cons of each solution, they can identify potential trade-offs and make informed decisions.

Furthermore, analytical thinkers understand that the evaluation process is not static. As they uncover additional data or gain further insights, they adapt their analysis accordingly. They remain open to revisiting and refining their assessments as they gather more data or perspectives. This flexibility allows them to consider evolving circumstances and make well-informed decisions that align with the current context.

Analytical thinkers are in high demand in the workforce, and their skills are only becoming more important as the world becomes increasingly complex. So how do you, as a BI professional, practice and enhance your analytical skills? Let us go through some different actions to take to help you build these:

- **Read books and articles on analytical thinking**: This will help you to learn about the distinct types of analytical thinking and how to apply them in different situations

- **Ask questions and seek feedback**: The more you ask questions and get feedback, the better you will become at analytical thinking

- **Take online courses or workshops on analytical thinking**: This is a terrific way to learn from experts and get feedback on your analytical skills

- **Play games that require critical thinking**: Some examples of these games include chess, sudoku, and Minesweeper

- **Solve puzzles and brain teasers**: You can improve your problem-solving abilities and have fun at the same time!

- **Get involved in activities that require you to think critically**: This could include volunteering, joining a debate team, or starting a business.

Here are some additional tips for improving your analytical thinking skills:

- Practice breaking down problems into smaller, more manageable pieces
- Learn to identify patterns and trends in data
- Develop the ability to think critically and ask probing questions
- Be open to innovative ideas and perspectives
- Communicate your findings clearly and concisely

Analytical thinking is closely tied to making sound decisions. By thoroughly understanding the components and relationships within a problem, individuals can assess the potential outcomes and implications of different options. They can weigh the risks and benefits, evaluate the trade-offs, and make informed choices based on a comprehensive understanding of the problem's intricacies. This ability to make sound decisions is crucial for BI professionals tasked with analyzing data, extracting insights, and providing actionable recommendations to support strategic and operational decision-making within organizations.

Analytical thinking is a critical skill for BI professionals as it enables them to break down complex problems, identify the relationships between components, and make sound decisions based on a comprehensive understanding of the problem at hand. By honing their analytical thinking abilities, BI professionals can effectively navigate the complexities of data analysis, derive meaningful insights, and contribute to the success of organizations in an increasingly data-driven world.

Problem-solving

Problem-solving is the process of identifying a problem, gathering information, brainstorming solutions, evaluating solutions, and implementing the best solution. It is a critical skill for success in all areas of life.

There are many different problem-solving techniques, but they all share some common steps. The first step is to identify the problem. This may seem obvious, but it is important to be clear about what the problem is before you can start looking for solutions. Once you have identified the problem, you need to gather information. This information can come from a variety of sources, such as your own experience, research (online or via a library), and talking to others.

The next step is to brainstorm solutions. This is where you produce as many viable solutions as you can, no matter how crazy they may seem. The more ideas you have, the better. Once you have a list of solutions, you need to evaluate them. This means considering the pros and cons of each solution and deciding which one is the best fit for the problem.

The last step is to implement the solution. This may involve taking some action, such as talking to someone, deciding what to do, or changing your behavior. It is important to follow through on your solution and make sure that it is working. If it is not, you may need to go back to the drawing board and produce a new solution.

Problem-solving is of utmost importance for BI professionals for the following reasons:

- **Identifying and defining problems**: BI professionals need strong problem-solving skills to identify and define the challenges and issues faced by an organization. They work closely with stakeholders to understand their needs, analyze business processes, and recognize areas that require improvement. Effective problem-solving helps in narrowing down the focus and ensuring that BI initiatives align with the organization's strategic objectives.

- **Data analysis and interpretation**: BI professionals are responsible for analyzing large volumes of data to uncover valuable insights. Problem-solving skills enable them to apply appropriate analytical techniques, identify patterns, correlations, and trends, and interpret data in a meaningful way. They use their problem-solving abilities to ask the right questions, make connections, and derive actionable insights from complex datasets.

- **Root cause analysis**: Effective problem-solving in BI involves going beyond surface-level observations and conducting root cause analysis. BI professionals dig deeper into the underlying factors contributing to the identified problems. They investigate various dimensions of the problem, such as data quality issues, process inefficiencies, or bottlenecks, to understand the root causes. This helps in developing targeted strategies and solutions that address the underlying issues rather than just treating the symptoms.

- **Developing data-driven solutions**: BI professionals use problem-solving skills to develop data-driven solutions that address the identified challenges. They leverage their analytical expertise, industry knowledge, and understanding of organizational goals to design effective data models, dashboards, and reports. Problem-solving skills enable them to translate complex data into meaningful insights and actionable recommendations that drive positive outcomes for the organization.

- **Decision support**: BI professionals play a vital role in providing decision support to stakeholders across the organization. They help leaders, managers, and teams make informed decisions by presenting relevant data, visualizations, and insights. Problem-solving skills enable them to analyze different scenarios, evaluate alternatives, and provide recommendations based on data-driven insights. By facilitating evidence-based decision-making, BI professionals contribute to improved performance, efficiency, and strategic alignment within the organization.

- **Continuous improvement**: Problem-solving is an ongoing process in business intelligence. BI professionals continuously strive to improve data collection processes, enhance data quality, refine analytical models, and optimize reporting mechanisms. They use their problem-solving skills to identify areas for improvement, implement changes, and monitor the impact of those changes. This iterative approach to problem-solving ensures that BI initiatives evolve with the changing needs of organizations and deliver sustained value over time.

Problem-solving skills are essential to BI professionals as they enable them to identify, analyze, and address the challenges faced by organizations. By effectively applying problem-solving techniques, BI professionals can uncover insights, develop data-driven solutions, and provide decision support that drives positive outcomes and helps organizations achieve their goals. Problem-solving is a skill that can be learned and improved with practice. The more you practice, the better you will become at identifying problems, gathering information, brainstorming solutions, evaluating solutions, and implementing solutions.

Leveraging online tools for problem-solving

Online tools are so important for BI developers today because they can help save time, improve productivity, and create better-quality code. Online tools can be used for a variety of tasks, including the following:

- Code editing and debugging
- Version control
- Unit testing
- Continuous integration and delivery
- Performance testing
- Security testing
- Documentation
- Collaboration

By using online tools, developers can focus on the creative aspects of their work and leave mundane tasks to machines. This can lead to a more efficient and productive development process, which can lead to better-quality software.

Here are some of the specific benefits for developers of using online tools:

- **Saving time**: Online tools can automate many of the tasks that developers would otherwise have to do manually, such as code linting, code formatting, and unit testing. This can save developers a significant amount of time, which they can then use to focus on more creative and strategic tasks.

- **Improving productivity**: Online tools can help developers to be more productive by providing them with a central repository to store their code, manage their projects, and collaborate with others. This can help developers to stay organized and on track, and it can also help them to get their work done faster.

- **Creating better quality code**: Online tools can help developers to create better quality code by providing them with features such as code linting, code formatting, and unit testing. These features can help developers to identify and fix errors in their code, which can lead to more reliable, bug-free software.

Overall, online tools can be an asset to developers and can help developers save time, improve productivity, and create better-quality code. Online tools are so important for BI professionals today because they can help them to do the following:

- **Access data from anywhere**: Online tools allow BI professionals to access data from anywhere, at any time. This is essential for businesses that operate in multiple locations or that have employees who work remotely.

- **Share data with stakeholders**: Online tools make it easy to share data with stakeholders, both inside and outside of the organization. This allows businesses to make better decisions faster by getting input from a wider range of people.

- **Collaborate on data analysis**: Online tools make it easy for BI professionals to collaborate on data analysis. This can be done by sharing datasets, visualizations, and reports.

- **Automate tasks**: Online tools can automate many of the tasks that BI professionals would otherwise have to do manually. This can save time and resources, and it can also help to improve the accuracy of data analysis.

- **Get insights from data**: Online tools can help BI professionals to get insights from data that would otherwise be difficult or impossible to obtain. This can help businesses to make better decisions, improve efficiency, and identify new opportunities.

In today's digital era, online tools have become an asset for BI professionals, revolutionizing the way organizations gather, analyze, and utilize data.

Web (Google) search

Google Search is a powerful tool that can be used to help solve data problems. Here are a few tips for using Google Search to your advantage:

- **Use keywords that are specific to your problem**: The more specific your keywords are, the more relevant the results will be.

- **Use quotation marks around phrases**: This will help Google to find results that contain the exact phrase, even if the words are in a different order.

- **Use the minus sign (-) to exclude results that contain certain words**: This can be helpful if you are getting too many results that are not relevant to your problem.

- **Use the advanced search features**: The advanced search features allow you to narrow down your results by date, location, and other factors.

- **Use Google Scholar**: Google Scholar is a specialized search engine that is designed to find academic research papers. This can be a great resource for finding information on data problems.

- **Use Google Books**: Google Books is a search engine that indexes books from all over the world. It can be a great resource for finding information on data problems that are not available online.

Stack Overflow

Stack Overflow is a question-and-answer site for professional and enthusiastic programmers. It is a great resource for finding answers to data problems. Here are a few tips for using Stack Overflow to your advantage:

- **Ask clear and concise questions**: The better your question, the more likely you are to get a helpful answer

- **Use keywords that are specific to your problem**: The more specific your keywords are, the more likely your question is to be seen by people who can answer it

- **Search the site before you ask a question**: There is a good chance that your question has already been answered

- **Be patient**: It may take some time for someone to answer your question

- **Mark your question as answered when it has been answered**: This will help other people who are searching for the same answer

- **Upvote and accept answers that are helpful**: This will help to ensure that good answers are seen by more people

By following these tips, you can use Stack Overflow to help you solve data problems. Here are some additional tips for using Stack Overflow:

- **Be respectful of other users**: Stack Overflow is a community of people who are trying to help each other. Be sure to be respectful of other users' time and expertise.

- **Use the right tags**: When you ask a question, be sure to use the right tags. This will help other users to find your question.

- **Provide context**: When you ask a question, be sure to provide as much context as possible. This will help other users to understand your problem and provide a helpful answer.

- **Do not be afraid to ask for help**: If you are stuck, do not be afraid to ask for help. There are many skilled developers and engineers on Stack Overflow who will be willing to help you.

AI chatbots (ChatGPT/Bard)

This entire section was generated using an AI chatbot. We simply prompted the AI chatbot to give us some output on why using it would be beneficial. Here is what it had to say:

Prompt #1 – how would we use an AI chatbot to help us solve data problems?

"AI chatbots are large language models which are trained to be informative and conversational. They are trained on terabytes of text data to communicate and generate human-like responses to prompts and questions. It can provide summaries or generate new stories very quickly.

Here are some ways you can use an AI chatbot to help you solve data problems:

- *Ask an AI chatbot questions about data*

- *An AI chatbot can help you analyze data. An AI chatbot can help you to identify patterns and trends in data and to develop insights that can be used to make decisions.*

- *An AI chatbot can help you visualize data. An AI chatbot can create charts and graphs that can help you to understand data more easily.*

- *An AI chatbot can help you communicate data. An AI chatbot can help you to draft reports and presentations that are clear and concise.*

Overall, an AI chatbot can be a valuable tool for anyone who needs to work with data. If you are facing a data problem, I encourage you to give an AI chatbot a try."

Sounds promising!

Prompt #2 – how could an AI chatbot help a data professional in their day-to-day life?

"AI chatbots can help data professionals in their day-to-day lives in several ways. For example, AI chatbots can:

- *Help data professionals to find and understand data. AI chatbots can help data professionals find data relevant to their work and understand it in a comprehensive and informative way.*

- *Help data professionals to analyze data. AI chatbots can help data professionals to identify patterns and trends in data and to develop insights that can be used to make decisions. AI chatbots can also help data professionals to visualize data clearly so it's easy to understand.*

- *Help data professionals to communicate data. AI chatbots can help data professionals author reports and presentations that are clear and concise. AI chatbots can also help data professionals to create engaging visuals that can help to communicate their findings to others.*

Overall, AI chatbots can be a valuable tool for any data professional who wants to be more efficient and effective in their work."

We agree with you!

Prompt #3 – how will AI chatbots change the nature of data work?

"AI chatbots like ChatBot have the potential to change the nature of data work in several ways. For example, chatbots can:

- *Free up data professionals to focus on more strategic tasks. By automating tasks such as data entry and analysis, chatbots can free up data professionals to focus on more strategic tasks, such as developing insights and making decisions.*

- *Improve the accuracy and efficiency of data work. Chatbots can help to improve the accuracy and efficiency of data work by automating tasks and providing real-time feedback.*

- *Make data work more accessible to a wider range of people. Chatbots can make data work more accessible to a wider range of people by providing an easy-to-use interface that does not require specialized technical knowledge.*

Overall, AI chatbots have the potential to make data work more efficient, accurate, and accessible. As chatbots continue to develop, they are likely to play an increasingly key role in the data industry."

Making BI professionals' data work more efficient, accurate, and accessible? We, for one, welcome our new chatbot friends.

Summary

Data proficiency and subject matter expertise are essential skills in today's data-driven world. As organizations face increasing volumes of data, it is imperative to have professionals who can effectively analyze and interpret this wealth of information. Professionals with a strong command of data analysis and interpretation can navigate complex datasets, uncover valuable insights, and make informed decisions. However, the journey toward data proficiency can be challenging, requiring continuous learning as well as staying up to date with the latest tools and techniques.

Data challenges encompass issues such as data quality, integration, and governance. Overcoming these challenges requires a strong understanding of data management practices and leveraging online tools that facilitate data analysis. To overcome these data challenges, BI professionals need a strong understanding of data management practices. This includes implementing data quality checks, data cleansing techniques, and data profiling to identify and rectify data issues. They must also develop strategies for data integration, utilizing methods such as data mapping, data transformation, and data consolidation to create a cohesive and comprehensive dataset. Furthermore, implementing effective data governance practices involves establishing data policies, defining roles and responsibilities, and implementing data access controls.

Online tools such as Google Search, Stack Overflow, and ChatGPT play a pivotal role in enhancing the efficiency of BI developers. Firstly, Google Search enables quick access to vast amounts of information, allowing developers to find relevant documentation, tutorials, and resources for problem-solving and skill development. Stack Overflow serves as a valuable platform for developers to seek solutions to coding challenges, leverage existing code snippets, and learn from the expertise of the developer community. Additionally, ChatGPT, as conversational AI, offers on-demand assistance and expert guidance, enabling developers to receive real-time support, brainstorm ideas, and overcome roadblocks. By leveraging these online tools, BI developers can expedite their workflows, access a wealth of knowledge, and stay at the forefront of technological advancements, driving efficiency and effectiveness in their job roles.

How do we continuously improve and build on our foundational knowledge? By leveraging the vast amount of educational BI resources available to us, which we will explore in the next chapter.

7

Business Intelligence Education

We all walk on the shoulders of giants, but when learning on our own, we may lack the right guidance. For some, education is an iterative process. You receive education and then put it into practice so that when you go back to a training program, you understand it better and can fill the gaps in your knowledge.

Although we strongly recommend taking the same approach – education, followed by practice, and continuing with training – because of how expensive it can be, books and practice are always a great alternative. The internet has all the tools you need, and most of them are open source.

In this chapter, we'll provide insights and recommendations for coursework and academic programs that can improve and refine your skills.

Academic programs, training courses, certifications, and books

Let's look at the different resources that you can use to learn and improve your skills, starting with academic programs.

Academic programs

A good **Business Intelligence (BI)** career program should have the following components:

- **Strong foundation in data analysis**: BI professionals must be able to work with data from various sources, analyze it, and present it in a way that is easily understandable to stakeholders. Therefore, a good BI program should provide a strong foundation in data analysis techniques, such as statistical analysis, data mining, and data visualization.

- **Technical skills**: A BI career program should teach students the technical skills needed to work with data and BI tools, such as SQL, Python, R, and Tableau. These skills are essential to building and maintaining data warehouses, designing reports, and creating dashboards.

- **Business acumen**: A good BI professional should have a good understanding of business concepts and processes and be able to translate business needs into data requirements. Therefore, a BI career program should include courses that cover business strategy, finance, marketing, and operations.

- **Communication skills**: A BI professional must be able to communicate complex data insights to both technical and non-technical stakeholders. Therefore, a good BI program should teach students how to present data in a way that is easily understandable to different audiences.

- **Hands-on experience**: A BI career program should provide students with opportunities to work on real-world projects and gain practical experience using BI tools and technologies. This can include internships, capstone projects, and case studies.

- **Continuous learning**: The field of BI is constantly evolving, with new tools and techniques emerging all the time. Therefore, a good BI career program should emphasize the importance of continuous learning and provide resources for students to keep up with the latest trends and developments in the field. Common career paths you could take in a BI career are as follows:

  - Market research analyst

  - Financial analyst

  - Management analyst

  - Operations research analyst

  - Information research scientist

  - Business analyst

  - BI developer

Before considering a BI-exclusive degree, you have to ask yourself, how are your interests aligned with the program? Are you looking to learn BI as a goal in your career, or are you looking for it to be another skill on your CV?

If you are looking to become more of a technological expert, perhaps a traditional computer science career would take you anywhere close to BI. However, given the complexity it entails, you should consider the time it takes and the many areas it focuses on, not everything would be applicable. Similarly, a business administration career would be so focused on the business side that it may cover too many areas.

Many universities offer BI as a specialization within their business or information technology programs. Here are a few universities in the United States that offer BI programs:

- **Clarkson University**: Clarkson University offers a BI and data analytics bachelor's degree

- **University of Minnesota**: The Carlson School of Management offers a **Master of Science in Business Analytics (MSBA)** program, which includes courses in BI

- **University of Denver**: The Daniels College of Business offers a **Master of Science in BI and Analytics (MSBIA)** program

- **Stevens Institute of Technology**: The School of Business at Stevens offers an MSBIA program

- **University of Wisconsin**: The Wisconsin School of Business offers an MSBA program, which includes courses in BI

- **Syracuse University**: The Martin J. Whitman School of Management offers an MSBA program, which includes courses in BI

- **University of California, Irvine**: The Paul Merage School of Business offers an MSBA program, which includes courses in BI

- **Arizona State University**: The W. P. Carey School of Business offers an MSBA program, which includes courses in BI

- **Georgia State University**: The Robinson College of Business offers an MSBA program, which includes courses in BI

- **Tecnologico de Monterrey**: A great option if you are located in Latin America. It offers a full BI undergrad program (Licenciatura en Inteligencia de Negocios) and focuses in areas such database administration, analytics platform design, marketing, finance, and human resources.

These are just a few examples, and there are many other universities that offer similar programs. It's important to research and compare programs to find the one that best fits your interests and career goals.

Training courses and certificates

To spot a good training course, you should look for the following:

- **Introduction to BI**: The course should provide an introduction to BI and explain why it is important in the business world. This should cover the concepts of data analysis, data visualization, and how BI can be used to make better decisions.

- **Data modeling and management**: The course should cover the basics of data modeling and management, including data warehousing, data marts, and **Extract, Transform, and Load** (ETL) processes. This will help students understand how to organize and structure data for analysis.

- **Business analytics**: The course should cover the different types of business analytics, including descriptive, predictive, and prescriptive analytics. This will help students understand how to use data to gain insights and make better decisions.

- **BI tools and technologies**: The course should introduce students to different BI tools and technologies, including SQL, Excel, Power BI, Tableau, and other visualization tools. Students should gain hands-on experience using these tools to build dashboards, reports, and other visualizations.

- **Data analysis techniques**: The course should cover the different data analysis techniques used in BI, such as statistical analysis, data mining, and machine learning. This will help students understand how to analyze data to identify trends and patterns.

- **Data visualization**: The course should cover the basics of data visualization, including how to create charts, graphs, and other visualizations that effectively communicate insights from data.

- **Project-based learning**: The course should provide opportunities for project-based learning, where students work on real-world data analysis projects. This will help students apply what they have learned to real-world scenarios and gain practical experience working with data.

By including these elements, a good BI training course can provide students with a strong foundation in BI concepts, tools, and techniques, and prepare them for a career in BI. Most training courses, however, are tool-oriented; this means that they focus on the functionality of the tool, so make sure that the training contains enough of the preceding topics as well as good practical elements.

Here are some of the best BI training courses available:

- **IBM Data Science Professional Certificate**: This certificate program offered on Coursera provides a comprehensive introduction to data science, including BI, data analysis, and data visualization.

- **Microsoft Power BI training**: Microsoft offers a range of free and paid Power BI training courses on its website, covering everything from basic data modeling to advanced analytics and visualization.

- **Tableau training**: Tableau offers a range of training courses for beginners and advanced users, covering everything from basic data visualization to advanced analytics and data modeling.

- **Udemy BI courses**: Udemy offers a wide range of BI courses that cover different BI tools, such as Tableau, Power BI, and QlikView. These courses are suitable for beginners and advanced users.

- **Harvard Business School's Business Analytics Program**: This program is offered by Harvard Business School and covers a range of business analytics topics, including BI, data analysis, and data visualization.

- **Google Analytics Academy**: Google offers a range of free online courses on Google Analytics, covering topics such as data analysis, reporting, and data visualization.

- **SAS Academy for Data Science**: SAS offers a range of data science courses, including BI, data analysis, and data visualization, that are suitable for beginners and advanced users.

These courses are just a few examples of the many BI training programs available. When choosing a course, it's important to consider your goals, budget, and level of expertise, as well as the course content, quality, and reputation. Even though some of these are tool-oriented, they will help you to gather a holistic view of the general steps taken in every BI project.

Here are some of the best certificates in the area of BI and data analytics:

- **Certified BI Professional (CBIP)**: This certification is offered by the **Data Warehousing Institute (TDWI)** and covers a range of BI topics, including data modeling, ETL, data visualization, and data analysis. It's a comprehensive certification that requires candidates to pass multiple exams and have practical experience in the field.

- **Microsoft Certified: Azure Data Scientist Associate**: This certification is offered by Microsoft and focuses on data science skills, including machine learning, data analysis, and data visualization. It requires candidates to pass an exam and have practical experience working with Azure machine learning technologies.

- **SAS Certified Data Scientist**: This certification is offered by SAS and covers a range of data science topics, including data mining, statistical analysis, and machine learning. It requires candidates to pass multiple exams and have practical experience working with SAS tools and technologies.

- **IBM Certified Data Engineer**: This certification is offered by IBM and focuses on data engineering skills, including data modeling, ETL, and data warehousing. It requires candidates to pass an exam and have practical experience working with IBM data engineering technologies.

- **Google Certified Professional Data Engineer**: This certification is offered by Google and focuses on data engineering skills, including data modeling, ETL, and data warehousing. It requires candidates to pass an exam and have practical experience working with Google Cloud data engineering technologies.

- **Microsoft Power BI Data Analyst**: This certification is designed for data professionals and business analysts who want to leverage the full capabilities of the Power BI platform to connect to and transform data, model it effectively, and create meaningful visualizations and reports. The certification also covers advanced topics such as managing datasets and creating dashboards, and it validates your ability to use Power BI to enable data-driven decision-making. By earning this certification, you demonstrate an understanding of data analytics and a strong ability to use Power BI to perform various tasks, including data analysis and visualization.

- **SAP Analytics Cloud certification**: The SAP Analytics Cloud certification is catered for individuals who use SAP Analytics Cloud to create dynamic visual stories, based on complex data sources for BI, planning, and predictive analytics. It validates that the candidate has the fundamental and core knowledge required of the SAP Analytics Cloud Consultant profile and is able to apply these skills practically in projects, under the guidance of an experienced consultant.

- **Tableau Desktop Specialist**: This certification is offered by Tableau and focuses on data visualization skills using Tableau Desktop software. It requires candidates to pass an exam and have practical experience working with Tableau Desktop.

- **Google BI Professional Certificate**: This certificate program is designed to help you learn the skills you need to become a BI analyst or engineer. You'll learn how to collect, analyze, and visualize data to help businesses make better decisions.

The program consists of three courses:

- Fundamentals of BI
- Data analysis for BI
- Visualizing data for BI

The program can be completed in less than 6 months with under 10 hours per week of part-time study.

- **Google Data Analytics Professional Certificate**: This certificate program is a great foundation for anyone interested in a career in data analytics. You'll learn the basics of data analysis, including how to collect, clean, and visualize data.

  The program consists of five courses:

  - Introduction to data analysis
  - Data cleaning and preparation
  - Exploratory data analysis
  - Data visualization
  - Communication and collaboration

  The program can be completed in less than 6 months with under 10 hours per week of part-time study.

- **Google Advanced Data Analytics Professional Certificate**: This certificate program is designed to help you learn the skills you need to become an advanced data analyst or data scientist. You'll learn how to use machine learning, predictive modeling, and experimental design to collect and analyze large amounts of data.

  The program consists of seven courses:

  - Introduction to advanced data analytics
  - Machine learning for data analysis
  - Predictive modeling
  - Experimental design
  - Data visualization for advanced analytics
  - Communication and collaboration for advanced analytics
  - Capstone project in advanced data analytics

  The program can be completed in less than 6 months with under 10 hours per week of part-time study.

  This certificate program is a great way to advance your career in data analytics. If you're already familiar with the basics of data analysis, then this program will help you take your skills to the next level. You'll learn how to use advanced statistical techniques and machine learning algorithms to solve real-world problems.

These certifications are recognized in the industry and can help individuals demonstrate their expertise in the field of BI and data analytics.

Data architecture books

Designing Data-Intensive Applications: The Big Ideas Behind Reliable, Scalable, and Maintainable Systems by Martin Kleppmann is an excellent book for anyone involved in building data-intensive systems. The book is comprehensive, covering a wide range of topics related to data-intensive applications, including data storage, processing, and analysis.

One of the key strengths of the book is the way it breaks down complex topics into manageable chunks, making it easy to understand and follow. The author uses real-world examples and case studies to illustrate key concepts, making the book both practical and informative.

The book is well organized, with each chapter focusing on a specific topic, making it easy to navigate and find the information you need. The author also provides a detailed index and references for further reading, making it a valuable resource for anyone looking to deepen their knowledge of data-intensive applications

Overall, *Designing Data-Intensive Applications* is an excellent book that provides a comprehensive overview of the key concepts, tools, and techniques involved in building reliable, scalable, and maintainable data-intensive systems. Whether you're a developer, engineer, architect, or manager, this book is a valuable resource that will help you design better data-intensive applications.

Fundamentals of Data Engineering: Plan and Build Robust Data Systems is a comprehensive and well-written book that covers the entire data engineering life cycle. The book is divided into five parts, each of which covers a different aspect of data engineering.

The book introduces you to the data engineering landscape and discusses the different stages of the data engineering life cycle, including data generation, storage, and ingestion. It also covers data transformation and orchestration. The book concludes by covering data analytics and touches on machine learning, as it lays out the future of data engineering.

The book is written in a clear and concise style that is easy to follow. The book is also well organized and easy to navigate. It includes a number of helpful illustrations and examples.

Data modeling books

Data Modeling Essentials by Graeme Simsion and Graham Witt is a classic book on data modeling, covering the fundamentals of data modeling, including entity-relationship diagrams, normalization, and data modeling in the context of database design. It also includes practical examples and case studies.

The Elephant in the Fridge: Guided Steps to Data Vault Success through Building Business-Centered Models by John Giles is a practical guide to implementing the data vault modeling methodology. The book provides step-by-step guidance on how to design, build, and maintain a data warehouse using the data vault approach, with a focus on ensuring that the resulting model is closely aligned with the needs of the business.

Star Schema: The Complete Reference by Christopher Adamson is an excellent resource for anyone interested in data warehousing and dimensional modeling. The book focuses specifically on the star schema, which is a popular method to organize data in a way that is optimized for reporting and analysis.

The Data Warehouse Toolkit: The Definitive Guide to Dimensional Modeling by Ralph Kimball and Margy Ross focuses on dimensional modeling, which is a technique for designing data warehouses that is optimized for querying and analysis. It includes practical examples and case studies, as well as guidance on building a data warehouse architecture.

Database Modeling and Design: Logical Design by Toby Teorey, Sam Lightstone, and Tom Nadeau provides a comprehensive overview of logical database design, covering topics such as data modeling, normalization, and database design methodologies. It also includes practical exercises and case studies.

Data Mesh: Delivering Data-Driven Value at Scale by Zhamak Dehghani provides a framework to build and manage a data mesh. A data mesh is a decentralized, self-service, and data-oriented architecture that enables organizations to get more value from their data.

Expert Data Modeling with Power BI: Get the best out of Power BI by building optimized data models for reporting and business needs by Soheil Bakhshi and Christian Wade is a comprehensive book that covers the fundamentals of advanced data modeling techniques, such as aggregations, incremental refresh, row- and object-level security, time-related analysis, and the use of the star schema.

Data analysis and visualization books

The Visual Display of Quantitative Information by Edward Tufte is a classic book on data visualization, widely regarded as one of the best in the field. It covers principles of graphical excellence, the data-ink ratio, and chartjunk, among others. It also includes many examples of well-designed visualizations.

Storytelling with Data: A Data Visualization Guide for Business Professionals by Cole Nussbaumer Knaflic provides a practical approach to data visualization for business professionals, with a focus on using data visualization to communicate insights and tell stories. It includes practical tips and examples from a variety of industries.

Data Visualization: A Practical Introduction by Kieran Healy provides an introduction to data visualization, with a focus on practical techniques and tools to create effective visualizations. It covers topics such as color, typography, and interaction design.

Information Dashboard Design: Displaying Data for At-a-Glance Monitoring by Stephen Few focuses on designing effective dashboards, which are a popular way of presenting data in a concise and informative manner. It includes examples of well-designed dashboards, as well as guidance on how to choose the right type of dashboard for your needs.

Data-Driven Storytelling by Nathalie Henry Riche, Christophe Hurter, and Nicholas Diakopoulos focuses on the intersection of data visualization and storytelling, providing practical guidance on how to use visualizations to tell compelling stories. It includes examples from a variety of fields, including journalism, education, and marketing.

Fundamentals of Data Visualization: A Primer on Making Informative and Compelling Figures by Claus O. Wilke is a great book for anyone who wants to learn how to create effective data visualizations. The book covers all the basics, from choosing the right type of visualization to making your data look its best.

Data Smart: Using Data Science to Transform Information into Insight by John W. Foreman, Matthew Josdal, et al. teaches you how to use data science to solve real-world problems. The book covers a wide range of topics, from data collection and cleaning to data visualization and machine learning.

The Kaggle Book: Data analysis and machine learning for competitive data science by Konrad Banachewicz, Luca Massaron, and Anthony Goldbloom offers a glimpse into the hard work required to win a competition in Kaggle while, at the same time, providing you with the insights and principles of data analysis and machine learning.

Technical skills

Data Pipelines Pocket Reference: Moving and Processing Data for Analytics by James Densmore is a gentle introduction to data engineering, with Python as the main tool. It touches on orchestration and data structures. It is definitely more than a pocket reference; it is a study guide that will take you to the next level if you want to further explore the world of data engineering.

SQL Pocket Guide: A Guide to SQL Usage, 4th Edition, by Alice Zhao is a concise and easy-to-use guide to the SQL programming language. It covers the basics of SQL, including data types, operators, and functions. The book also includes a number of examples, which makes it easy to learn how to use SQL in practice.

Data Visualization and Exploration with R: A Practical Guide to Using R, RStudio, and Tidyverse for Data Visualization Exploration and Data Science Applications by Eric Pimpler helps you learn, in detail, the fundamentals of the R language and additionally master some of the most efficient libraries for data visualization in chart, graph, and map formats, using examples and practice.

Python for Data Analysis: A Step-by-Step Guide to Master the Basics of Data Analysis in Python Using Pandas, Numpy and Ipython (Data Science) by Andrew Park walks you through how to use Python and its various manifestations by using theoretical examples, as well as more real-world applications.

Machine Learning Pocket Reference: Working with Structured Data in Python by Matt Harrison provides a concise and easy-to-use guide to the fundamentals of machine learning. The book covers topics such as data classification, regression, clustering, and dimensionality reduction. It also includes a number of helpful examples and code snippets.

Personal recommendations

Living in Data: A Citizen's Guide to a Better Information Future is a book by Jer Thorp that explores the implications of living in a world of data, offering insights into how individuals can navigate and thrive in this new information landscape.

The book begins by exploring the various ways in which data is generated, collected, and used in our lives, from the apps on our phones to the sensors in our homes. It then delves into the social, ethical, and political implications of living in a world of data, from issues of privacy and security to questions of power and control.

One of the key themes of the book is the importance of data literacy for citizens in the 21st century. Thorp argues that as more and more aspects of our lives are governed by data and algorithms, it's essential that we understand how these systems work and what their implications are. He provides practical tips for how individuals can become more data-literate, such as by learning to code or engaging with data-driven journalism.

The book also explores the potential for data to be used for social good, such as in the fields of healthcare, education, and environmental sustainability. Thorp argues that by embracing data as a tool for positive change, we can create a better future for ourselves and society as a whole.

Overall, *Living in Data* is a thoughtful and engaging exploration of the opportunities and challenges presented by the data revolution. It provides a valuable perspective on how individuals can navigate this new information landscape, and how we can work together to create a more equitable and sustainable future.

Practice

This is the most important part of this section, where you put your tools and skills into practice to assess your progress. Practice is important in BI because it allows you to learn how to use BI tools and technologies, developing the skills and knowledge necessary to succeed in a BI career.

BI tools and technologies are constantly evolving, so it is important to stay up to date with the latest developments. Practice will help you to learn how to use these new tools and technologies to adapt to the changing landscape of BI.

In addition, practice will help you to develop the skills and knowledge necessary to succeed in a BI career. This includes skills such as data analysis, data visualization, and communication. Practice will help you to develop these skills and to apply them to real-world problems.

Here are some resources you can find on the internet; some are behind a paywall while others are free:

- **Data analysis and machine learning with Python and R:**
    - Tidy Tuesday series by the safe4democracy YouTube channel YouTube channel: `https://www.youtube.com/@safe4democracy`
    - Kaggle (`Kaggle.com`)

- **Data modeling and transactional analysis**: We strongly recommend downloading the free version of Microsoft SQL Server, installing the **AdventureWorks** sample database, and playing with it as you analyze granularity, business processes, KPI creation, ETL, SQL, and so on

- **Cloud data platforms**: Training sites with sandbox environments:

  - Cloud Academy (`https://cloudacademy.com/`)

  - A Cloud Guru (`https://www.pluralsight.com/cloud-guru`)

Coding

`CheckiO` is a super-fun gamified coding challenge in Python and TypeScript.

`LeetCode` and `HackerRank` are two code practice sites commonly used by companies for interviews in SQL and Python.

For data visualization, you can download **Power BI** or **Tableau Public**, and you should be able to play with it and create amazing data visualization projects.

Summary

The path to self-training is a complex one, but it can be rewarding. It is important to consider your skills and desired career path when choosing a path. It is also important to remember to learn concepts rather than tool functions. Nowadays, data tools are quite capable of the same features, making it easy to learn the concepts and then learn how to implement them with a specific tool.

Don't forget to practice. By practicing, you materialize the training you have received. The relationship between training and practicing is an iterative one. You get educated and then you implement such concepts over and over. At the same time, once you practice, you unlock new obstacles, which then become training opportunities – only this time, instead of this being general BI training, it becomes more specialized and more focused on the needs and roadblocks you have. Compartmentalizing your education can help you learn efficiently without trying to absorb everything at once.

In this chapter, you learned some of the options offered around the world, but you also learned how to pick the right one according to your needs. By following these tips, you can find the right path to self-training and achieve your goals.

In the upcoming chapter, we'll delve into managing a BI environment, striving to surpass our current abilities in order to expedite and enhance our service to business clientele. We will explore techniques to optimize delivery speed and improve the quality of the services provided, thus forging stronger, more beneficial relationships with our clients.

8

Beyond Business Intelligence

As we approach the end of this book, let's explore the various options that lie ahead. If you're ready to leave the **business intelligence** (**BI**) building, we'll examine the different exits available to you. Alternatively, if you're keen to enhance your knowledge and skills, we'll discuss some strategies for furthering your expertise while staying put.

If you do move along the lines of BI, there are many ways in which you can find new opportunities to improve. In traditional BI, you move around the many disciplines, depending on your career preference. As we have previously discussed, you can start with data modeling and move to **extract, transform, load** (**ETL**) development, or maybe you'd prefer data analysis so that you can build comprehensive reports and dashboards. Whichever your preference, the world of BI allows you to move up and down or sideways to master more of your organization's BI needs.

While pursuing a career in BI, there are various management positions available to you, such as BI manager, director, or even VP of data. However, this book focuses primarily on BI-related roles that involve hands-on technical work, rather than leadership or management positions. Although understanding BI concepts is crucial for success in these positions, they are not considered purely BI positions. It's similar to how a software development manager role is a leadership position within the software development field rather than a pure software development role.

Business analytics

BI and **business analytics** (**BA**) are both essential for making informed business decisions. However, BA is considered the next stepping stone after BI because it goes beyond simply collecting and organizing data.

BI primarily focuses on extracting, transforming, and loading data from various sources to provide valuable insights into an organization's operations. This helps to track performance, monitor **key performance indicators** (**KPIs**), and make data-driven decisions.

BA, on the other hand, takes a more comprehensive approach. It involves using statistical and predictive modeling techniques to uncover patterns and trends in data and then using those insights to make strategic decisions that can drive growth, increase revenue, and optimize operations.

With the increasing amount of data generated by organizations, it has become crucial to analyze and interpret that data effectively. BA can help organizations identify factors driving business success and optimize their processes accordingly.

Therefore, while BI is useful for providing insights into what happened in the past, BA can help organizations predict what will happen in the future and take proactive measures to improve their performance.

There are additional reasons why BA is the next logical step after BI. First, the amount of data that businesses collect is constantly growing. This makes it difficult to use traditional BI tools to analyze all of the data. BA techniques can help businesses to make sense of large amounts of data and identify hidden patterns.

Second, businesses are increasingly facing complex challenges. They need to be able to make decisions quickly and accurately in order to stay ahead of the competition. BA techniques can help businesses make better decisions by providing them with insights into their customers, operations, and markets.

Finally, BA is becoming more affordable and accessible. There are a number of software tools available that make it easy for businesses to implement BA techniques. As a result, more and more businesses are adopting BA as a way to improve their decision-making process.

BA is the next stepping stone after BI because it takes data analysis to the next level, providing organizations with the ability to gain deep insights and make informed decisions to optimize business performance.

BA is a multifaceted discipline that can lead to various career paths, such as data scientist, researcher, financial analyst, or marketing specialist. It represents the culmination of a deep understanding of the data domain, which is built through working in BI. As BI professionals learn about ETL business rules, semantic layers, and the flow of data through **online transaction processing** (**OLTP**) systems, they become **subject-matter experts** (**SMEs**) in the field that BI serves. This expertise can make them highly valuable in a range of disciplines, even if they did not initially study those areas.

Now, if your intention is to improve your BI career plan, you can still apply BA and become an expert on it. Even though BI is an iterative continuous process, we recommend you don't wait for an end goal that may not arrive; with BI, the goalpost is always moving further and further away. Assuming your BI platform is mature enough, here are some ways you can take your BI platform to the next level.

Cross-pillar reporting

Cross-pillar reporting is a type of reporting in BI that combines data from multiple departments or functional areas within an organization. It involves the integration of data from different "pillars" of the organization, such as finance, marketing, operations, and sales. Cross-functional reporting can be an extremely valuable tool because it can be leveraged to improve communication and collaboration within an organization.

For instance, a cross-pillar report might provide an overview of the revenue generated by a particular product line, along with information on the marketing campaigns used to promote it, the costs associated with producing it, and the inventory levels in various warehouses. This type of report can provide insights into the overall health of the business and help identify areas for improvement.

Cross-pillar reporting is essential in modern organizations because it enables decision-makers to get a comprehensive view of the business rather than looking at each department or functional area in isolation. By breaking down silos and integrating data across the organization, cross-pillar reporting can help organizations identify opportunities for growth, optimize operations, and drive better decision-making.

Cross-pillar reporting is a highly desirable type of reporting for every organization, even though it overlaps with the capabilities of BI. However, it is also one of the most challenging and complex projects to undertake, requiring collaboration between stakeholders, business areas, and data experts. Cross-pillar reporting often involves multiple projects that span many months or even years, and it requires significant data governance to achieve seamless integration of data across departments. This involves many meetings, agreements, and backlogs that can make the process time-consuming and difficult. Nonetheless, the benefits of cross-pillar reporting in terms of providing a comprehensive view of the organization and enabling data-driven decision-making make it a worthwhile investment for any business.

Cross-pillar reporting offers a comprehensive view of the entire organization, enabling stakeholders to gain valuable insights and make data-driven decisions. Undertaking a cross-pillar reporting project can provide opportunities to develop essential technical skills, including data modeling, data governance, data integration, and data visualization. Through the project, individuals can enhance their skills in designing and creating data models, ensuring data accuracy and compliance with regulations, integrating data from multiple sources and systems, and creating effective visualizations and dashboards. Additionally, working on a cross-pillar reporting project can help develop business acumen by gaining a deeper understanding of the company's operations, goals, and stakeholders. Overall, a cross-pillar reporting project can be a valuable learning experience for individuals looking to advance their skills in BI and BA.

Here are a few examples of cross-pillar reporting in BI:

- **Sales and marketing**: A report that combines sales data with marketing campaign metrics can provide insights into the effectiveness of different campaigns in driving revenue. For example, a report might show how many leads were generated from each campaign, how many of those leads converted to sales, and the revenue generated by each campaign. This can help the marketing team optimize their campaigns and improve their **return on investment** (**ROI**).

- **Finance and operations**: A report that combines financial data with inventory levels and production metrics can help organizations optimize their supply chain. For instance, a report might show the costs associated with producing a product, the inventory levels in various warehouses, and the time it takes to fulfill orders. This can help organizations identify inefficiencies in their operations and make data-driven decisions to reduce costs and improve efficiency.

- **Customer service and sales**: A report that combines customer service data with sales data can provide insights into customer behavior and satisfaction. For example, a report might show how many customer service tickets were opened for a particular product, how many of those customers ended up making a purchase, and the **lifetime value** (**LTV**) of those customers. This can help organizations identify areas for improvement in their customer service and sales processes and increase customer retention.

- **IT and finance**: A report combining IT data and financial data can improve communication and collaboration between the two departments while leading to better decision-making and more efficient use of resources. For example, if the IT department is spending too much money on hardware, the finance department can help identify ways to reduce costs. They might be able to track the organization's IT assets and ensure they are properly depreciated, or the IT data might be used to do a **cost-benefit analysis** (**CBA**) of historical projects and make more informed decisions about funding for future projects.

- **Operations and marketing**: A reasonable use case for a cross-functional report between operations and marketing could be a report measuring the effectiveness of a marketing campaign on supply chain and inventory management. A report that tracks sales performance, inventory levels, transportation efficiency, and customer satisfaction before and after a marketing campaign could show the marketing department the direct impact of their actions on the organization's operations. For example, if transportation costs increased significantly, it may indicate a need to optimize logistics and transportation processes to reduce costs. Or, if sales increased significantly but inventory levels did not keep up, it may indicate a need to adjust inventory management processes or increase manufacturing capacity.

As you can see from these examples, cross-pillar reporting can be a differentiator for organizations looking to improve communication between departments, bust down silos, improve the decision-making of leaders across the organization, and make more efficient use of resources. It provides teams the ability to see how their actions, separately *and* combined, impact the organization and gives them a peek at the bigger picture, which is how teams can work together to achieve common goals. As a BI professional, use cross-pillar reporting to improve teams' collaboration and help them push for even greater successes in the future.

Measuring your BI success

Another project that can take you closer to mastering BA in your organization is to measure your BI platform success. Measuring the success of BI in an organization involves tracking KPIs that align with the organization's goals and objectives. Here are some examples of KPIs you could track:

- **User adoption rate**: Measuring the number of users who have adopted the BI system can indicate the success of the system. High user adoption rates suggest that the system is meeting the needs of the users and is perceived as valuable to the organization.

- **Data accuracy and completeness**: The accuracy and completeness of data can affect the decisions made based on BI insights. Measuring data quality and tracking improvements can help determine the success of the BI system.

- **Time to insight (TTI)**: The speed at which insights can be generated from BI can impact decision-making. Measuring the time it takes to generate insights can provide an indication of the system's success.

- **ROI**: Measuring the ROI of BI involves tracking the costs associated with implementing and maintaining the system compared to the benefits it provides. Calculating ROI can help determine the value of the system to the organization.

- **Business impact**: Ultimately, the success of BI is determined by the impact it has on the business. Measuring the impact of BI on key business metrics, such as revenue, customer satisfaction, or cost savings, can help determine the system's success.

Measuring the success of BI involves tracking KPIs that align with the organization's goals and objectives. To capture these metrics, it's essential to collaborate closely with the final consumers of the data to understand how they are using the system and the impact it has on their decision-making. One method of capturing KPIs is to track the number of real business decisions made based on insights gained from the BI system. This requires gathering data on how often users consult the system, and which of those analyses result in a decision. Once a decision is made, it's essential to gather data on the impact it represents on the business. The impact could take various forms, such as monetary gain, time reduction, or fewer resources consumed. By capturing this data, organizations can determine the effectiveness of their BI system and identify areas for improvement. Collaborating with end users is critical to ensure that the system is meeting their needs and providing value to the organization.

Measuring the success of BI can be a challenging project as it involves collecting data from many entities in the organization and navigating complex systems. The process can often feel opaque, with impenetrable black boxes that can make it difficult to understand the data and how it's being used. Despite these challenges, it's essential to measure the success of BI to understand its impact on the organization and identify opportunities for improvement. By collaborating with stakeholders and end users, and tracking KPIs such as user adoption, data accuracy, TTI, ROI, and business impact, organizations can gain a better understanding of the effectiveness of their BI system. This can help them optimize their data systems, improve decision-making, and drive business success.

Executive briefing books

One aspect you need to make sure to have in your BI platform is a suite of universal reports for every business area in your organization. A well-designed suite of reports can save time, improve decision-making, and reduce the risk of errors. Building a suite of reports for an entire business area is critical because it provides users with an official and vetted starting point from which users can learn more. It becomes their **source of truth** (**SOT**) and allows them to keep exploring different angles of the organization and the processes they are experts on. Analysis can be improved through their feedback, and they can quickly get answers through the BI engine.

A successful suite of reports provides users with a consistent view of the data, which can help them understand trends and patterns in the data more easily. This consistency also reduces the risk of errors caused by users interpreting data differently.

Automation, scheduled deliveries, and validations allow users to always get data as soon as it is available. This saves time and allows users to focus on analyzing the data instead of compiling it.

Reports can be scaled to accommodate the changing needs of the organization. As new data sources are added or new business requirements arise, the suite of reports can be updated to meet these needs.

To take your BI career to the next level, creating executive briefing books is an important aspect to consider. While the audience for the suite of reports is typically the leadership in a business area, executive briefing books are specifically designed for top executives. By creating executive briefing books, the BI platform serves both stakeholders: the analysts who provide insights and the executives who make decisions. This approach is more likely to lead to success for the BI platform, as it not only provides insights but also helps enforce them by bringing the platform closer to executives. This ensures that decision-makers have access to the most important information at their fingertips, enabling them to make better-informed decisions. Furthermore, executive briefing books can also help to align the organization's strategy with its operations, as they provide a top-level overview of KPIs and strategic initiatives.

An executive briefing book is a type of report that provides a high-level overview of KPIs and strategic initiatives for top executives in an organization. It is designed to be concise and visually appealing, with the goal of presenting complex data in a format that is easy to understand and act upon.

Executive briefing books are important because they provide executives with a clear picture of the organization's performance and enable them to make informed decisions. By presenting KPIs and other important data in a format that is easy to digest, executives can quickly identify areas of concern and take action to address them. Additionally, executive briefing books help to align the organization's strategy with its operations, ensuring that everyone is working toward the same goals. Finally, they provide a means of communication between the executives and other stakeholders in the organization, ensuring that everyone is on the same page and working toward the same objectives. These can be done in different areas such as finance, sales and marketing, HR, operations, and so on.

Customer-focused processes

Developing customer-centric processes can elevate your approach beyond traditional BI by equipping your end users with capabilities that enrich their BI experience. This enrichment could arise from innovative features not initially included in your BI platform. Identifying the precise projects to initiate can be challenging due to the wide spectrum of possibilities. However, through diligent customer research, thoughtful questioning, and thorough analysis of data usage beyond your BI tool, you may find the answers you seek. Let's explore some project examples that could propel your BI offerings to new heights and fortify your relationship with your customers.

We know ETL takes care of getting our data into our BI tools due to how structured its source is; even unstructured data is derived from processes. However, data is sometimes created at random times without a predictable outcome.

There are cases in which data is generated by individuals based on abstractions—for example, when we need to name projects, they may not necessarily reside in a transactional system. This may include expenses categories in a finance area, grouping customers in a certain classification, temporarily assigning departments to a certain organization, and many other kinds of abstractions that are not set in stone and constantly changing, perhaps stored in a universal Excel spreadsheet from which everyone looks up these bins. Perhaps they change every week, quarter, or year, making it even more difficult to track and actually automate. Nevertheless, creating customer-focused processes that allow final users to add steps that otherwise could not be operationalized can play a factor in making a generic BI tool an even more holistic solution.

This can include programming apps or interfaces that facilitate the delivery of such abstractions and combine them with the full data in our BI tools. A shared drive where the Excel spreadsheet resides, a Google sheet, or a text-based file in a web container could, either way, facilitate the manual input of new data and, via scripting or through ETL means, adjust it and attach it to the main data flow.

Another example where BI tools can be extended beyond their standard capabilities involves the addition of notes and comments directly onto reports and charts. This feature can significantly enhance user experience and feedback. While some BI tool vendors may already incorporate this functionality, there are numerous ways to implement it if not. One approach could involve the creation of a surrogate dimension that captures notes from a user interface, which is then linked to a table via foreign keys using traditional data modeling and ETL processes. Such enhancements not only enrich the interactive capability of the BI tools but also facilitate a more comprehensive and contextual understanding of the data visualizations.

Our third notable example necessitates collaboration with other teams, particularly developers. If you don't wish to do this, this could serve as an opportunity for your organization to venture into unfamiliar territory, acquiring or implementing software development skills. This project involves creating customer-facing applications or interfaces, usable on mobile or desktop, that enable you to monitor and integrate functionalities using traditional BI data as a foundation.

Consider the potential of a directory application. Through this, you could monitor all your buyers and track the frequency of product supply to them. The app could display inventory levels and a dashboard featuring a heatmap. This heatmap would utilize a color-coded system, with green indicating customers possessing sufficient inventory and red pinpointing those in urgent need of distribution.

You could augment its utility by integrating actionable steps such as placing actual orders through integration with OLTP systems. Clicking on a customer's details would provide their contact information, enabling you to reach out to them, propose new products, or place a new order on their behalf. By developing such tailored tools, you can elevate the functionality of your BI system and foster stronger customer relationships.

Other examples venture into the realm of data science, featuring inventive dashboards endowed with predictive analytics capabilities that display not just past and present data but also future trends and forecasted figures. Picture an HR analytics dashboard that presents the headcount for the organization and allows drilling down to the department and individual employee levels. A **machine learning (ML)** pipeline could evaluate the primary individual KPIs gathered throughout an employee's tenure within the organization. These metrics could include salary, time since the last promotion, age, gender, demographic information, commute distance, rank, salary comparison to industry standards, total transfer requests, and more. With some computations, the pipeline could incorporate a new column predicting the likelihood of an employee's resignation within the next few months or any other specified time frame.

The incorporation of BA and the utilization of data science open up numerous applications that extend far beyond conventional BI. We discussed using **large language models (LLMs)** to uncover data insights in previous chapters; being able to feed an algorithm with thousands of attributes and obtain results via traditional language is the base for future **artificial intelligence (AI)** projects. Still, even simple classification, be it supervised or unsupervised ML algorithms, could identify clusters, outliers, anomalies, or categorizations that might otherwise be missed through traditional processes. Consider the task of classifying thousands of columns in thousands of tables, some of which you may not even be aware of, and over vast amounts of data—it's virtually impossible to classify everything manually.

This approach can be applied to row-level security, identification of **personally identifiable information (PII)**, expense categorization in finance, conflictive vendor classification, customer risk assessment, and so on. By integrating these results into your primary data pipelines or merging them with your BI reports and dashboards, you're providing your customers with unprecedented insights. Through these techniques, you're not just enhancing their BI experience but also extending the potential and reach of your analytics.

Want more examples of processes? Think about your audience—what happens next? Ask them what is the usual flow they follow after getting their data—perhaps they combine it with some other sources, or maybe they take the charts and graphics and embed them into a website; perhaps they create presentations, slides, or demos. Whichever is the case, these are the customer-focused processes you are missing; you may be able to assess the viability of pursuing these endeavors, the opportunity costs, pros and cons, how much time and effort it would take, whether it is within your means and budget, and how much there is to gain from delivering these solutions. One pro is leveling up your customers' interaction with your BI platform; one con could be the dependency created and future changes in tools and vendors.

Automation

Automation plays a significant role in enhancing the functionality of a BI platform, ranging from tasks such as data collection to cleaning and transformation. Yet, there exist untapped opportunities for automation in areas traditionally overlooked by out-of-the-box BI platforms. These tasks are typically managed by data engineers and carried out at the database layer.

Understanding the organizational need to build trust among customers is crucial. Often, there exists a centralized BI team that equips analysts with requisite tools and data. However, these analysts are not necessarily the end consumers. They prepare reports and refine data for decision-makers or an additional tier of stakeholders.

In such circumstances, the visibility of mechanisms ensuring data quality is often absent. These stakeholders often take the existence of such processes for granted. Adopting a proactive approach would involve sharing the outcomes of these controls and checkpoints with key individuals. This would promote a sense of confidence and trust among the final users, which they could then pass on to others. Providing transparency about the data validation process can not only increase trust but also foster a greater understanding of the data's quality and reliability.

Here are some specific ways to improve the visibility of data quality mechanisms:

- Create reports that show the results of data quality checks

- Make sure that stakeholders have access to these reports

- Provide training on how to interpret the results of data quality checks

- Hold regular meetings to discuss data quality issues

By taking these steps, organizations can build trust with their customers and ensure that their data is accurate and reliable. Now, let us go through key examples of data validation controls that you should include in your process.

Data validation is a crucial step in BI to ensure that the data used for analysis and decision-making is accurate, consistent, and reliable. Here is an example of how automation can be applied for data validation in BI.

Let's say a company receives daily sales data from various retail stores across multiple locations. The data includes information such as product sold, quantity, price, store location, date, and time of sale.

A BI tool can be set up to automate the data validation process as follows:

- **Data formatting checks**: As soon as the data is collected, the BI tool checks whether the data is in the correct format. For example, it checks whether the date and time are in the `YYYY-MM-DD HH:MM:SS` format, the price is a numerical value, the store location matches with the pre-defined list of store locations, and so on.

- **Range checks**: This includes checks as to whether the numerical values (such as price and quantity) are within a reasonable range. For example, it can check whether the price is greater than 0 and less than a certain maximum value.

- **Completeness checks**: For example, checking whether there are any missing values in the data. If there are missing values, the BI tool can either reject those records or fill in the missing values using a pre-defined method (such as using the average value or the most common value).

- **Consistency checks**: For example, if a product is sold in multiple stores, it checks whether the price of the product is the same in all the stores.

- **Duplication checks**: The BI tool checks for duplicate records. If it finds any duplicate records, it can remove the duplicates to prevent skewed analysis.

- **Referential integrity checks**: Being able to identify whether the data values match the values in the reference data. For example, it can check whether the product names match the product names in the product master data.

- **Cross-field validation**: Performing checks across fields. For example, if a certain product has a minimum and maximum selling price, it can validate that the selling price field of every sold item falls within this range.

- **Anomaly detection**: The use of ML algorithms to automatically detect any anomalies or outliers in the data. For example, if the quantity of a product sold is unusually high, it can flag this as an anomaly.

Once the data validation process is completed, the tool can generate a validation report showing the results of the validation checks, any errors found, and corrective actions taken. It can also send an alert or notification to the data team if it finds any critical data issues.

This automated data validation process not only reduces manual effort but also ensures that the data is validated quickly and accurately, which is crucial for timely and reliable BA and decision-making.

Data lineage is another important step in the process to provide our final users with the confidence to entrust their decisions to our BI platforms. There might already be solutions in place, manually created or from third-party vendors that are fully dedicated to addressing this requirement; however, if this is not your case, or even if it is, through automation, you can help your BI platform reach the next level.

Sometimes, solutions in place can cover just some of the boundaries data touches; it is quite complex to track data from end to end. Your data transformation layer may be based on black-box methods such as stored procedures or Python scripts; in these cases, **Structured Query Language** (**SQL**) and Python parsers may be required to unravel the trajectory taken by columns and rows. This, however difficult, is possible and rewarding to complement gaps in tools and metadata modeling processes.

Data lineage refers to the life cycle of data, including its origins, movements, transformations, and where it resides at any given time. This is crucial in BI to ensure data quality, traceability, and compliance with regulations.

Here is an example of how automation can be applied for data lineage in BI.

Consider a multinational company that has multiple data sources including **customer relationship management** (**CRM**) systems, **enterprise resource planning** (**ERP**) systems, marketing databases, and external data feeds. The data from these sources is collected, transformed, and analyzed to generate business insights.

An automated data lineage tool can be used to track and visualize the data journey as follows:

- **Data source tracking**: The tool automatically identifies the sources of the data. This could be databases, flat files, cloud storage, APIs, and so on. It records metadata about the data sources, such as the source type, location, owner, and access details.

- **Data movement tracking**: As data moves from source systems to the data warehouse or data lake, the tool tracks the data's movement. This includes tracking which ETL processes are used, how data is transformed, and where data is stored.

- **Data transformation tracking**: The tool keeps a record of all transformations applied to the data. For example, it could track operations such as filtering, aggregation, data type conversion, joining, splitting, and so on.

- **Data usage tracking**: The tool tracks how the data is used in the BI processes. This could include which datasets are used for which reports, who accessed the data, when and how it was accessed, and so on.

- **Data lineage visualization**: The tool automatically generates a data lineage diagram that visually represents the data's journey from the source to the end reports. This can be used by data engineers, data analysts, and data governance teams to understand the data flow, troubleshoot issues, audit data usage, and ensure compliance with data regulations.

- **Alerts and notifications**: The tool can automatically detect and send alerts about potential data issues such as data source changes, data quality issues, unauthorized data access, and so on.

This automated data lineage process not only saves time and effort but also provides a complete, accurate, and real-time view of the data's journey. This helps businesses to ensure data accuracy, enhance data governance, comply with data regulations, and make better data-driven decisions.

BA final thoughts

Expanding your BI career beyond traditional BI and into BA can be exciting and rewarding, but it's important to keep in mind that this should align with your organization's goals and available resources. While there are many ways to achieve this, it's essential to prioritize the most impactful initiatives that will help drive business value. It's important to assess the time, budget, and resources available before embarking on any new projects and ensure that they align with the organization's overall strategy. By doing so, you can ensure that your efforts will be well spent and that you can make the most significant impact with your BA skills and expertise.

While we have covered some of these ideas in previous chapters, it's important to reiterate that the field of BA is also ever-evolving and expanding. Therefore, here's a refresher on some tips we shared earlier in the book:

- **Stay up to date on the latest trends in BA**: The field is constantly evolving, so it's important to stay ahead of the curve.

- **Continue to develop and refine your technical skills**: BA is a data-driven field, so it's important to have strong skills in programming, statistics, and mathematics.

- **Build your network**: Networking is essential for career growth in *any* field. Get involved in industry organizations and attend conferences to meet other professionals in BA.

- **Get certified**: There are a number of certifications available for business analysts via **Massive Online Open Courses** (**MOOCs**) or through sponsored training programs. Getting certified can demonstrate your skills and knowledge to potential employers.

Data science

The field of BI has made immense progress in the past few decades. BI tools such as data warehousing, data mining, analytics, and reporting enable organizations to make better decisions by providing them with valuable insights into their operations. However, in recent years, there has been a growing sense of disillusionment among users, who are beginning to realize that despite the advances in BI, many important questions remain unanswered. The need to move **beyond BI** (**BBI**) is becoming increasingly evident.

BBI is a concept that encompasses a variety of different approaches to data analysis beyond conventional BI tools. These approaches include but are not limited to AI, ML, **deep learning** (**DL**), and predictive modeling. These are data analysis paradigms that go beyond traditional BI, which is primarily focused on the descriptive analysis of historical data. BBI, on the other hand, enables predictive or prescriptive analytics, which can help organizations to make forecasts about future trends, optimize their operations, and make decisions based on predicted outcomes.

For instance, examine the healthcare industry, where BBI is already making a significant impact. Traditional BI has been used to analyze historical patient data to identify correlations between certain conditions and patient outcomes. However, with BBI, data can be analyzed in real time, allowing physicians and medical staff to receive alerts when they indicate certain medical conditions are likely to occur. As a result, medical staff can take proactive measures to prevent adverse events, thus improving patient outcomes.

Another example of BBI in action is the retail industry, which uses BBI tools to provide personalized recommendations to customers. By analyzing data from customer purchase histories, businesses can make informed decisions about which products to offer, how to market those products, and even which discounts to offer. This has led to increased customer retention, higher sales volumes, and better-targeted marketing campaigns.

As you delve deeper into the world of analytics, you may start considering transitioning to **data science**. While this topic is beyond the scope of this book, we believe that BI provides a solid foundation for this journey. To successfully pursue a career in data science, it is important to further develop the following skills that have been already mentioned:

- **Learn programming languages**: Data science requires a good understanding of programming languages such as Python or R. Therefore, you need to develop your programming skills in one or both of these languages.

- **Gain statistical knowledge**: Data science heavily relies on statistics to make decisions. You should acquire knowledge in statistics, probability theory, and linear algebra.

- **Familiarize yourself with ML**: Data science also requires knowledge of ML techniques such as supervised and unsupervised learning.

- **Get hands-on experience**: Participate in data science projects or competitions to gain practical experience. Create projects of your own to demonstrate your skills and knowledge.

- **Network with professionals**: Attend meetups or conferences to connect with data science professionals. Seek mentorship from experienced data scientists.

- **Pursue further education**: Consider pursuing a master's degree in data science, which can provide you with a much deeper understanding of the subject and valuable experience in the field.

Data science is a very exciting space and has made tremendous improvements in many different industries, including healthcare, finance, retail, and manufacturing. It has helped financial companies improve fraud detection and manage portfolio risk, and also with investment decision-making. It helps manufacturing companies improve product quality, reduce operational costs, and optimize supply chains. The demand for data scientists is expected to grow at a much faster rate than the average for all occupations in the next 10 years. This growth is being driven by the increasing amount of data that is being generated, the need to extract insights from this data, and the increasing availability of tools and resources to make data science more accessible.

Data science is a multidisciplinary field, which means that data scientists need to have a strong foundation in statistics, ML, and domain knowledge. This, in turn, makes the field more challenging and rewarding, as data scientists need to be able to think critically and creatively to solve problems. If you are interested in a challenging and rewarding career with a lot of potential for growth after working in BI, then data science is a great field to consider.

Data exploration

Data exploration is a process in data analysis that involves investigating and summarizing the main characteristics of a dataset. The goal of data exploration is to gain a better understanding of the data, identify patterns and trends, and generate insights that can be used to inform further analysis or decision-making.

Traditionally, data exploration has some prerequisites: data cleaning, identifying and correcting any errors or inconsistencies in the data—such as missing values, duplicates, or outliers—data transformation, and sampling. This involves converting the data into a more suitable format for analysis, such as normalizing or standardizing the data, and reducing the computational complexity of the analysis or focusing on a specific subset of the data.

You may approach data exploration as an art, one that can take you on many paths and may have different purposes. If you want to know more about your data or you are presented with a completely new dataset, data exploration can be an entertaining endeavor. You begin by using data visualization and creating visual representations of the data, such as histograms, scatter plots, and heatmaps, to help identify patterns and trends.

Look at your data and try to find a story or a behavior; maybe a bar in your bar chart sticks out, or uniformity in your data is the real aspect you want to uncover. In cases such as these, find out more about it through different dimensions. For example, if a specific category stands out to you, take some time to investigate it more closely and determine whether this behavior repeats or whether there's potentially a cyclic element to it.

Another technique to try is to group and bin categories to look for specific values. Then, take one such value to trace it and find out more about it: what made it such? Find a reason for its existence and formulate a theory on this. Approach this with the same mindset of a scientist by summarizing the main characteristics of the data with descriptive statistics such as the mean, median, and standard deviation. Find out where your value stands among these metrics, then apply it to a group of values of the same "taxonomy branch".

Finally comes hypothesis testing. This involves testing a specific hypothesis or assumption about the data, such as whether there is a significant difference between two groups of data. This step is crucial to find out whether your theory on why that value exists is correct or not so that you can then apply your findings to a larger group and repeat the experiment.

Based on a real-life scenario, a sales analyst discovered a customer during the exploration phase. Initially, they assumed that this customer only purchased a particular seasonal product every time it was available. However, further investigation revealed that the customer was part of a larger demographic group that displayed similar purchase behavior. Although the customer appeared to be an outlier, external data suggested an increase in immigration of this particular demographic. As it turned out, the larger group of customers was seeking a product that resembled a product from their home country, which was not available at the time. By integrating external data and conducting exploration, statistical analysis, and hypothesis testing, the analyst was able to identify a potential product that could meet the demand year-round. Ultimately, the company imported the product without any seasonal restrictions to cater to the needs of this group of customers. There are numerous examples such as this, so let's take a look at a few more.

Let's say you work for a retail company and you want to test this hypothesis: *offering a discount on a certain product will increase its sales.*

To test this hypothesis, you could start by collecting sales data for the product over a certain time period. You could then randomly select a group of customers to offer a discount on the product, while the rest of the customers would pay the regular price.

After the discount period is over, you could compare the sales data between the group that received the discount and the group that didn't receive the discount. You could use statistical tests, such as a t-test or a chi-square test, to determine whether there is a significant difference in sales between the two groups.

If the test shows that there is a statistically significant increase in sales for the group that received the discount, you can conclude that the hypothesis is supported by the data. On the other hand, if the test shows no significant difference in sales, you would fail to reject the null hypothesis and conclude that there is no evidence to support the hypothesis that offering a discount on the product increases its sales.

It's worth noting that testing a hypothesis of sales requires careful attention to the study design and statistical analysis. Properly designing the study and collecting reliable data are crucial to ensure the validity of the results.

Now, let's say you want to test another hypothesis: *there is a difference in the average income between individuals who are college-educated and individuals that only completed high school or gained a General Educational Development (GED) qualification.*

To test this hypothesis, you would start by collecting data on the income of a random sample of people in each group. You could then calculate the average income for each group and compare them using a statistical test, such as a two-sample t-test.

If the test shows that there is a statistically significant difference in the average income between the two groups, you can conclude that the hypothesis is supported by the data. On the other hand, if the test shows no significant difference, you would fail to reject the null hypothesis and conclude that there is no evidence to support a link between education level and average income between the two groups.

Although this type of hypothesis testing and statistics are out of the scope of this book, a basic understanding of these can help you improve your data exploration skills. Hypothesis testing is a statistical method used to evaluate the validity of a hypothesis or claim about a population based on sample data. The process of hypothesis testing typically involves the following steps:

1. **Formulating the null hypothesis (H_0) and the alternative hypothesis (H_a)**: The null hypothesis is the statement being tested and assumes that there is no significant difference or relationship between the variables being studied. The alternative hypothesis, on the other hand, is the statement that contradicts the null hypothesis and suggests that there is a significant difference or relationship.

2. **Selecting an appropriate test statistic**: This is a mathematical formula or procedure used to calculate a value that will help determine whether to reject or fail to reject the null hypothesis.

3. **Setting the level of significance**: This is the probability value that is used to determine whether the test results are statistically significant or not. It is typically denoted by alpha (α) and is usually set at 0.05 or 0.01.

4. **Collecting and analyzing sample data**: This involves collecting data from a sample and using it to calculate the test statistic.

5. **Comparing the test statistic with the critical value**: The critical value is the value that separates the rejection and non-rejection regions of the sampling distribution. If the test statistic falls within the rejection region, the null hypothesis is rejected in favor of the alternative hypothesis.

6. **Drawing conclusions**: Based on the test results, a conclusion is drawn as to whether the null hypothesis should be rejected or not.

Let's summarize the chapter and look at the key takeaways.

Summary

This chapter aims to elevate your proficiency, enabling you to provide your end users with functionalities that extend beyond the standard features offered by every tool. It's important to recognize that as we delve deeper, the complexity increases. This can be illustrated through a chart correlating the progression of time with the level of programming required to achieve these advancements.

Remember—BI is not a final destination; it's a journey. There isn't a single linear path; rather, it's a road that diverges, intersects, and loops back onto itself. Sometimes, it extends endlessly. BI is not a one-way street; it evolves with the advent of new technologies and emerging requirements. BA takes a more proactive approach in the quest for insights. Data science, meanwhile, is a comprehensive effort involving a dedicated team and specialized tools to explore both the industry and the organization itself.

Ultimately, it's essential to understand that your journey may involve enhancing your existing BI platform or branching out into parallel or complementary pursuits. Either path will lead you beyond the confines of conventional BI.

9

Hands-On Data Wrangling and Data Visualization

For the final component of this book, we will go through two quick hands-on exercises. First, we will perform some data wrangling, cleaning, and manipulation with Python using the pandas and NumPy libraries, and build some simple data visualizations using Matplotlib and Seaborn. Second, we will build a Tableau dashboard using a publicly available dataset.

The purpose of these tutorials is to provide you with a comprehensive understanding of how to approach and analyze unfamiliar datasets. We aim to guide you through the process of assessing data, applying basic data wrangling techniques, and emphasizing the significance of data manipulation in preparing a dataset for in-depth analysis. Furthermore, we intend to equip you with the skills to create reports using a widely recognized and established **business intelligence (BI)** tool.

In these tutorials, we will delve into the initial stages of data exploration, enabling you to gain insights into the characteristics and structure of the dataset. We will cover techniques for understanding the data's variables, identifying missing values, and assessing data quality. By addressing these crucial aspects, you will be better equipped to make informed decisions regarding data cleaning and transformation.

The tutorials will then focus on data wrangling techniques to refine and shape the dataset. We will introduce you to powerful tools and libraries such as Python's pandas library, all of which offer a range of functions for filtering, aggregating, and transforming data. By demonstrating practical examples, you will learn how to handle missing values, remove duplicates, and apply necessary data transformations for accurate analysis.

To help you showcase your analysis effectively, we will provide step-by-step guidance on utilizing a popular and established BI tool called Tableau. With its user-friendly interface, we will explore how to create visually appealing and interactive reports using the tool's drag-and-drop functionality. You will learn how to select appropriate visualizations and customize the appearance of their reports to effectively convey their findings.

Finally, we will guide you on how to merge individual reports into a cohesive and comprehensive dashboard. Through this process, you will learn how to synthesize multiple reports into a single view, allowing stakeholders to gain a holistic understanding of the data and its insights. We will highlight best practices for dashboard design, including layout, interactivity, and storytelling techniques, enabling you to present your analyses in a compelling and influential manner.

By the end of these tutorials, you will have a holistic understanding of the entire data analysis process, from initial data assessment to advanced visualization techniques. You will be equipped with the knowledge and skills to confidently explore unknown datasets, apply data wrangling techniques, create insightful reports using a renowned BI tool, and effectively merge their reports into a coherent and impactful dashboard.

Technical requirements

To follow along with the tutorials in this chapter, you will need to have the following applications/ programs installed on your machine (there are versions available for both Windows and macOS):

- Python (`https://www.python.org/`)
- The Jupyter Notebook library (`https://jupyter.org/`)
- Tableau Desktop (`https://www.tableau.com/products/trial`)

The GitHub URL containing the Jupyter Notebook and the Tableau workbook is `https://github.com/PacktPublishing/Business-Intelligence-Career-Master-Plan`.

Data analysis using Python

Python is a high-level programming language that was first released in 1991 by Guido van Rossum. It is known for its simplicity, readability, and versatility, making it one of the most popular programming languages in the world. Python's design philosophy emphasizes code readability, with its syntax utilizing indentation and whitespace, which contributes to its clean and intuitive structure.

Python has a broad range of applications and is widely used in various domains, including web development, data analysis, scientific computing, artificial intelligence, machine learning, automation, and more. Its versatility stems from the extensive collection of libraries and frameworks available, which provide pre-built functionalities for various tasks and domains.

Python's simplicity and readability make it an excellent language for beginners as it allows them to focus on problem-solving rather than getting caught up in complex syntax. It has a large and active community that contributes to its growth and provides support through forums, online resources, and extensive documentation.

We could have created this data wrangling tutorial using R, SQL, Scala, MATLAB, or Java. We decided to use Python for our data wrangling tutorial because of its importance and widespread adoption by

BI professionals. It is a powerful programming language that is widely used in various industries and domains, making it an excellent choice for beginners and experienced developers alike.

Here are some additional reasons why Python is so widely used by BI professionals:

- **Versatility**: Python is a versatile programming language that offers a wide range of libraries and tools specifically designed for data wrangling and visualization, such as pandas, NumPy, Matplotlib, Seaborn, and Plotly. These libraries provide powerful functions and methods to manipulate and analyze data and create interactive and informative visualizations.

- **Data integration**: Python facilitates the integration of diverse data sources. BI professionals often deal with data from various systems and in different formats, including databases, spreadsheets, CSV files, APIs, and more. Python's extensive libraries and modules make it easier to import, preprocess, and transform data from diverse sources, enabling analysts to combine and merge datasets seamlessly.

- **Data cleaning and transformation**: Data obtained for BI purposes often requires cleaning and transformation to ensure its accuracy and consistency. Python offers robust libraries such as pandas, which provide efficient tools for handling missing values, removing duplicates, filtering, sorting, and transforming data. These capabilities are crucial for preparing data for analysis and generating reliable insights.

- **Statistical analysis**: Python's extensive ecosystem of libraries enables BI professionals to perform advanced statistical analysis. With packages such as SciPy and StatsModels, analysts can conduct statistical tests, perform regression analysis, calculate descriptive statistics, and derive meaningful insights from data.

- **Visualization capabilities**: Python libraries such as Matplotlib, Seaborn, and Plotly provide rich visualization capabilities, allowing BI professionals to create a wide range of charts, graphs, and interactive visualizations. Visualizations are instrumental in presenting complex data in a more accessible and understandable manner, enabling stakeholders to grasp insights quickly and make informed decisions.

- **Automation and reproducibility**: Python's scripting capabilities make it ideal for automating data wrangling and visualization tasks. By writing reusable and scalable code, BI professionals can streamline their workflows, saving time and effort in repetitive tasks. Additionally, Python promotes reproducibility, ensuring that analyses and visualizations can be easily recreated and shared with others, enhancing collaboration and transparency.

- **Community and support**: Python has a vast and active community of data scientists, analysts, and BI professionals. This thriving community contributes to the development of new libraries, shares best practices, and provides support through forums, online communities, and extensive documentation. Access to this collective knowledge makes Python a reliable choice for data wrangling and visualization tasks.

Overall, using Python for data wrangling and visualization empowers BI professionals with a powerful and flexible toolkit to efficiently explore and analyze data, communicate insights effectively, and drive data-driven decision-making within organizations. For this reason, we will use Python in our tutorial.

Data wrangling and visualization with Python

In this tutorial, we will walk through the process of cleaning the *Data Science Job Posting* dataset, which is available here: https://www.kaggle.com/datasets/rashikrahmanpritom/data-science-job-posting-on-glassdoor?resource=download.

The dataset contains information about job postings related to data science on the Glassdoor platform. Glassdoor is a popular website where individuals can find job listings, read company reviews, and access salary information. It includes a variety of fields that describe data science job postings. These fields provide details such as job titles, company names, job locations, job descriptions, required qualifications, salary information, employee reviews, and other attributes. With this dataset, you could potentially perform analyses or extract insights related to data science job trends, job requirements, salary distributions, or even sentiment analysis based on company ratings.

Once you have Python and Jupyter Notebooks installed on your computer, you can begin following along with the following tutorial.

Step 1 – loading the dataset

First, let's start by importing the libraries we will be using during the data wrangling portion of the tutorial. We will start with `pandas` and `numpy`, which are two very typical data analysis libraries. We will read the data file into memory and load the data into a pandas DataFrame:

```
Import pandas as pd
import numpy as np
```

Next, we will read the file using the `read_csv` function in the `pandas` library and store it in a DataFrame called `ds_df` (data science DataFrame):

```
ds_df = pd.read_csv('data files/Uncleaned_DS_jobs.csv')
```

Inspect the first five rows of the dataset using the `head()` function. We must do this to confirm the data file was loaded correctly and to get a sense of what the dataset looks like:

```
ds_df.tail()
```

This will print out the following output:

Out[3]:

index		Job Title	Salary Estimate	Job Description	Rating	Company Name	Location	Headquarters	Size	Founded	Type of ownership	Industry	Sector
667	667	Data Scientist	$105K – 167K$ (Glassdoor est.)	Summary\n\n\nWe're looking for a data scientist ...	3.6	TRANZACT\n3.6	Fort Lee, NJ	Fort Lee, NJ	1001 to 5000 employees	1989	Company - Private	Advertising & Marketing	Business Services
668	668	Data Scientist	$105K – 167K$ (Glassdoor est.)	Job Description\nBecome a thought leader withi...	-1.0	JKGT	San Francisco, CA	-1	-1	-1	-1	-1	-1
669	669	Data Scientist	$105K – 167K$ (Glassdoor est.)	Join a thriving company that is changing the w...	-1.0	AccessHope	Irwindale, CA	-1	-1	-1	-1	-1	-1
670	670	Data Scientist	$105K – 167K$ (Glassdoor est.)	100 Remote Opportunity As an AINLP Data Scient...	5.0	ChaTeck Incorporated\n5.0	San Francisco, CA	Santa Clara, CA	1 to 50 employees	-1	Company - Private	Advertising & Marketing	Business Services
671	671	Data Scientist	$105K – 167K$ (Glassdoor est.)	Description\n\n\nThe Data Scientist will be part...	2.7	1-800-Flowers\n2.7	New York, NY	Carle Place, NY	1001 to 5000 employees	1976	Company - Public	Wholesale	Business Services

Figure 9.1 – The last five rows of the Data Science Job Posting dataset

Next, let's explore the dataset.

Step 2 – an initial exploration of the dataset

In the previous step, we printed out the last five rows of the dataset to give us a better sense of the data structure and what it looks like. We noticed a duplicate `index` column that already exists in the DataFrame (the `index` column is the very first column with the bold lettering), so we can remove this before continuing. We can do this with the `df.drop()` function in `pandas`. We will use `inplace=True` so that the DataFrame saves this change for the rest of the notebook:

```
ds_df.drop('index', axis=1, inplace=True)
```

Next, let's check the dimensions of the dataset to get a sense of the size and complexity of the dataset we will be working with:

```
print('Dataset Dimensions:', ds_df.shape)
Dataset Dimensions: (672, 14)
```

The dataset's dimensions provide insights into the size and scale of the dataset. Knowing the number of rows and columns helps us estimate the overall volume of data and the computational resources required for processing and analysis. This information is crucial for optimizing memory usage and selecting appropriate data manipulation and analysis techniques.

Since we intended this tutorial to be a straightforward exercise, we chose a simple dataset with a small number of variables and not too many rows. You will work with much more complex datasets in future work, but rest assured the techniques we use here can be used when wrangling larger tables with millions of records and hundreds of variables.

Now that we know the dataset is manageable and will not take up many resources on our computer, we can check the column names to see what *kind* of data we can analyze. We can sort the column names in alphabetical order using the `sort_values()` function so it is a little easier to see what is available to us versus printing them out in the order that they appear in the DataFrame:

```
print('Column Names:\n')
for i in ds_df.columns.sort_values():
    print(i)


Output: Column Names:

Company Name
Competitors
Founded
Headquarters
Industry
Job Description
Job Title
Location
Rating
Revenue
Salary Estimate
Sector
Size
Type of ownership
```

In the preceding code block, we pulled out the DataFrame columns and then did a simple loop to print each of the column names in a new row. Here is a simple data dictionary that we can put together based on the output:

- `Company Name`: The company that posted the job
- `Competitors`: Companies that are direct competitors
- `Founded`: The year the company was founded or established
- `Headquarters`: Location of company headquarters
- `Industry`: Industry of the company
- `Job Description`: The full job description for the job posting
- `Job Title`: Title of the position in the job posting
- `Location`: Job location
- `Rating`: Rating of that post

- Revenue: Total revenue for the company

- Salary Estimate: Salary range for that job

- Sector: Sector of the company

- Size: Total number of employees at the company

- Type of ownership: Public/private/non-profit

Now that we have an idea of *what* kind of data we have, we can start analyzing it. Let's get a better sense of the data's completeness and what kind of data types are in the dataset. We have a couple of diverse ways we can accomplish these using pandas, but we are going to take advantage of one of the many prebuilt functions and call df.info():

```
print(ds_df.info())


<class 'pandas.core.frame.DataFrame'>
RangeIndex: 672 entries, 0 to 671
Data columns (total 14 columns):
 #   Column            Non-Null Count  Dtype
---  ------            --------------  -----
 0   Job Title         672 non-null    object
 1   Salary Estimate   672 non-null    object
 2   Job Description   672 non-null    object
 3   Rating            672 non-null    float64
 4   Company Name      672 non-null    object
 5   Location          672 non-null    object
 6   Headquarters      672 non-null    object
 7   Size              672 non-null    object
 8   Founded           672 non-null    int64
 9   Type of ownership 672 non-null    object
 10  Industry          672 non-null    object
 11  Sector            672 non-null    object
 12  Revenue           672 non-null    object
 13  Competitors       672 non-null    object
dtypes: float64(1), int64(1), object(12)
memory usage: 73.6+ KB
None
```

This tells us a great deal about the data we will be working with:

- The total number of rows (entries) in the DataFrame.

- The total number of columns in the DataFrame.

- The names of each column (called "column names" or "column labels").

- The data type of each column. This includes information about whether the column contains numeric data (integers, floats), text data (strings), dates, or other specialized types.

- The number of non-null values in each column. This indicates how many values are present and not missing (NaN) in each column.

- The memory usage of the DataFrame. This represents the approximate amount of memory used by the DataFrame in bytes.

We can see that there are no NULL values anywhere in the dataset, which is normally something that we would need to handle, either via extrapolation or by removing those records. According to this function, none of the columns contain any null or missing data.

> **Note**
>
> This should be the first indication that there may be something going on with the missing values in the dataset. It is exceedingly rare to encounter a dataset that is complete and contains records for every single row and column (and if you ever encounter one, you are one of the lucky ones!). We will have to dig a little deeper into the data to see what is truly going on.

We can see that the data types are object, which means they will be text data/string values. The Rating column is a floating-point value that tells us there must be decimals included in the rating calculation. The Founded column is an integer, which means that this is simply just the year the company was founded.

One of the limitations of this dataset is there is no date field to indicate *when* the job posting was placed, so we cannot get a sense of how old this data is at the time of writing this tutorial. However, considering the dataset was published in 2021, we can infer that it was scraped from Glassdoor around that time.

When utilizing publicly available data, a notable challenge arises as it may not encompass all the necessary data points required for conducting an analysis. Consequently, the responsibility falls on the analyst to exercise their discernment in choosing a dataset that aligns with their analysis objectives.

> **Note**
>
> If we did want to deal with missing values, there are a few handy functions we can use. For example, we could drop columns with a high missing value percentage by setting a threshold and using the dropna () function:
>
> ```
> threshold = 0.75
> ds_df = ds_df.dropna(thresh=threshold * len(ds_df), axis=1)
> ```
>
> Alternatively, we could fill in empty values with our own fix using the fillna () function:
>
> ```
> ds_df['Sector'] = data['Sector'].fillna('Not Available')
> ```

Step 3 – remove duplicate rows

Our next step is to review the dataset for any duplicate records and remove those. We can do this using the df.duplicated() function and summing to get the count of duplicate rows:

```
ds_df.duplicated().sum()
```

```
13
```

There are only 13 duplicate rows in the dataset, but we should still remove them by running df.drop_duplicates(). We will also reset the index on the DataFrame since we are dropping rows and do not want to lose track of the new row count:

```
ds_df.drop_duplicates(inplace=True)
```

Then, we will print the shape to see the new DataFrame dimensions and confirm that the 13 duplicate rows are gone:

```
ds_df.shape()
```

```
(659, 14)
```

Removing duplicate rows from a dataset is essential for maintaining data accuracy, ensuring consistent analysis results, improving computational efficiency, preserving data integrity, obtaining reliable insights, optimizing database performance, and achieving data consistency in merged datasets. By eliminating duplicates, analysts can work with clean and reliable data, enabling accurate and meaningful analysis.

Step 4 – cleaning and transforming data

Now, we will move on to the longest and most challenging part of the tutorial: cleaning and transforming the data to ensure consistency and uniformity. Cleaning and transforming address issues related to data quality. Datasets often contain errors, inconsistencies, missing values, or outliers that can affect analysis results. By cleaning the data, you can rectify these issues, ensuring data accuracy and reliability.

Cleaning and transforming data can also reveal patterns, trends, and relationships that might not be apparent in raw, unprocessed data. By transforming variables, aggregating data, or creating derived features, you can uncover deeper insights and enhance the interpretability of the data.

To start, let's look at the first five rows of data to see if there are manipulations or clean-up steps we should take before proceeding:

```
ds_df.head()
```

This prints out the following output:

Out[11]:

Job Description	Rating	Company Name	Location	Headquarters	Size	Founded	Type of ownership	Industry	Sector	Revenue	Competitors
Description\n\nThe Senior Data Scientist is re...	3.1	Healthfirst\n3.1	New York, NY	New York, NY	1001 to 5000 employees	1993	Nonprofit Organization	Insurance Carriers	Insurance	Unknown / Non-Applicable	EmblemHealth, UnitedHealth Group, Aetna
Secure our Nation, Ignite your Future\n\nJoin ...	4.2	ManTech\n4.2	Chantilly, VA	Herndon, VA	5001 to 10000 employees	1968	Company - Public	Research & Development	Business Services	1to2 billion (USD)	-1
Overview\n\n\nAnalysis Group is one of the lar...	3.8	Analysis Group\n3.8	Boston, MA	Boston, MA	1001 to 5000 employees	1981	Private Practice / Firm	Consulting	Business Services	100to500 million (USD)	-1
JOB DESCRIPTION:\n\n\nDo you have a passion for ...	3.5	INFICON\n3.5	Newton, MA	Bad Ragaz, Switzerland	501 to 1000 employees	2000	Company - Public	Electrical & Electronic Manufacturing	Manufacturing	100to500 million (USD)	MKS Instruments, Pfeiffer Vacuum, Agilent Tech...
Data Scientist\nAffinity Solutions / Marketing...	2.9	Affinity Solutions\n2.9	New York, NY	New York, NY	51 to 200 employees	1998	Company - Private	Advertising & Marketing	Business Services	Unknown / Non-Applicable	Commerce Signals, Cardlytics, Yodlee

Figure 9.2 – The first five rows of the Data Science Job Posting dataset

There are a few observations we can make from the first five rows in the dataset:

- The `Salary Estimate` column has a lot of extra characters that we can clean up, and we could format this in a better way to highlight a range.

- The `Company Name` column has a newline, `\n`, and the company rating following it (due to a parsing error); we should remove anything after `\n` so that we only have the company name.

- Finally, the `Competitors` column has `-1` in a few different rows. If we recall our earlier analysis, we saw that there were no null or empty values in the dataset. Instead, this is what is supposed to represent a `NULL` or empty value; we will need to look more in-depth at the different columns in the dataset to see how many rows contain this value before we decide what to do.

Let's start with the company name since this will be a straightforward fix. We can start by just printing the column out to confirm `\n#.#` appears on every row:

```
Input:
ds_df['Company Name']
Output:
0                    Healthfirst\n3.1
1                      ManTech\n4.2
2                Analysis Group\n3.8
3                      INFICON\n3.5
4            Affinity Solutions\n2.9
                    . . .
667                  TRANZACT\n3.6
668                         JKGT
```

```
669                      AccessHope
670       ChaTeck Incorporated\n5.0
671             1-800-Flowers\n2.7
Name: Company Name, Length: 659, dtype: object
```

The pandas library has a variety of diverse ways to do this. First, we can use the str.split() method to pull apart each element in the Company Name column. Then, we can overwrite the original column by assigning it back to the column:

```
ds_df['Company Name'].str.split('\n', expand=True)
```

```
                         0     1
0               Healthfirst   3.1
1                   ManTech   4.2
2            Analysis Group   3.8
3                   INFICON   3.5
4        Affinity Solutions   2.9
..                      ...   ...
667                TRANZACT   3.6
668                    JKGT  None
669              AccessHope  None
670     ChaTeck Incorporated   5.0
671            1-800-Flowers   2.7

[659 rows x 2 columns]
```

Then, we can grab the company name by only selecting the first element, which in Python starts with [0]. After, we can reassign this to the Company Name column so that we replace the original company name with what we transformed it into:

```
ds_df['Company Name'] = ds_df['Company Name'].str.split('\n',
expand=True)[0]
```

For all our transformations, we want to print out the results of our work to confirm our code is performing the transformations as we expect:

```
ds_df['Company Name']
```

```
0               Healthfirst
1                   ManTech
2            Analysis Group
3                   INFICON
4        Affinity Solutions
                    ...
667                TRANZACT
```

```
668                    JKGT
669                AccessHope
670      ChaTeck Incorporated
671              1-800-Flowers
Name: Company Name, Length: 659, dtype: object
```

Now, let's look at the `Industry` column and see if there is anything strange happening there. We can do this very quickly by counting the values to see what comes up:

```
ds_df['Industry'].value_counts()[0:10]

Industry
Biotech & Pharmaceuticals                66
IT Services                              61
-1                                       60
Computer Hardware & Software             56
Aerospace & Defense                      46
Enterprise Software & Network Solutions  43
Consulting                               38
Staffing & Outsourcing                   36
Insurance Carriers                       28
Internet                                 27
Name: count, dtype: int64
```

We can see `-1` in this dataset. Remember what we observed earlier when inspecting the first five rows of the DataFrame; this dataset is using `-1` in place of `NULL` or an empty value. We will need to replace this `-1` with a more suitable value to help our analysis (especially for numeric fields).

For this example, let's replace `-1` with `Unknown Industry` using the `str.replace()` function:

```
ds_df['Industry'] = ds_df['Industry'].str.replace('-1', 'Unknown
Industry')
```

Let's confirm the transformation was successful. We can just look at the top 10 industries to confirm it worked:

```
ds_df['Industry'].value_counts()[0:10]

Industry
Biotech & Pharmaceuticals                66
IT Services                              61
Unknown Industry                         60
Computer Hardware & Software             56
Aerospace & Defense                      46
Enterprise Software & Network Solutions  43
```

```
Consulting                          38
Staffing & Outsourcing              36
Insurance Carriers                  28
Internet                            27
Name: count, dtype: int64
```

The transformation was successful, and now we do not have a −1 industry to confuse our stakeholders.

Next, let's look at the `Salary Estimate` column. This is an extremely useful column for analysis but in its current format, it is a bit of a mess. We can start by counting how many salary ranges there are and seeing what we will need to strip out:

```
ds_df['Salary Estimate'].value_counts()[0:10]
```

```
Salary Estimate
$75K-$131K (Glassdoor est.)      32
$79K-$131K (Glassdoor est.)      32
$99K-$132K (Glassdoor est.)      32
$137K-$171K (Glassdoor est.)     30
$90K-$109K (Glassdoor est.)      28
$56K-$97K (Glassdoor est.)       22
$79K-$106K (Glassdoor est.)      22
$90K-$124K (Glassdoor est.)      22
$92K-$155K (Glassdoor est.)      21
$138K-$158K (Glassdoor est.)     21
Name: count, dtype: int64
```

Based on our observations of the first 10 different salary estimates, it looks like our best bet here is to use a regular expression (regex) to strip out any of the non-numeric values, then create two columns with the minimum and maximum salaries for each row. We can use the `str.extract()` function with a simple regex to only pull the first element in the salary range, which is the minimum salary.

> **Note**
>
> A **regular expression** (**regex**) is a sequence of characters that define a search pattern. They are used for pattern matching and string manipulation tasks in text processing. Regular expressions provide a powerful and flexible way to search, extract, and manipulate specific patterns within strings.

We can also multiply the salary number by `1000` since the salary range is in the thousands for a more accurate representation:

```
ds_df['Min Salary'] = ds_df['Salary Estimate'].str.extract('\$(\d+)
K').astype(float)*1000
```

We can perform the same with `Max Salary`, but this time pulling out the second element in the salary range to get the maximum salary. We will also multiply this number by `1000`:

```
ds_df['Max Salary'] = ds_df['Salary Estimate'].str.extract(r'\$(\d+)
K-\$(\d+)K')[1].astype(float)*1000
```

Let's print out a few elements from each newly created column to confirm the transformations were successful:

```
print(ds_df[['Min Salary', 'Max Salary']])

     Min Salary  Max Salary
0       137000.0    171000.0
1       137000.0    171000.0
2       137000.0    171000.0
3       137000.0    171000.0
4       137000.0    171000.0
..          ...         ...
667     105000.0    167000.0
668     105000.0    167000.0
669     105000.0    167000.0
670     105000.0    167000.0
671     105000.0    167000.0

[659 rows x 2 columns]
```

Now, we can analyze the salary ranges more effectively. Now that we have these columns in a better format for performing calculations, let's do a simple one to add an `Average Salary` column to the dataset so that we can slice `Min Salary`, `Max Salary`, and `Average Salary` by job.

To do this, we can use the `mean()` function on our two columns and specify `axis=1` so that the calculation is performed on every row. If we do not make that specification in the function call, it will give us the average for all of the minimum and maximum salaries, which is a good summary statistic but not our intention:

```
ds_df['Average Salary'] = ds_df[['Min Salary', 'Max Salary']].
mean(axis = 1)
```

We can print out a few sample values to confirm the average calculation was performed on every row and looks good:

```
ds_df['Average Salary']

0       154000.0
1       154000.0
2       154000.0
```

```
3        154000.0
4        154000.0
            . . .
667      136000.0
668      136000.0
669      136000.0
670      136000.0
671      136000.0
Name: Average Salary, Length: 659, dtype: float64
```

Now that we have a salary in a more suitable format for analysis, let's look at the `Size` column by printing the value counts:

```
ds_df['Size'].value_counts()

Size
51 to 200 employees        134
1001 to 5000 employees     104
1 to 50 employees           86
201 to 500 employees        84
10000+ employees            80
501 to 1000 employees       77
5001 to 10000 employees     61
Unknown                     17
-1                          16
Name: count, dtype: int64
```

Notice that `employees` is repeated on every line and that there are a few -1s that we should take care of; we can transform them into `Unknown` because our earlier observation of the dataset tells us −1 is replacing NULLs or blank values, so we can categorize these as Unknown company sizes:

```
ds_df['Size'] = ds_df['Size'].str.replace('-1', 'Unknown')
```

Now, let's remove `employees` from all of the entries so that it looks a little better:

```
ds_df['Size'] = ds_df['Size'].str.split(' employees', expand=True)[0]
```

Let's print out the value counts to see if the transformations were successful:

```
ds_df['Size'].value_counts()

Size
51 to 200        134
1001 to 5000     104
1 to 50           86
```

```
201 to 500          84
10000+              80
501 to 1000         77
5001 to 10000       61
Unknown             33
Name: count, dtype: int64
```

Let's look at the year the company was founded and use this to calculate how old the company is. To start, we should see if there are any strange values in the Founded column by also looking at value counts:

```
ds_df['Founded'].value_counts()[0:10]

Founded
-1          107
 2012        34
 2011        24
 2010        22
 1996        22
 1999        22
 2015        21
 2006        16
 2013        16
 2000        15
Name: count, dtype: int64
```

-1 is back; because this column is an integer, and we want to use it to perform a simple calculation to subtract it from the current year of 2023, we can just replace it with a 0, then perform the calculation:

```
ds_df['Founded'] = ds_df['Founded'].replace(-1, 0)
```

To do the calculation correctly, we must account for all the companies we set to 0. We can build a simple lambda function for this: if the year = 0, then just set the age of the company to 0; otherwise, subtract it from 2023 to get the number of years of the company:

> **Note**
>
> In Python, a lambda function is a small, anonymous function that can be defined without a name. It is also known as an "anonymous function" because it does not require a standard function definition using the def keyword. Instead, lambda functions are created using the lambda keyword followed by a list of arguments, a colon (:), and an expression that defines the function's logic.
>
> ```
> ds_df['Age of Company'] = ds_df['Founded'].apply(lambda x: 2023-
> x if x != 0 else x)
> ```

Print the results to see if the transformations worked:

```
ds_df['Age of Company'].value_counts()[0:10]

Age of Company
0       107
11       34
12       24
13       22
27       22
24       22
8        21
17       16
10       16
23       15
Name: count, dtype: int64
```

There are many young companies in this dataset; data science still has some room for growth soon! For the sake of time and brevity, we will perform a few more data wrangling techniques before we try visualizing the data. Let's look at the Ratings column and see if anything can be transformed there:

```
print(ds_df['Rating'].value_counts().reset_index()[0:10])

   Rating   count
0     3.5      58
1     3.3      41
2     4.0      41
3     3.9      40
4     3.8      39
5     3.7      38
6     5.0      36
7     4.5      32
8     3.6      31
9     3.4      31
```

We can see that -1 appears again. We have a couple of approaches we can take:

- We could filter out any rows with -1 in them but then we lose out on some of the other data that would be useful for analysis

- We could impute a value here based on the mean of the Rating column

- We could impute a NULL or empty value since the data type is float

Let's go with the last approach here; this is the safest bet to accurately represent that the `Ratings` data is missing for those rows and will not affect the min, max, and average calculations:

```
ds_df['Rating'] = ds_df['Rating'].replace(-1, np.NaN)
```

Now, let's show the average rating since we have replaced the -1s with NULL:

```
print('The average Rating after replacing -1 with NULL is:', ds_
df['Rating'].mean().astype(str))

The average Rating after replacing -1 with NULL is: 3.8812903225806448
```

As we can see, there are some very highly regarded companies hiring data scientists – this is good news for us BI professionals. Next, we need to look at the job locations and see if there is any strange or missing data there:

```
ds_df['Location'].value_counts()

Location
San Francisco, CA     58
New York, NY          50
Washington, DC        26
Boston, MA            24
Chicago, IL           22
                      ..
Lehi, UT               1
Culver City, CA        1
Lake Oswego, OR        1
New Orleans, LA        1
Irwindale, CA          1
Name: count, Length: 207, dtype: int64
```

Nothing major stands out here just yet. Let's start by pulling out just the state abbreviations and disregarding the cities:

```
ds_df['Location'].apply(lambda x: x.split(",")[-1]).value_counts()

Location
 CA            154
 VA             89
 MA             62
 NY             52
 MD             40
 United States  11
 NJ             10
```

```
CO                 10
OK                  6
WI                  6
Remote              5
New Jersey          2
SC                  2
OR                  2
UT                  2
Utah                2
NH                  2
MS                  1
KS                  1
Texas               1
DE                  1
California          1
WV                  1
Name: count, dtype: int64
```

Now that we've looked at just the state abbreviations, we can see that a few of the job locations have the full state name or USA in them. We will create a simple function to deal with these job locations that do not adhere to the two-letter standard for state abbreviations. Let's start by creating a state column so that we still maintain the original Location column:

```
ds_df['Job State'] = ds_df['Location'].apply(lambda x: x.split(",")
[-1].strip())
```

We could do this a little more programmatically if we had multiple states (we would want to change them by using a simple mapping table) but for this exercise, we will keep it simple and just change the values to ones that seem appropriate:

- California to CA

- New Jersey to NJ

- Texas to TX

- Utah to UT

- United States to USA

- Remote to All:

```
ds_df['Job State'] = ds_df['Job State'].replace(['California', 'New
Jersey', 'Texas', 'Utah', 'United States', 'Remote'],['CA', 'NJ',
'TX', 'UT', 'USA', 'All'])
```

Then, we can print out the `Job State` column to confirm our transformations were successful:

```
ds_df['Job State'].value_counts()[0:5]

Job State
CA     154
VA      89
MA      62
NY      52
MD      40
Name: count, dtype: int64
```

Now, let's look at the job titles in each of the descriptions and see if we can do some quick work on them. We will start by looking at what the counts are for the `Job Title` column:

```
ds_df['Job Title'].value_counts()[0:8]

Job Title
Data Scientist                                 326
Data Engineer                                   26
Senior Data Scientist                           19
Machine Learning Engineer                       15
Data Analyst                                    12
Senior Data Analyst                              6
Data Scientist - TS/SCI FSP or CI Required       4
Data Science Software Engineer                   4
Name: count, dtype: int64
```

It looks like the vast majority of the postings use the first five titles or some form of them.

The best way to determine what the true job title for each listing is to do the following:

- Set all of the characters in the job title string to lowercase
- Look to see if the job titles we are interested in analyzing appear in the `Job Title` text
- Return the job title with the appropriate casing
- Set all others to `Unknown Job Title`

We are doing this to simplify the analysis a bit and have bigger buckets from which to work with. To do this, we can create a super simple function and then apply it to the `Job Title` column:

```
def job_title_transformation(title):
    title = title.lower()
    if 'data scientist' in title:
        return 'Data Scientist'
```

```
    elif 'data analyst' in title:
        return 'Data Analyst'
    elif 'data engineer' in title:
        return 'Data Engineer'
    elif 'machine learning' in title:
        return 'Machine Learning Engineer'
    elif 'director' in title:
        return 'Director'
    elif 'manager' in title:
        return 'Manager'
    elif 'vice president' in title:
        return 'Vice President'
    elif 'analyst' in title:
        return 'Data Analyst'
    else:
        return 'Unknown Job Title'
```

Now, we can apply the function to the Job Title column and create a new column called Job Title Transformed:

```
ds_df['Job Title Transformed'] = ds_df['Job Title'].apply(job_title_
transformation)
```

Let's confirm the new column looks as expected:

```
ds_df['Job Title Transformed'].value_counts()

Job Title Transformed
Data Scientist              444
Unknown Job Title            68
Data Analyst                 55
Data Engineer                46
Machine Learning Engineer    35
Manager                       7
Director                      3
Vice President                1
Name: count, dtype: int64
```

Much better! We can also see that there are only 68 jobs that are in that miscellaneous bucket, so it helps to bucket them all.

The last step in the transformation process is to search for the most popular skills in the Job Description column. To fit this book's theme, we will pick some job skills and technologies that we presume we will see come up often:

- Python
- Spark
- SQL
- Excel
- Tableau
- Power BI
- AWS

To do this effectively, we will need to create Boolean columns that indicate whether any of the skills show up in the job description. Again, we can do this with a simple function:

```
def create_flag_columns(df, columns):
    for column in columns:
        df[column.title()] = df['Job Description'].str.lower().str.
contains(column).astype(int)
```

The create_flag_columns function takes two parameters: df (the DataFrame) and columns (a list of column names to create flags for) and does the following:

- It iterates over each column in the columns list
- For each column, it converts the values in that column into lowercase using str.lower(), enabling case-insensitive comparisons
- It checks if the column name is present in the lowercase column values using str.contains(column)
- The result of str.contains() is cast to int using astype(int), converting True to 1 and False to 0
- The resulting binary values are assigned to the respective columns in the df DataFrame

Let's test out the function:

```
columns = ["python", "excel", "tableau", "power bi", "aws", "sql",
"spark"]
create_flag_columns(ds_df, columns)
```

Here, we're passing the ds_df DataFrame and a list of column names to the create_flag_columns function. This will create flag columns for each specified column in ds_df, indicating whether the corresponding keyword is present in the respective column's values. We can print one of the columns to confirm it worked successfully:

```
ds_df['Python'].value_counts()


Python
1    479
0    180
Name: count, dtype: int64
```

Let's check that all the new columns were created:

```
ds_df.columns


Index(['Job Title', 'Salary Estimate', 'Job Description', 'Rating',
       'Company Name', 'Location', 'Headquarters', 'Size', 'Founded',
       'Type of ownership', 'Industry', 'Sector', 'Revenue',
'Competitors', 'Min Salary', 'Max Salary', 'Average Salary', 'Age
of Company','Job State', 'Job Title Transformed', 'Python', 'Excel',
'Tableau','Power Bi', 'Aws', 'Sql', 'Spark'],dtype='object')
```

Let's print the first five rows of the DataFrame as one final check to confirm our transformations have been applied successfully:

```
ds_df.head()
```

This will print out the following output:

Out[49]:

Rating	Company Name	Location	Headquarters	Size	Founded	Type of ownership	...	Age of Company	Job State	Job Title Transformed	Python	Excel	Tableau	Power Bi	Aws	Sql	Spark
3.1	Healthfirst	New York, NY	New York, NY	1001 to 5000	1993	Nonprofit Organization	...	30	NY	Data Scientist	0	0	0	0	1	0	0
4.2	ManTech	Chantilly, VA	Herndon, VA	5001 to 10000	1968	Company - Public	...	55	VA	Data Scientist	0	0	0	0	0	1	0
3.8	Analysis Group	Boston, MA	Boston, MA	1001 to 5000	1981	Private Practice / Firm	...	42	MA	Data Scientist	1	1	0	0	1	0	0
3.5	INFICON	Newton, MA	Bad Ragaz, Switzerland	501 to 1000	2000	Company - Public	...	23	MA	Data Scientist	1	1	0	0	1	1	0
2.9	Affinity Solutions	New York, NY	New York, NY	51 to 200	1998	Company - Private	...	25	NY	Data Scientist	1	1	0	0	0	1	0

Figure 9.3 – The first five rows of the Data Science Job Posting dataset

In this step, we applied various cleaning and transformation operations to specific columns. We replaced salary ranges with a unified format, extracted minimum and maximum salary values, and cleaned and transformed the `Rating`, `Size`, `Founded`, `Type of ownership`, `Industry`, and `Sector` columns using regular expressions and string manipulations.

Step 5 – saving the cleaned dataset

Let's save the cleaned dataset to a new file for further analysis.

By executing this code, we will save the cleaned dataset to a new CSV file called `Glassdoor_DS_Jobs_Final.csv`:

```
ds_df.to_csv('data files/Glassdoor_DS_Jobs_Final.csv', index=False)
```

Congratulations! You have completed the data cleaning process for the *Data Science Job Posting* dataset. The cleaned dataset can now be used for further analysis or visualization tasks.

Remember that data cleaning is an iterative process, and you can apply additional cleaning techniques based on the specific requirements of your analysis.

Step 6 – load the cleaned dataset

Let's load the cleaned dataset so that we can perform simple visualizations to showcase our data engineering efforts. Instead of loading the original data file, now, we can load the cleaned dataset we saved in the previous step:

```
ds_vis_df = pd.read_csv('data files/Glassdoor_DS_Jobs_Final.csv')
```

Let's confirm the dataset looks like the one we just saved by checking the first few rows:

```
ds_vis_df.head()
```

The output is as follows:

Out[68]:

Rating	Company Name	Location	Headquarters	Size	Founded	Type of ownership	...	Age of Company	Job State	Job Title Transformed	Python	Excel	Tableau	Power BI	Aws	Sql	Spark
3.1	Healthfirst	New York, NY	New York, NY	1001 to 5000	1993	Nonprofit Organization	...	30	NY	Data Scientist	0	0	0	0	1	0	0
4.2	ManTech	Chantilly, VA	Herndon, VA	5001 to 10000	1968	Company - Public	...	55	VA	Data Scientist	0	0	0	0	0	1	0
3.8	Analysis Group	Boston, MA	Boston, MA	1001 to 5000	1981	Private Practice / Firm	...	42	MA	Data Scientist	1	1	0	0	1	0	0
3.5	INFICON	Newton, MA	Bad Ragaz, Switzerland	501 to 1000	2000	Company - Public	...	23	MA	Data Scientist	1	1	0	0	1	1	0
2.9	Affinity Solutions	New York, NY	New York, NY	51 to 200	1998	Company - Private	...	25	NY	Data Scientist	1	1	0	0	0	1	0

Figure 9.4 – The first five rows of the Data Science Job Posting dataset

It looks just like the dataset we just saved, so we are ready to build some nice visualizations using this cleaned-up data.

Step 7 – creating visualizations to summarize the data

Let's do some simple visualizations to summarize the data and draw some simple conclusions. Let's start by importing the libraries we will need to create the visualizations:

```
import matplotlib.pyplot as plt
import seaborn as sns
```

matplotlib is a popular Python library for creating static, animated, and interactive visualizations. It provides a wide range of functions and tools for generating high-quality plots, charts, and graphs. Matplotlib is widely used in data analysis, scientific research, and data visualization tasks.

seaborn is a Python data visualization library built on top of Matplotlib. It provides a high-level interface for creating attractive and informative statistical graphics. Seaborn is widely used for exploratory data analysis, statistical modeling, and presenting data visualizations in a visually appealing and concise manner.

In this section, we are going to make extensive use of creating functions using the two libraries we just imported. To start, let's create a simple function to generate a bar plot to showcase which skills are being called out, based on the Boolean columns we created in the previous step of the data engineering process:

```
def plot_skill_appearances(df, skill_columns):
    counts_1 = [len(df.loc[df[column] == 1, column]) for column in
skill_columns]
    counts_0 = [len(df.loc[df[column] == 0, column]) for column in
skill_columns]

    x = skill_columns
    y1 = counts_1
    y2 = counts_0

    sns.set()
    plt.figure(figsize=(10, 6))
    sns.barplot(x=x, y=y1, color='b')
    sns.barplot(x=x, y=y2, bottom=y1, color='r')
    plt.xlabel('Technical Skill')
    plt.ylabel('Skill Appearances')
    plt.show()
```

The `plot_skill_appearances` function takes two parameters: `df` (the DataFrame) and `skill_columns` (a list of skill columns to plot) to do the following:

- It uses list comprehensions to compute the counts of appearances for each skill (1s and 0s) in the DataFrame.

- The resulting counts are stored in `counts_1` and `counts_0`.

- The x variable is set to `skill_columns` to define the X-axis labels.

- The `y1` and `y2` variables are set to the counts of appearances for 1s and 0s, respectively.

- The function then creates a bar plot using `plt.bar()`, where `y1` represents the bars for 1s and `y2` represents the bars for 0s. The bottom parameter is used to stack the bars.

- The plot is customized with axis labels and displayed using `plt.show()`.

We call the function on the DataFrame to show the bar graph with the skills columns we generated earlier:

```
skills = ['Python', 'Excel', 'Sql', 'Tableau', 'Power Bi', 'Aws',
'Spark']
plot_skill_appearances(ds_vis_df, skills)
```

This will generate the following plot:

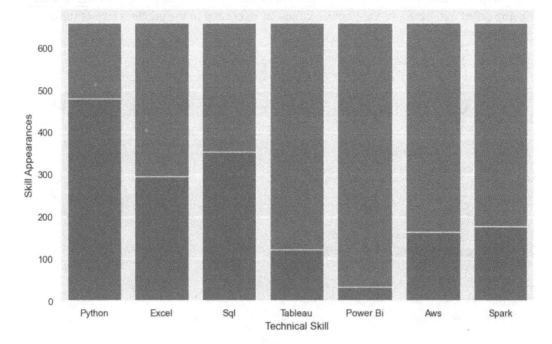

Figure 9.5 – Number of job postings by technical skills bar graph

What kinds of conclusions can you draw from this visualization? Feel free to jot some down in the margins or a separate document.

Next, let's look at how the job titles are distributed in this dataset. We can create a simple pie chart to demonstrate the percentage of each job title. We will create a function to help us produce the pie chart:

```
def plot_job_title_distribution(df, column):
    category_distribution = df[column].value_counts(normalize=True)

    # Create a pie chart using seaborn
    plt.figure(figsize=(8, 8))
    sns.set()
    category_distribution.plot(kind='pie', autopct='%1.1f%%')
    plt.title('Job Title Distribution')
    plt.ylabel('')
    plt.show()
```

The plot_category_distribution function takes two parameters: df (the DataFrame) and column_name (the column containing the job categories to visualize):

- It calculates the proportion of jobs in each category using value_counts(normalize=True)
- The resulting proportions are used to create a pie chart using Seaborn
- The Seaborn styling is set using sns.set() to enhance the aesthetics of the plot
- The plot is displayed using plt.show()

Let's call the function and see what the pie chart looks like:

```
plot_job_title_distribution(ds_vis_df, 'Job Title Transformed')
```

This will generate the following pie chart:

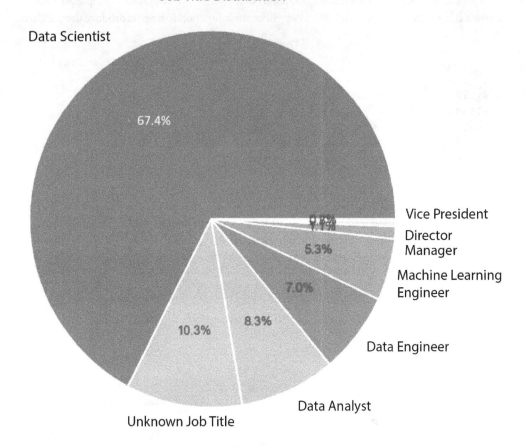

Figure 9.6 – Job Title Distribution pie chart

One thing that you might see is that because the Vice President, Director, and Manager roles make up such a small amount of the job postings, the titles and percentages overlap one another. This is one of the unfortunate limitations of using the Python and Seaborn libraries for plotting.

What kinds of conclusions can be drawn from this? Feel free to jot some down.

Next, let's plot the top 10 industries that appear in the Glassdoor results:

```python
def plot_top_industries(df, n=10):
    top_industries = df['Industry'].value_counts().nlargest(n).index
    data_filtered = df[df['Industry'].isin(top_industries)]

    plt.figure(figsize=(12, 6))
    sns.countplot(data=data_filtered, y='Industry', order=top_
industries)
    plt.title(f'Top {n} Industries')
    plt.xlabel('Count')
    plt.ylabel('Industry')
    plt.show()
```

The `plot_top_industries` function takes a DataFrame (`df`) and an optional parameter, n (defaulted to 10), as input.

It calculates the top *n* industries based on the frequency using `value_counts().nlargest(n).index`:

- The DataFrame is filtered to include only the rows with the top industries

- `countplot` is created using `sns.countplot()` from Seaborn, with `data_filtered` as the input data and `y='Industry'` to specify the column for the industries

- The order parameter is set to `top_industries` to order the bars according to the top industries

- The figure size, title, *X*-label, and *Y*-label are labeled to help provide context

- The plot is displayed using `plt.show()`

Let's call the function and see what the top 10 industries are by using the default number we established in the function:

```python
plot_top_industries(ds_vis_df)
```

This will print out the following plot:

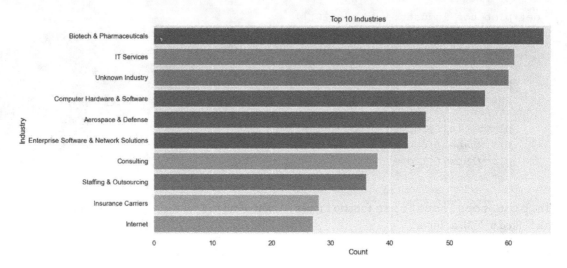

Figure 9.7 – Top 10 industries appearing in the job posting bar graph

What kinds of conclusions can be drawn from this visualization?

Next, let's take a look at the salary information and get an idea of the distribution of salaries:

```
def plot_salary_distribution(df):
    plt.figure(figsize=(10, 6))
    sns.histplot(data=df, x='Average Salary', kde=True)
    plt.title('Distribution of Salaries')
    plt.xlabel('Average Salary')
    plt.ylabel('Count')
    plt.show()
```

The plot_salary_distribution function takes a DataFrame (df) as input:

- The histogram plot is created using sns.histplot() from Seaborn
- The x parameter is set to Average Salary to specify the column for the salary values
- Setting kde=True adds a kernel density estimate plot to the histogram
- The plot is displayed using plt.show()

Call the function and see what the distribution of salaries looks like:

```
plot_salary_distribution(ds_vis_df)
```

This prints out the following bar chart:

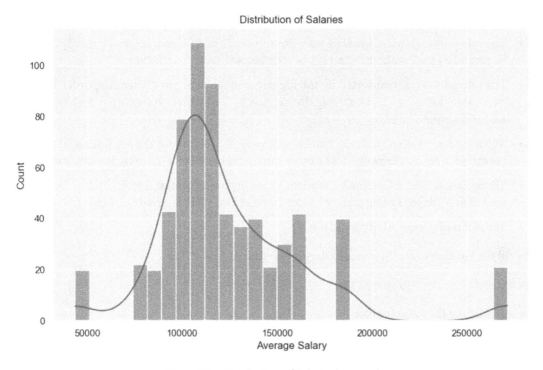

Figure 9.8 – Distribution of Salaries bar graph

What kind of conclusions can be drawn from this visualization? Jot some down.

Next, let's plot the average salary by job title using the transformed job title column we created earlier in this tutorial:

```
def plot_average_salary_by_title(df):
    filtered_data = df[df['Job Title Transformed'] != 'Unknown Job
Title']
    sorted_data = filtered_data.sort_values('Average Salary',
ascending=False)

    plt.figure(figsize=(12, 6))
    sns.barplot(data=sorted_data, x='Job Title Transformed',
y='Average Salary')
    plt.title('Average Salary by Job Title')
    plt.xlabel('Job Title')
    plt.ylabel('Average Salary')
    plt.xticks(rotation=45)
    plt.show()
```

The `plot_average_salary_by_title` function takes a DataFrame (`df`) as input:

- The bar plot is created using `sns.barplot()` from Seaborn

- The data is filtered to exclude rows with `Unknown Job Title` using `filtered_data = data[data['Job Title'] != 'Unknown Job Title']`

- The filtered data is then sorted by the highest average salary in descending order using `sorted_data = filtered_data.sort_values('Average Salary', ascending=False)`

- The x parameter is set to `Job Title` to specify the column for the job titles, and the y parameter is set to `Average Salary` to specify the column for the average salary values

- The figure size, title, X-label, and Y-label are added to provide context, and the X-axis labels are rotated by 90 degrees using `plt.xticks(rotation=90)` to avoid overlapping

- The plot is displayed using `plt.show()`

Let's call the function to see the average salary by job title:

```
plot_average_salary_by_title(ds_vis_df)
```

This will print out the following plot:

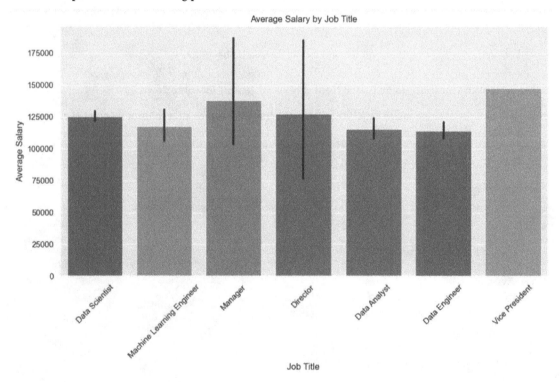

Figure 9.9 – Average Salary by Job Title bar graph

What conclusions can be drawn from this visualization? Jot some down.

Finally, let's look at the average salary by the size of the company to see if there is any significant relationship between the number of employees and the average salary for data science jobs:

```python
def plot_average_salary_by_size(data):
    plt.figure(figsize=(12, 6))
    sns.boxplot(data=data, x='Size', y='Average Salary', order=['1 to
50', '51 to 200', '201 to 500', '501 to 1000', '1001 to 5000', '5001
to 10000', '10000+'])
    plt.title('Average Salary by Company Size')
    plt.xlabel('Company Size')
    plt.ylabel('Average Salary')
    plt.xticks(rotation=45)
    plt.show()
```

The `plot_average_salary_by_size` function takes a DataFrame (`df`) as input:

- The bar plot is created using `sns.boxplot()` from Seaborn, with the x parameter set to `Size` to specify the column for company size, and the y parameter set to `Average Salary` to specify the column for the average salary

- The `order` parameter is set to specify the desired order of company sizes for better visualization

- The figure size, title, X-label, and Y-label are set accordingly

- The rotation parameter is used to rotate the X-axis labels for better readability

- The plot is displayed using `plt.show()`

Let's call the function to show the relationship between average salary and company size:

```python
plot_average_salary_by_size(ds_vis_df)
```

This will print out the following plot:

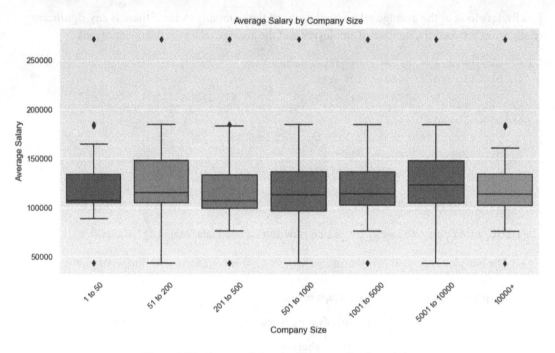

Figure 9.10 – Average Salary by Company Size box plot

There are unlimited ways to visualize this data and draw conclusions from the dataset. These are just some samples of graphs that can be created using the cleaned-up dataset. Take some time to practice on your own and develop your own analysis!

Tableau for data visualization

Tableau is a powerful and widely used BI and data visualization tool. It provides an intuitive and user-friendly interface that enables users to connect to various data sources, visualize data, and create interactive and visually appealing dashboards, reports, and charts. Tableau is designed to simplify the process of exploring and analyzing data, making it accessible to both technical and non-technical users.

Tableau is widely adopted across industries for data analysis, reporting, and decision-making. It caters to a broad spectrum of users, including business analysts, data scientists, and executives, enabling them to uncover patterns, trends, and insights hidden within their data. The tool's versatility, user-friendly interface, and powerful visualization capabilities make it a popular choice for organizations seeking to transform data into actionable insights.

Tableau offers a rich set of visualization options, allowing users to create charts, graphs, maps, and other visual representations of data. It provides a drag-and-drop interface that makes it easy to build visualizations without writing complex code. With Tableau, users can combine multiple visualizations into interactive dashboards. Dashboards enable users to explore data dynamically, filter and drill down into specific details, and interact with the visualizations to gain deeper insights.

Using Tableau for data visualization offers several advantages for BI professionals:

- **User-friendly interface**: Tableau provides a user-friendly and intuitive interface that allows BI professionals to create visualizations without extensive coding or technical expertise. Its drag-and-drop functionality enables users to quickly build interactive dashboards and reports, making it accessible to a wider audience within an organization.

- **Wide range of visualizations**: Tableau offers a comprehensive set of visualization options, including charts, graphs, maps, and other interactive elements. This versatility allows users to present data in various formats, making it easier to uncover patterns, trends, and insights that might be overlooked with traditional tabular representations.

- **Real-time data connections**: Tableau supports real-time data connections, enabling BI professionals to connect directly to databases, cloud services, and other data sources. This capability allows for dynamic and up-to-date visualizations, ensuring that users have access to the most current information.

- **Interactive and exploratory analysis**: Tableau facilitates interactive and exploratory data analysis by allowing users to filter, drill down, and slice data easily. BI professionals can create interactive dashboards that enable users to interact with the data, dynamically change parameters, and explore different perspectives, empowering them to make more informed decisions.

- **Collaboration and sharing**: Tableau provides robust collaboration and sharing features, allowing BI professionals to share visualizations and insights with colleagues, stakeholders, and decision-makers. Users can publish dashboards to Tableau Server or Tableau Public, making them accessible to a wider audience and promoting collaboration and knowledge sharing within an organization.

- **Scalability and performance**: Tableau is designed to handle large and complex datasets efficiently. It employs intelligent data querying and caching techniques to optimize performance, ensuring that visualizations remain responsive and interactive even with extensive data. Tableau's scalability allows it to handle the evolving data needs of growing organizations.

- **Integration with other tools**: Tableau integrates seamlessly with other BI tools, databases, and data sources. It can connect to a wide range of data systems, including spreadsheets, SQL databases, cloud services, and big data platforms. This integration flexibility enables BI professionals to leverage existing data infrastructure and incorporate Tableau into their existing workflows.

- **Community and support**: Tableau has a vibrant and active user community that offers extensive support, resources, and knowledge sharing. The Tableau community provides access to forums, blogs, tutorials, and training materials, allowing BI professionals to learn, collaborate, and stay updated with the latest best practices and techniques.

Overall, Tableau's intuitive interface, diverse visualization options, real-time data connections, interactive capabilities, collaboration features, scalability, and community support make it a valuable tool for BI professionals looking to create compelling visualizations and deliver actionable insights for their organizations.

Tableau dashboard hands-on

To follow along with this tutorial, please have Tableau Desktop downloaded and installed on your machine (the version does not matter). For this Tableau tutorial, we will use the Airbnb data from the Boston, Massachusetts area, which is available on Kaggle (`https://www.kaggle.com/datasets/airbnb/boston`). There are three distinct datasets we will be using:

- `Listings.csv` (information about the listings themselves and their review scores)

- `Calendar.csv` (information about the availability and pricing for each listing for each day)

- `Reviews.csv` (information about each reviewer and their commentary on each listing)

Let's start creating the dashboard:

1. Download the dataset from `https://www.kaggle.com/datasets/airbnb/boston` and extract the files from the ZIP folder. You will see three CSV files when you unzip the download:

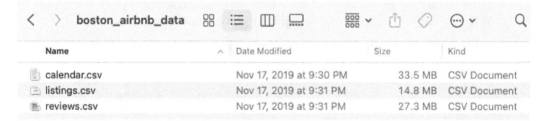

Figure 9.11 – Boston Airbnb CSV files

2. Now that we have the data, let's fire up Tableau Desktop. When we have the application open, we'll want to **Connect** to a data source; in this case, this is the CSV files we just downloaded:

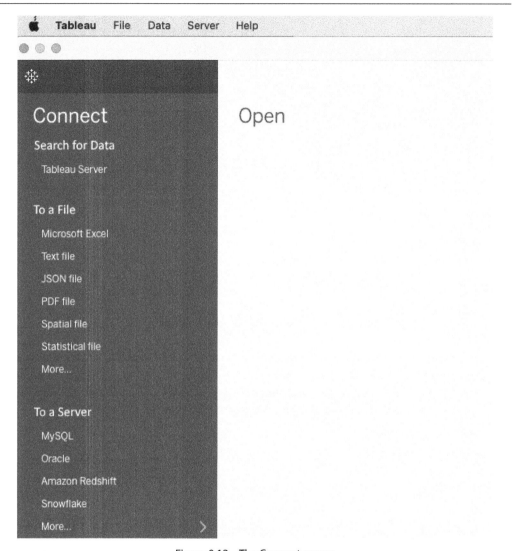

Figure 9.12 – The Connect screen

3.   Select the listings.csv file first, then click **OK**. This will be our "base" table.

4.   This will bring us to the **Data Modeling** window in Tableau Desktop. From here, we'll be able to join the data together by building the JOINS (relationships) needed to create visualizations, and ultimately, a dashboard from these three datasets.

5. Let's double-click on the `listings.csv` box; this will open a new window. Then, drag the `calendar.csv` file next to the `listings.csv` file to create a relationship:

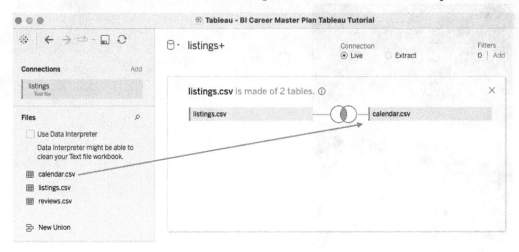

Figure 9.13 – The Tableau data modeling screen

6. Let's change the relationship that Tableau pre-selected for us; Tableau will sometimes try to guess what the correct JOIN logic is, but unfortunately for us, it got it incorrect. We do not want to join on price because it is not a unique identifier. There could be several listings with the same price, so we would see many rows repeated in the dataset:

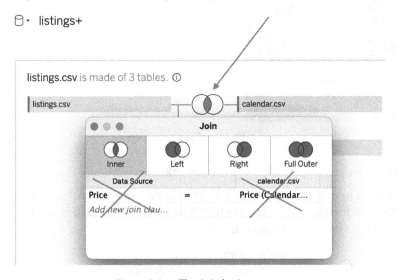

Figure 9.14 – The Join logic screen

7. Select **Listing ID** from the dropdown box under `calendar.csv` to create an INNER JOIN on **Listing.Id = Calendar.Listing Id**:

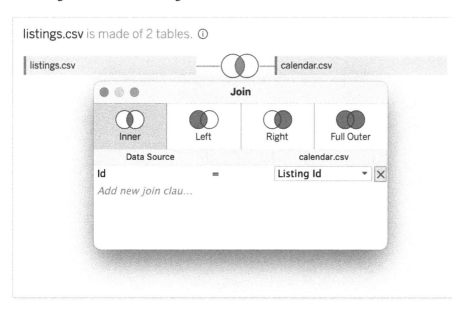

Figure 9.15 – The Join screen

8. We can follow an identical process for the `reviews.csv` data. Again, we will do an INNER JOIN on the **Listing.Id = Reviews.Listing Id** field:

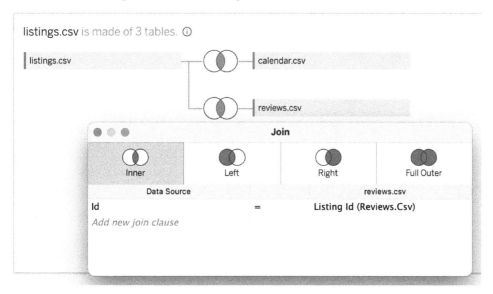

Figure 9.16 – The Join screen

Our final data model will look like this:

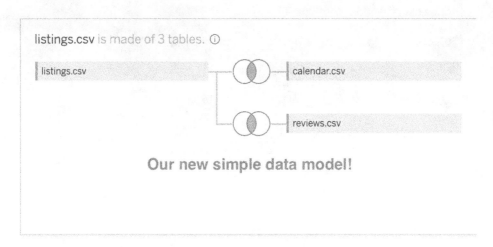

Figure 9.17 – We will see this simple data model, which is needed to build the dashboard

9. Now, we have the data correctly set up with the right relationships needed to build out the reports. Let's click on the **Sheet 1** tab to build our first analysis! It will open a blank sheet for us.

10. Let's start by building a visualization to capture **Average AirBnB Price per Zip Code** using Tableau's built-in functionality for creating maps. Conveniently, Tableau has a feature to create a visualization of a map using the **Latitude** and **Longitude** fields, which get automatically generated when an address is included in the dataset. Drag the **Longitude** and **Latitude** marks into **Columns** and **Rows**, respectively:

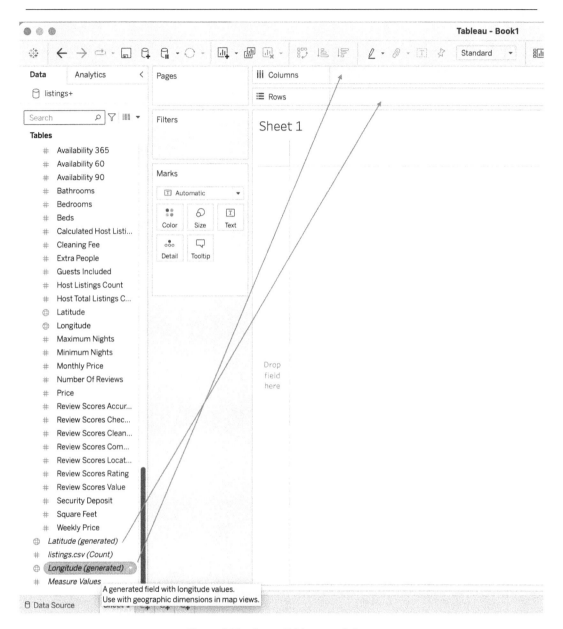

Figure 9.18 – A new Tableau worksheet

11. We will see that an empty map is created at first, which is not very helpful! Let's add some data points to flesh this visualization out by pulling the **Zip Code** dimension to the **Label** and **Color** marks. As we mentioned earlier, we want to display **Average Airbnb Price by Zip Code**:

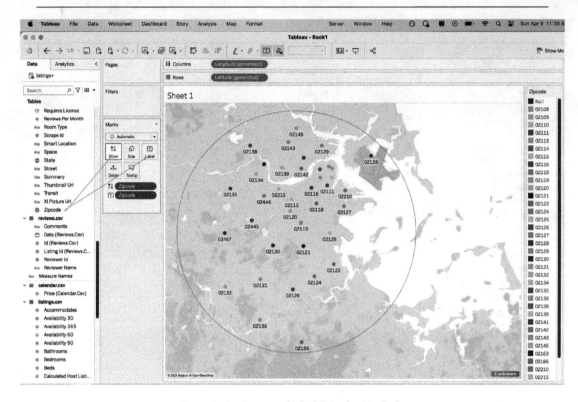

Figure 9.19 – Average AirBnB Price by Zip Code

12. Now, let's pull the **Price** measure over the **Label** mark and change it from **SUM** to **AVG**. Right-click on **Price** and search for Average in the drop-down menu:

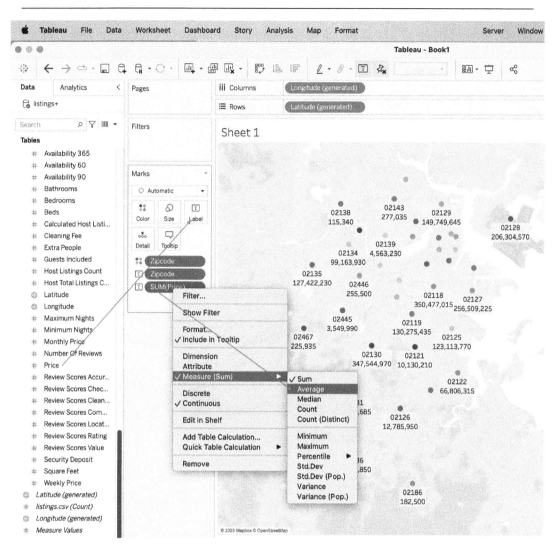

Figure 9.20 – The drop-down menu for adjusting measure calculations

13. Let's clean this up a bit by changing the default number formatting of **Price** to look a little more intuitive for our business stakeholders. Right-click on the **Price** measure and select **Currency (Custom)**:

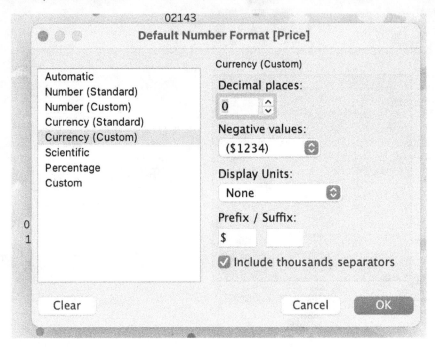

Figure 9.21 – The Currency (Custom) option

Remove the decimals by setting them to 0 and keep the standard prefix for USD ($):

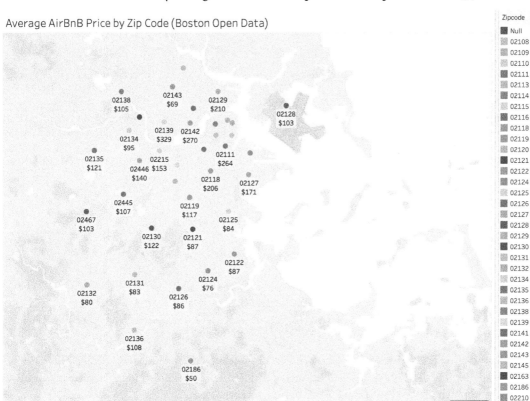

Figure 9.22 – Map showing Average Airbnb Price by Zip Code

Time series data is extremely important for reporting trends, so let's try this out with our dataset by building out a time series line graph:

1. Let's open a new sheet by clicking right next to **Sheet 1** and adding a new sheet.

2. Then, let's drag the **Price** measure and **Date** dimension into **Columns** and **Rows**, respectively.

3. We will see that Tableau is automatically slicing this by year, but that's not as helpful as seeing this broken out by week. To make this adjustment, we can simply right-click on the **YEAR(Date)** dimension and change it to **WEEK (Number)**:

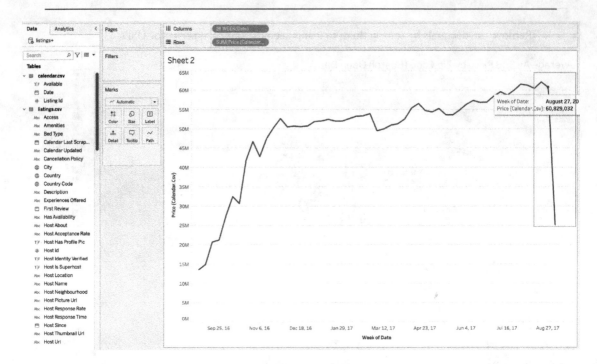

Figure 9.23 – Airbnb revenue per week

Now we are getting somewhere! But as savvy BI professionals, we notice something odd in the visualization: there is a drop-off after August 27th. This drop-off is due to incomplete data and could potentially be confusing for our business stakeholders.

4. We can remove the incomplete data by filtering by week. Right-click on the **WEEK(Date)** dimension in the **Columns** section and select **Filter**:

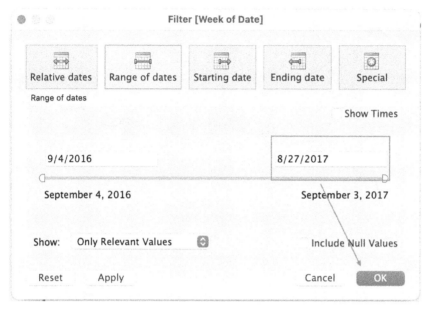

Figure 9.24 – Filter [Week of Date]

Drag the slider until you see the last date in the range of dates of 8/27/2017 and click on **OK**. This should give you the following result:

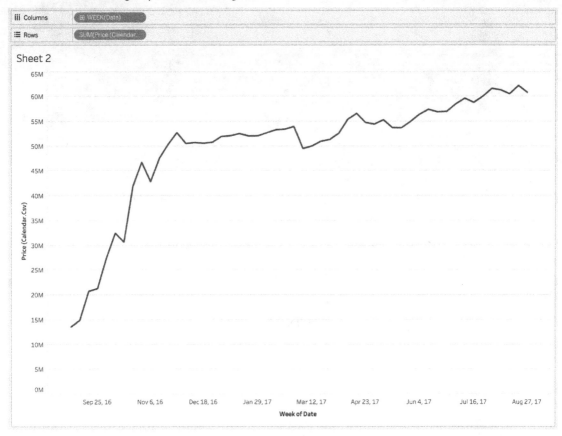

Figure 9.25 – Airbnb revenue by week

5. Let's add a title and change the formatting of the *Y*-axis. First, right-click on **Sheet 2** and select **Rename**. Rename the graph **Airbnb Revenue Per Week (Boston Open Data)**.

6. Then, right-click on the *Y*-axis and select **Format**.

7. Then, go to **Numbers** and change this to **Currency - Custom**:

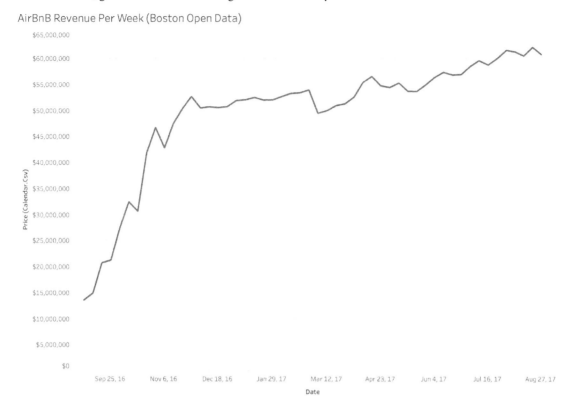

AirBnB Revenue Per Week (Boston Open Data)

Figure 9.26 – Airbnb Revenue Per Week (Boston Open Data)

Let's do one more visualization to close out this dashboard:

1. Next, let's create an **Average Airbnb Price per Bedroom** visualization to see how having additional bedrooms affects the price of an Airbnb listing. Drag the **Bedrooms** and **Price** measures into **Columns** and **Rows**, respectively; what you will notice is that because **Bedrooms** is a measure, it makes for a poor visualization. No worries – we will fix that momentarily!

2. To improve the bar graph visualization, change the **Bedrooms** measure to **Discrete Dimension**. Right-click the measure and select **Dimension**. Then, right-click the measure again and select **Discrete**.

3. As savvy BI professionals, we realize that NULL values do not add any helpful context to this visualization – let's remove those by filtering them out. Right-click **Bedrooms** and select **Filter**. Uncheck the box next to **Null** to remove nulls and click **OK**:

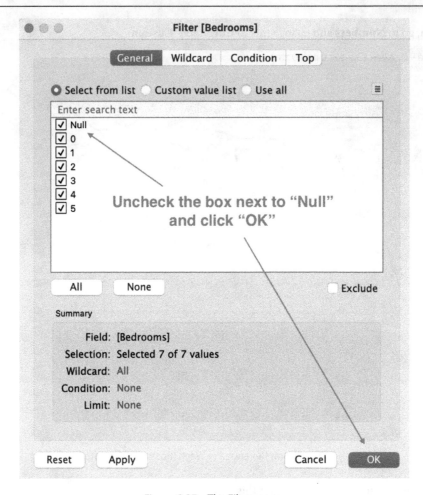

Figure 9.27 – The Filter menu

4. Now, let's change **SUM(Price)** to **AVG(Price)** and add labels to each bar.

5. Drag **Price** to the **Label** card. Then, right-click **SUM(Price)** and change it to **Average** to reflect the average price.

6.   Now, let's make the graph **Fit Width** so it fills the whole page:

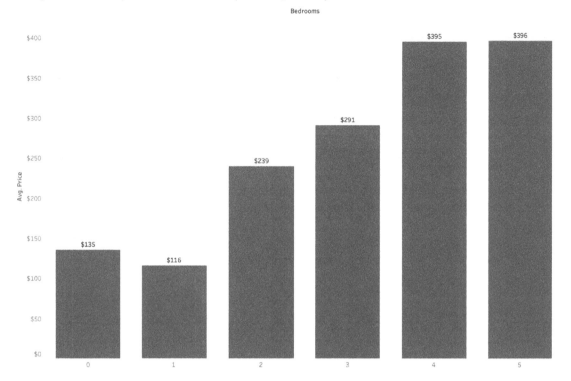

Average AirBnB Price by Number of Bedrooms (Boston Open Data)

Figure 9.28 – Average Airbnb Price by Number of Bedrooms

Let's create a dashboard to bring it all together:

1.   Start by clicking on **New Dashboard** near the bottom. Find the **New Dashboard** tab, which looks like four squares with a plus (+) symbol:

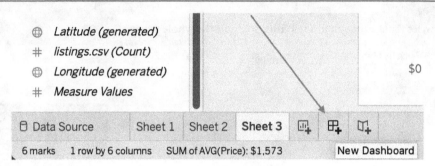

Figure 9.29 – The New Dashboard tab

2. This will open a new dashboard page, which we can use to bring the visualizations together. Let's adjust the size a bit to 1250px x 850px to give us a bigger canvas to work with.

3. Drag **Average Airbnb Price by Number of Bedrooms (Sheet 3)** in first and see what it looks like. Drag the sheet over to the **Drop sheets here** text:

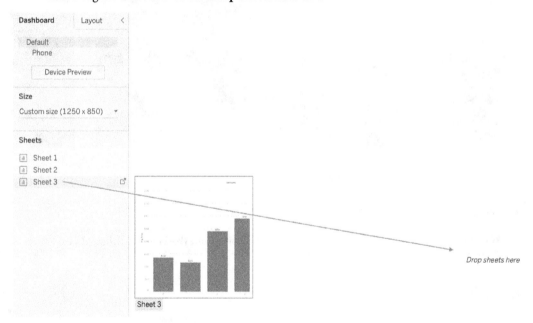

Figure 9.30 – The dashboard layout screen

4. Drag in the **Average Airbnb Price by Zip Code** visualization (**Sheet 1**) and place it below the bar graph. We will have two sheets on top of each other on the dashboard layout screen:

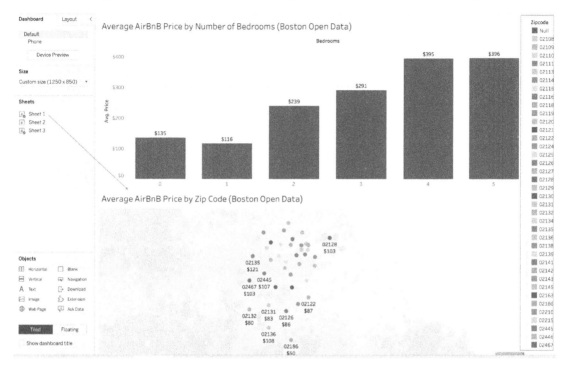

Figure 9.31 – The dashboard layout screen

5. Let's move the legend closer to the **Zip Code** visualization so it's not taking up so much space. Pull the **Zip Code** legend down next to the map to make it more presentable:

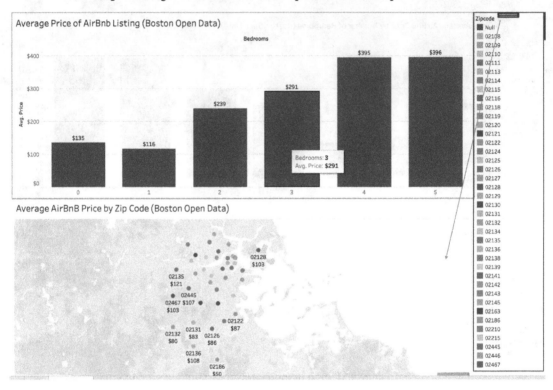

Figure 9.32 – The dashboard layout screen

6. We're almost there! Let's grab **AirBnB Revenue Per Week** and put it to the left of the **Average AirBnb Price by Zip Code** visualization. Pull **Airbnb Revenue Per Week (Sheet 2)** to the left of the map visualization:

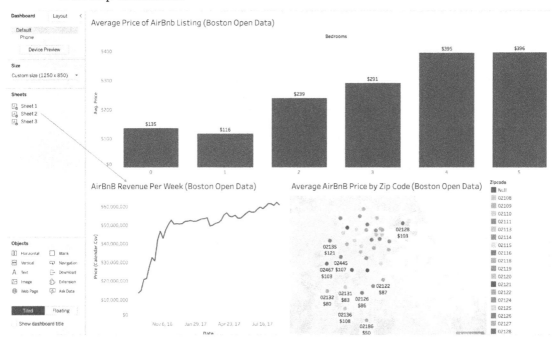

Figure 9.33 – The dashboard layout screen

The final dashboard will look like this:

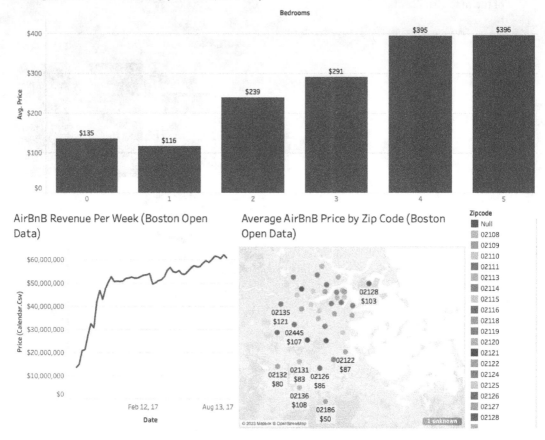

Figure 9.34 – The completed Airbnb dashboard

The dashboard is ready for publishing and feedback from business stakeholders. There are potentially hundreds of different visualizations that can be explored with this dataset; we hope that this very simple hands-on tutorial introduced you to how quickly and easily a Tableau dashboard can be set up to deliver insights to business stakeholders.

The datasets and workbook can be found here: `https://github.com/PacktPublishing/Business-Intelligence-Career-Master-Plan/tree/main/ch9`. Feel free to explore them and try them out on your visualizations!

Summary

The tutorials featured in this chapter dove into data wrangling techniques, emphasizing the use of powerful tools and libraries such as Python's pandas. These tools provided a variety of functions for filtering, aggregating, and transforming data. Through practical examples, you have gained the skills to effectively handle missing values, eliminate duplicates, and apply essential data transformations, ensuring accurate and reliable analysis.

We also empowered you to present your analysis compellingly by offering detailed instructions on leveraging Tableau, a widely adopted BI tool. With its intuitive interface, we guided you in creating visually appealing and interactive reports using drag-and-drop functionality. Through this process, you learned how to choose suitable visualizations and personalize the appearance of your reports, ensuring you can effectively communicate your findings.

Finally, we guided you on merging your reports into a cohesive and comprehensive dashboard. Through this process, you learned how to synthesize multiple reports into a single view, allowing stakeholders to gain a holistic understanding of the data and its insights.

Conclusion

The field of BI is constantly evolving, driven by advances in technology, changes in business needs, and increasing demands for data-driven decision-making. This book has explored the foundations of BI, including data warehousing, data mining, and data visualization, as well as the latest trends and techniques for extracting insights from data.

We have seen that successful BI initiatives require a clear understanding of business goals, strong collaboration between IT and business units, and a focus on delivering actionable insights. The importance of data quality, security, and governance cannot be overstated as they underpin the reliability and trustworthiness of the insights generated.

We took a look at the next steps to improve your career and even go beyond traditional BI. As with everything in life, BI, analytics, data science… it's all iterative and requires continuous improvement and learning. Your skills are going to improve if you focus your attention on aligning your career preferences and your organization's goals.

We hope that this book has provided you with a comprehensive overview of BI, its benefits and challenges, and practical guidance for implementing successful BI initiatives. As we move toward an increasingly data-driven world, the ability to extract insights from data will become a crucial competitive advantage for organizations of all sizes and sectors. We encourage you to continue to explore and innovate in the field of BI and embrace the opportunities and challenges that lie ahead.

Index

www.packtpub.com

Subscribe to our online digital library for full access to over 7,000 books and videos, as well as industry leading tools to help you plan your personal development and advance your career. For more information, please visit our website.

Why subscribe?

- Spend less time learning and more time coding with practical eBooks and Videos from over 4,000 industry professionals

- Improve your learning with Skill Plans built especially for you

- Get a free eBook or video every month

- Fully searchable for easy access to vital information

- Copy and paste, print, and bookmark content

Did you know that Packt offers eBook versions of every book published, with PDF and ePub files available? You can upgrade to the eBook version at www.packtpub.com and as a print book customer, you are entitled to a discount on the eBook copy. Get in touch with us at customercare@packtpub.com for more details.

At www.packtpub.com, you can also read a collection of free technical articles, sign up for a range of free newsletters, and receive exclusive discounts and offers on Packt books and eBooks.

Other Books You May Enjoy

If you enjoyed this book, you may be interested in these other books by Packt:

Data Modeling with Tableau

Kirk Munroe

ISBN: 978-1-80324-802-8

- Showcase Tableau published data sources and embedded connections
- Apply Ask Data in data cataloging and natural language query
- Understand the features of Tableau Prep Builder with the help of hands-on exercises
- Model data with Tableau Desktop using examples
- Formulate a governed data strategy using Tableau Server and Tableau Cloud
- Optimize data models for Ask and Explain Data

Tableau Desktop Specialist Certification

Adam Mico

ISBN: 978-1-80181-013-5

- Understand how to add data to the application
- Explore data for insights in Tableau
- Discover what charts to use when visualizing for audiences
- Understand functions, calculations and the basics of parameters
- Work with dimensions, measures and their variations
- Contextualize a visualization with marks
- Share insights and focus on editing a Tableau visualization

Packt is searching for authors like you

If you're interested in becoming an author for Packt, please visit authors.packtpub.com and apply today. We have worked with thousands of developers and tech professionals, just like you, to help them share their insight with the global tech community. You can make a general application, apply for a specific hot topic that we are recruiting an author for, or submit your own idea.

Share your thoughts

Now you've finished *Business Intelligence Career Master Plan*, we'd love to hear your thoughts! Scan the QR code below to go straight to the Amazon review page for this book and share your feedback or leave a review on the site that you purchased it from.

https://packt.link/r/1801077959

Your review is important to us and the tech community and will help us make sure we're delivering excellent quality content.

Download a free PDF copy of this book

Thanks for purchasing this book!

Do you like to read on the go but are unable to carry your print books everywhere?

Is your eBook purchase not compatible with the device of your choice?

Don't worry, now with every Packt book you get a DRM-free PDF version of that book at no cost.

Read anywhere, any place, on any device. Search, copy, and paste code from your favorite technical books directly into your application.

The perks don't stop there, you can get exclusive access to discounts, newsletters, and great free content in your inbox daily

Follow these simple steps to get the benefits:

1. Scan the QR code or visit the link below

https://packt.link/free-ebook/978-1-80107-795-8

2. Submit your proof of purchase
3. That's it! We'll send your free PDF and other benefits to your email directly